Giant Book of Bread Machine Recipes

Giant Book of Bread Machine Recipes

Norman A. Garrett

Sterling Publishing Co., Inc.
New York

10 9 8 7 6 5 4 3 2 1

Published by Sterling Publishing Company, Inc
387 Park Avenue South, New York, N.Y. 10016
Material in this collection was adapted from
Favorite Bread Machine Recipes Norman A. Garrett
Great Bread Machine Recipes Norman A. Garrett
Quick & Delicious Bread Machine Recipes Norman A. Garrett
Specialty Breads in Your Bread Machine Norman A. Garrett

Distributed in Canada by Sterling Publishing
c/o Canadian Manda Group, One Atlantic Avenue, Suite 105
Toronto, Ontario, Canada M6K 3E7
Distributed in Great Britain and Europe by Cassell PLC
Wellington House, 125 Strand, London WC2R 0BB, England
Distributed in Australia by Capricorn Link (Australia) Pty Ltd
P.O. Box 6651, Baulkham Hills, Business Centre, NSW 2153, Australia

Sterling ISBN 0-8069-1743-1

CONTENTS

GETTING TO KNOW YOUR BREAD MAKER

Basic Operations

Although bread machines come in various shapes, sizes, capacities, and capabilities, they all share common characteristics and principles of operation. They are all designed to make bread making easy, quick, and complete. Except for placing the proper ingredients in the baking pan, pressing a few buttons, and removing the bread when it is finished (and slicing it, of course), the machine does all the work.

After ingredients are placed in the pan and you start the machine, the following cycles are completed:

1. The initial mix cycle

2. The first rise

3. The "punch down"

4. The second rise

5. The bake

6. The cool down

The length of each cycle depends on the make and model of your machine. Some machines skip the second rise and bake after the first rise. Other machines have alternate settings that let you select a double or single rise (often called the "quick bread" cycle). Some of the new machines have cycles especially created for whole grain breads, which generally require longer rising cycles. In addition, some machines have added capabilities, such as special cycles for cooking rice, jam, quick breads (batter breads), and cakes.

Whatever your machine's configuration, you need to become familiar with the way it works so you can tap its full potential for making delicious loaves of bread.

Capacities and Limitations

Each machine has a maximum capacity and limitation. Capacities are usually either 1 pound or 1½ pounds, with a few machines accommodating loaf sizes of 2 pounds. It is not wise to exceed the rated capacity of your machine, because overloading the machine can cause motor damage or dough overflows.

I have seen ads for machines that can bake "3 pound loaves," but the fine print will usually reveal that this will only work in the case of a dense bread that doesn't rise much. I would not recommend baking loaves much larger than your machine can handle, as it could cause damage to your machine, particularly the mixing motor.

What about baking a loaf smaller than the rated capacity? On most machines, that will work fine. The recipes in this book are presented in 1 pound, 1½ pound, and 2 pound sizes. If you have a 1 pound machine, limit yourself to baking the 1 pound loaves. If you have a larger, 1½ pound machine, feel free to try both 1 and 1½ pound recipe sizes.

Table 1 shows the basic capacity differences among bread machines currently on the market. You can determine the capacity of your machine from the owner's manual or determine the capacity by checking the white bread recipe that came with the machine. If the recipe calls for 2 cups of bread flour, you have a 1 pound machine. If it calls for 3 or more cups, you have a 1½ pound (or greater) capacity machine.

Table 1. Bread Machine Capacities: Basic White Bread Recipe

Flour Amount	1 lb	1½ lb	1½+ lb
2 cups	X		
2.5 cups	X		
3 cups		X	
3.5 cups			X
3 to 4 cups			X

Note: Determine the amount of flour called for in the basic white bread recipe for your machine. This chart will tell you the capacity of your machine based on that amount. If you do not have access to the basic white bread recipe that came with your machine, assume that it has a 1 pound capacity.

Baking the Dough Yourself

All machines let you bake the dough yourself in the oven by extracting it from the machine after the first rise is complete. If your machine has a dough setting, it will beep when it is time to remove the dough. You can then punch the dough down, knead it, place it in a bread pan or on a cookie sheet for a final rise, and bake in an oven, rather than in the machine itself.

Adding Ingredients

Some machines have a "mix bread" setting, which will beep when it is time to add raisins, seeds, or other ingredients to the dough. Since not all machines have this capability, I have developed the recipes in this book so all ingredients can be placed in the pan in the beginning. However, if you have a "mix" cycle, you can alternatively use that cycle, particularly in the recipes calling for seeds, nuts, or raisins. The advantage to adding these ingredients in a mix cycle is that the machine will tend to pound them less in the mixing process. Raisins, for example, will be more likely to remain whole when added in the mix bread cycle.

The timing of rising cycles varies somewhat from machine to machine. Some of the newer machines have separate cycles for whole wheat bread, which extends the rising time for the bread, giving a better rising loaf. Still other machines are programmable, allowing you to determine rise time yourself.

Crusts

The baking times vary on bread machines. Most machines offer you the option of selecting the darkness of your crust. The control for this will usually determine the baking temperature of your bread, and will not alter the length of the baking cycle. Selecting darker crusts will cause the bread to bake hotter. I found when using one machine, for example, that turning the dial to the lightest crust setting actually caused some breads to have uncooked dough in the middle. It will probably take a few loaves for you to determine the optimum setting to accommodate both your machine's capabilities and your personal tastes. Once you determine that setting, make a note of it, because you will probably want to bake all of your loaves with that same setting.

Knowing Your Own Machine

You will need to get used to your particular machine. In testing for my books I have found considerable variations among the different machines I have used. You will need to become familiar with two parts of the baking process as they apply to your specific machine: the optimum consistency of your dough and the sound of your machine as it goes through the cycles.

Dough Consistency

Dough consistency, and each machine's ability to deal with different dough consistencies, is important and varies greatly. Some machines will use a runnier dough (more liquid content); others have powerful motors that can easily handle stiffer doughs. Observe your bread as it is mixed. Make a mental note of the dough consistency. Then, when the bread is finished, note the texture of the bread. Learn to compare the finished texture to the consistency of the dough. Soon, you will be able to accurately predict the texture of the bread by looking at the dough immediately after mixing. This skill is important if you want to make any recipe modifications.

Machine Sounds

As you use your machine, also note the typical sounds it makes as it progresses through its various cycles. If you become familiar with the "normal" sounds, you will be aware when the motor is being overworked and the sounds the machine is making are unusual, which may indicate a process is potentially damaging.

Service and Cleaning

Cleaning

If you want consistently good bread from your machine, make sure it remains clean. Taking two or three minutes after each loaf has baked to clean the machine will yield consistently better loaves and will assure that your machine stays in peak operating condition.

How hard a machine is to clean depends on its design. Some machines use a bucket with the beater drive mechanism built in. Consequently, cleaning is simply a matter of removing the bread from the bucket, removing the beater, and cleaning the bucket with warm water. On other machines, the beater drive mechanism is not part of the bucket and must be cleaned after each use. This cleaning is more difficult and sometimes results in crumbs in the bottom of the baking chamber. To clean crumbs from the baking chamber, I have found that a damp kitchen washcloth will pick up most of them. I have tried mini-vacuums, canned air, and other methods such as turning the whole unit upside down and shaking it, but I find the simple washcloth the best (and least messy).

All machines have a special nonstick surface in the bread pan. Take care with this surface. Do not use any abrasive cleaners or scouring pads on the inside of the bread pan, or you will damage the nonstick surface. Try not to pry stuck breads with knives, forks, or other hard objects that may scratch the surface. If you must pry, use a rubber or soft plastic device of some kind, like a rubber spatula. If you take care of your bread pan, it will give you many future loaves of bread.

The machines that have the beater mechanism designed into the housing, rather than the bread bucket, also have a small plastic washer. Take great care with this washer. Don't lose it, and rinse it off and dry it after each loaf of bread. Without this washer, you will not have a good seal between your bucket and the bottom of your baking chamber, and leakage will result.

If you have an accident with your bread (such as dough overflow or another big mess), wait until the machine cools down, and take your time cleaning it. Most baked-on bread can be removed with warm water, and that is the recommended cleanup. I have had my share of disasters, but have managed to clean all of them up without even having to use any soap. Simple warm water and a washcloth have always been all that is needed.

Lost and Damaged Parts

There are generally no user-serviceable components in the bread machine, other than the standard cleaning of the parts just mentioned. However, there are parts that are easily lost or damaged that you can replace yourself. Most prominent on that list is the mixer beater. Since it is a small, removable part, it is easily misplaced. Make sure that you replace the beater in the bucket after each cleaning; that will minimize its potential for being lost.

On machines in which a plastic washer fits beneath the bread bucket, the washer will wear out over time. It is important to keep it clean, and it might not be a bad idea to order a replacement to have on hand, since it is an inexpensive item.

Bread Pan

The other major removable component is the bread pan. The most likely place of damage is its nonstick surface. If its surface is damaged to the point where bread is sticking to it, replace the bread pan. If small scratches seem to have no negative effect on your being able to remove the bread from the pan, you have probably not damaged the surface enough to worry about it.

Major Repairs

If any other problems arise with your machine, it is likely it will have to be sent in for repair. The control panel, for example, will sometimes cease to function and will need to be replaced. You should obtain an estimate of repairs before authorizing any major repairs on your machine because it is possible that the cost of repairs will exceed the cost of the machine, especially since the price of new machines will continue to fall for the foreseeable future as manufacturers achieve economy of scale. The likelihood is that your machine will have a long, productive life, and that it will give you many hours of trouble-free bread baking if you will simply keep it clean and ready for the next loaf.

Troubleshooting Guide

There are numerous variables that can affect your bread. Those listed below are all problems I have experienced while making bread in my bread machines. You may also encounter some not listed here. Before you write off the bread machine completely, send it out to repair, or blame the recipe, think the problem through and make sure that you have accounted for all other possible reasons for the problem. That would include crust settings, proper baking cycles, measuring ingredients properly, using fresh ingredients, checking for power outages during baking (which may recycle your machine), and, finally, curious children pushing buttons.

Stuck Dough Beater

If your dough beater is difficult to remove after baking a loaf of bread, try using some shortening on the shaft before installing the beater, and place dry ingredients in the pan first. In the machines where the beater is self-contained in the pan, soak the beater in water for a few minutes after removing the bread. In some types of machines, the beater will stay with the loaf of bread. In those types of machines, the beater is rarely a problem to remove.

Leakage of Liquid

This might be a problem on the machines whose pans have a hole in the bottom to accommodate the dough beater. If you have this kind of machine, place the dry ingredients in the bread pan first. Liquids should be added last. Also, check to make sure you have the rubber sealing washer in the proper position before locking the pan in place, and then make sure the pan is securely locked before adding ingredients.

Recipe Flop

Make sure you have added the proper quantities of ingredients. It is easy to become distracted while setting up a recipe and miscount your ingredients. Also, check to make sure you chose the correct settings when baking the bread. Finally, be sure your ingredients are fresh and that the proper type of ingredient has been used. A frequent culprit in recipe flops is yeast that is not fresh.

Loaf-Size Variation

The size of your loaf will vary according to the ingredients. Although the weight of two loaves of bread may be the same, their size and appearance may vary greatly. This is due to the different ingredients used. In general, breads using gluten-rich bread flour will rise more than breads using flours with less gluten content. Rye breads, for example, will be small, with dense texture, and will bake with a darker crust. The loaf sizes of the recipes in this book refer to weight, not to finished size.

Spoiled Ingredients

The two ingredients you must be cautious with are fresh eggs and fresh milk. Do not use either of these ingredients in a "delay bake" cycle (available on some machines), where you set the timer to start the bread at a later time. Milk would be all right if the delay were not more than an hour or two, but I would not recommend that eggs be used in any recipe that will not immediately be started. If you want to use a recipe calling for eggs on a delay bake, consider using powdered eggs instead of fresh eggs. If you want to use milk in a delayed recipe, use dry milk and add the proper amount of water to compensate.

Collapsing Dough

If your dough collapses, it dough probably rose too long. Since the timer cycles are not programmable on many machines, you may consider reducing the yeast by ½ teaspoon to get less rising. You also should check to make sure that the machine was not recycled during the process. Recycling can occur from brief power outages, or from children (or curious adults) pressing machine buttons. If a power outage occurs and you are aware of it, you can remove the dough from the machine and finish the process by hand, baking the bread in the oven. If your machine is programmable, set the rise cycle for a shorter time the next time you bake that recipe.

Strong Yeast Flavor

It is possible that too much yeast was added. Cut the yeast down by ½ teaspoon and try again.

Failure to Rise

This can be a complex problem with many possible causes. Any of the following will contribute to a loaf not properly rising:

• Using flour with low gluten content (pure rye flour, wheat flour, etc.)

• Too much salt in the recipe. Salt is a yeast inhibitor.

• Too little sugar in the recipe. Sugar feeds yeast and promotes rising.

• Yeast is old. Yeast expires. Check your yeast supply and make sure you are using fresh yeast. Old yeast will not activate and rise properly.

• Yeast is dead. This may be caused by adding hot ingredients. For example, if your recipe calls for some ingredients to be boiled before being added to the mix, do not add them until they have had time to cool. Adding ingredients that are too hot will kill your yeast.

Uneven Top

This usually indicates too little liquid in the recipe, but on some breads, such as rye breads, where less rising takes place, this may be a normal occurrence.

Collapsed Top

This is usually caused by too much liquid in the recipe. Cut the liquid back by two tablespoons and try again. Be careful not to make your bread dough too stiff, however, as some machines have underpowered motors that will not be able to handle stiffer dough, particularly in the 1½ pound recipes. Also be aware that some recipes use ingredients that are going to add liquid to the dough during the baking cycle, and a collapsed top might be normal. I found that breads using fresh cheeses generally fall into this category.

Rancid Taste

Check your whole grain ingredients. Whole grain flours, wheat germ, and similar ingredients should be kept in the freezer. They spoil rapidly when left at room temperature. White flours are not subject to the same type of spoilage and can be left in the cupboard for storage.

White Spots

These are from flour that has stuck to the side of the pan during the mixing process and has not mixed into the dough. This problem seems to occur more frequently in square pans than in round ones. When the bread rises and bakes, this flour sticks to the outside of the loaf. While not a taste problem, spots can present a cosmetic problem. The solution is to look into the baking pan after the mixing has taken place. If there is flour stuck to the sides of the pan, take a rubber spatula, remove it from the sides, and mix it in with the dough.

Soggy Crust

You left the bread in the pan too long after the baking cycle completed. Some machines have cooling cycles that cool the bread and help remove the moisture. Soggy crust is not as great a problem on these machines, but it is still a good idea to remove the bread and place it on a cooling rack as soon as the final beep is heard.

Improper Mix

This happened to me one time when I had forgotten to replace the dough beater after cleanup from the previous loaf. My solution to this is now to watch the initial mix for a minute or so when I first turn the machine on. I can see the mixing taking place. If the motor is running, but no mixing is happening, check your dough beater. If it has been left out, stop the machine, replace the beater, and start the cycle over.

Inconsistent Size and Texture

If you bake the same recipe and get different results, blame the weather. Weather is actually a large factor in baking, as temperature and humidity have substantial control over the amount of dough rising that will take place. Make notes as you bake and you will soon learn to make seasonal adjustments for your particular climate.

Lost Dough Beater

Check the last loaf of bread, particularly if your machine is of the variety where the beater stays in the loaf of bread when it is removed from the baking pan. I had a loaf of bread ready to give to a friend for testing, only to realize that I was about to give away the dough beater too! Get in the habit of cleaning your pan right away and putting everything back in the machine, and your beater will always be where you want it: In the pan, ready to bake.

CONVERTING EXISTING RECIPES

After you have had time to get used to your bread machine, you will probably want to try out some of your favorite bread recipes. When you look at them, however, you will notice that they were not designed to work in a bread machine. Practically any yeast bread recipe can be converted to work in your bread machine as long as you want to go to the effort of making the conversion. The key is to make sure the recipe is yeast-based. Although today we enjoy yeast which is reliable and easy to use, this is a relatively recent development. Recipes that are over 40 or 50 years old will likely use a chemical, rather than an organic, leavening. Chemical leavenings include baking soda and baking powder, and they do not have the same properties as yeast. Do not attempt to convert recipes that are not yeast-based for use in your bread machine.

Some machines have a cycle for "quick breads." These cycles are specifically designed for non-yeast baking (in fact, some of the machines can bake cake too!). Often called "batter breads," quick breads are breads that use batter with a consistency similar to pancake batter or cake batter. Quick breads are raised by means other than yeast. However, since most bread machines do not have these cycles, discussions regarding quick bread recipes are really beyond the scope of this book. We will stick to only yeast breads here.

Converting a standard bread recipe to work in your machine is not difficult, but is computationally intensive work, so have a calculator handy if you want to attempt a conversion. A sheet or two of paper will also be necessary, so you can write down the totals and the new, converted recipe.

This chapter will take you through the steps for converting a "regular" (non-machine) recipe to one you can try in your machine. It may take one or two trials to perfect the recipe, but the chances are good that you can successfully make the conversion. Before converting a recipe, make sure that it is a yeast bread recipe. As mentioned above, most bread machines are not designed to handle batter breads or breads using chemically based leavenings such as baking powder and baking soda.

Basic Steps

The four basic steps to convert a recipe are:

1. Cut the recipe down so it will make one loaf. Many recipes are designed to make two loaves and you will need to cut these in half because you will need a single-loaf recipe.

2. Determine the parameters of your particular bread machine.

3. Determine the liquidity ratio of the recipe. This is the "stiffness" of the dough. This is important because your machine has a rather narrow range of doughs it can handle.

4. Determine the overall bulk of the recipe. You do not want a recipe that is too large for your machine.

Let's look at each of these steps in turn, with particular attention to the details involved in each step. Once you have accomplished a few conversions, you will no longer need to refer to this book because the steps are not really so complex as they might seem at first.

Step One: Reduce the Recipe Size

Most recipes will tell you how many loaves they make. Some will even tell you the approximate size of each loaf. Cut the recipe down so it will make one loaf. This may involve some calculations on your part, so a good technique is to write down the new recipe as you reduce it from the original.

If the recipe doesn't say how many loaves it makes, you can make a rough judgment by looking at the amount of flour required. A one-pound loaf of bread will require about two cups of flour. Thus, if your recipe calls for six cups of all-purpose flour, you can probably figure that it will make three 1-pound loaves, or two 1½-pound loaves, or three 2-pound loaves.

Step Two: Determine the Parameters of Your Machine

Since each machine varies in its capacity and motor power, you must determine the acceptable ranges for your machine in two categories: liquidity ratio and bulk. Table 2 shows the acceptable liquidity ratio ranges. To find your machine's range, look at the basic white bread recipe that came with the machine. Determine the number of cups of flour called for, and follow that column until you find the row that shows the number of ounces of liquid (water or milk) called for in the recipe. In that box you will find the ratio range for your machine. Highlight or write down that ratio range (see page 126, where you can write down information about your bread machine.)

Bulk is also simply calculated by determining the number of cups of flour called for in the basic white bread recipe for your machine. If the recipe calls for 2-2½ cups of flour, you have a 1-pound machine. If the recipe calls for 3-4 cups of flour, you have a 1½ pound (or greater) machine.

Once you have written this information down, you will, in the future, be able to skip this step and move right from step one to step three.

Table 2. Bread Machine Liquidity Ratios

| oz liq. | Cups of Flour | | | |
	2 C*	2½ C	3 C	3½ C
5	2.9–3.5	3.6–4.4	4.3–5.3	5.0–6.2
6	**2.4–3.0**	3.0–3.6	3.6–4.4	4.2–5.2
7	**2.1–2.5**	2.6–3.2	3.1–3.7	3.6–4.4
8	1.8–2.2	2.3–2.8	2.7–3.3	3.2–3.9
9	1.6–2.0	2.0–2.4	**2.4–3.0**	2.8–3.4
10	1.4–1.8	1.8–2.2	**2.2–2.6**	2.5–3.1
11	1.4–1.7	1.6–2.0	2.0–2.4	2.3–2.8

Notes: *1 C (1 cup) = 8 ounces. Underlined entries show the most common bread machine ratio ranges. The ratio is computed by dividing dry ingredients by liquid ingredients. Higher ratios indicate stiffer dough; lower ratios indicate more liquid dough.

Step Three: Determine the Liquidity Ratio

Now you must determine the liquidity ratio (dough stiffness) of the recipe you are trying to convert. Table 3 (page 26) is a handy chart that you can duplicate and use each time you convert a recipe. To use the chart, simply fill in the ingredients and the amount called for in the original recipe. Write the amount in decimals (so your calculator can add them later) in the appropriate column. For example, if the recipe calls for 2½ cups of flour, enter 2.5 in the DRY Cup column. You will have to make a judgment as to whether the ingredient is dry or wet. In general, use the form that the ingredient is in when you add it. An exception to this would be an ingredient that is going to melt when heat is applied. They are considered liquids. Typical ingredients in this category would include butter, margarine, fresh cheeses, and shortening.

Some ingredients should not be computed. Do not include the following ingredients in the calculation:

1. Yeast

2. Raisins or nuts added at the mix cycle

3. Seeds added at the mix cycle

You should count raisins, nuts and seeds added initially as dry ingredients. The general rule is that if the ingredient will add to the stiffness of the dough, count it as a dry ingredient.

After you have entered all the ingredients, total each column and place the sum in the subtotal box. Then multiply each subtotal by the multiplier specified and place the result in the total box. Add the totals for dry ingredients together for a grand total (in teaspoons) and do the same for wet ingredients. Finally, divide the dry grand total by the wet grand total to compute the ratio for this recipe.

For best results, the ratio should fall within the liquidity ratio range designation for your machine (see step 2). If it only misses by a few points, it will probably be satisfactory. If the ratio for the recipe is below the range, your dough might be too wet. Try a slight reduction in liquid ingredients or an increase in dry ingredients and recalculate. If the ratio is above the range, it is too dry. Either reduce the dry ingredients slightly, or add liquid.

Chances are, you will still need to experiment to get the recipe just right, but this calculation will give you a good start and place you well beyond the "trial and error" stage.

Step Four: Determine the Overall Bulk

You certainly do not want to overflow your machine with your test recipe, so make sure the bulk does not exceed the capacity of your machine. If you have a 1 pound machine, you should make sure your recipe does not call for more than 2½ cups of flour. If you have a 1½ pound machine, 3½ to 3¾ cups of flour are about the limit. For a 2 pound machine, 4 to 5 cups would be the limit. If you need to adjust the recipe, make sure you make equal adjustments of wet and dry ingredients to maintain the liquidity ratio of the recipe.

Improving and Tailoring Your Recipes

After your initial attempt at your newly converted recipe, you may want to adjust the recipe to increase or decrease bulk, reduce or increase rise, or alter texture or taste. Experiment with the recipe until you have perfected it. Part of the enjoyment of a bread machine is being able to try new and exciting recipes and to be creative. Although the conversion process, as presented here, may seem somewhat better suited to a mathematician than an artist, science and art go hand in hand in bread baking. Once you get to know your machine and your ingredients, you will feel comfortable making substitutions, or even trying brand new creations, made from scratch.

Table 3. Dough Liquidity Calculation Worksheet

Ingredient	DRY			WET			
	t	T	C	t	T	C	oz
Subtotal							
Multiplier		3	48		3	48	6
TOTAL							
GRAND TOTAL							
Liquidity Ratio							

Instructions: 1. Use decimals for fractions (.5 teaspoon, etc.). 2. Subtotal each column. 3. Multiply the subtotal by the multiplier to obtain the total. Add the dry totals and the wet totals separately to obtain the wet and dry grand totals. 5. Divide the dry grand total by the wet grand total to get the liquidity ratio.

RECIPE POINTERS

Recipe Sizes

Three sizes are given for each of the recipes in this book, although smaller, and some larger, sizes are possible. I found in experimenting with a possible ¾ pound size loaf that the machines tended to overbake the small loaves, and that they typically were too dry. Consequently, I decided to present here only the three sizes that will be accommodated by virtually all bread machines.

Recipe sizes refer to finished weight, not dimensions. The finished dimensions of the bread will depend to a great extent on baking conditions, amounts of yeast used, and types of ingredients. A 1-pound loaf of white bread, for example, might be larger than a 1½-pound loaf of rye bread, which tends to be more densely textured.

Modifications for Specific Machines

I have tried to include recipes that will work in any machine. On the 1-pound recipes, I found virtually no difference when testing the recipes in different machines. With the larger loaves, however, I noticed that some machines will not tolerate a stiff dough as well as others. If your machine's motor seems to be laboring with a certain dough, you might consider adding an extra tablespoon or two tablespoons more liquid. This will lower the liquidity ratio slightly, making the dough less stiff. As mentioned previously, you will come to recognize the "normal" sounds of your machine and will be able to identify those situations when slight recipe modifications are needed.

The other major difference between machines is in their rise cycles and the amount of yeast called for. I have tried to optimize the amount of yeast in the recipes to be suitable to all machines. If your machine has a dispenser or other device that causes a change in the amount of yeast normally used, you should make the modification to the amount of yeast in the recipe.

Many machines have "rapid bread" cycles that allow you to bake a loaf faster (single rise, rather than the usual double rise). When using the rapid bread cycle on your machine, double the amount of yeast that is normally called for, or consult your owner's manual for the proper yeast adjustment.

Ingredients

There is a wide variety of ingredients called for in these recipes. Many are available at your local supermarket, but some must be purchased at health food stores. Some mail order sources are available if you do not have a health food store nearby. Here is a summary of important information about some of the main ingredients used in the recipes in this book.

White Flours

All wheat-based flours are made from various combinations of three different varieties of wheat: hard wheat, soft wheat, and durum wheat. Of the three, hard wheat is highest in protein content and best for bread-making. Soft wheat makes finer flour with less protein content. Durum wheat is used for semolina flour, which is a high-protein flour specifically used for pasta making. Flours vary by the combination of these wheat types used.

There are two main types of white flours, *all-purpose flour* and *bread flour*. All-purpose flour is made from about 80% hard wheat and 20% soft wheat. Bread flour is made from 100% hard wheat, giving it slightly better breadmaking characteristics. Both varieties are available in most grocery stores. Bread flour is slightly higher in gluten content than all-purpose flour and will usually rise more. You should try to use the type of flour called for in the recipe. Substituting all-purpose flour for bread flour is permissible; however, it may slightly change the texture of the bread and cause it to rise less.

You will also note that all-purpose flour is available both in *bleached* and *unbleached* varieties. Bleached flour is treated during the milling process with chlorine, which shortens the processing time in whitening the flour. Unbleached flour is refined without the chlorination, but takes longer to process as a result, and will generally cost more. If the process has been speeded up by the addition of a chemical called bromate, the flour will be labeled as "bromated" flour.

On supermarket shelves you will often see pastry flour, cake flour, and self-rising flours. Pastry flour and cake flour are very finely ground flours and are made from 100% soft wheat. They are not suitable for breadmaking. Self-rising flour contains salt and baking soda and is not useful for breadmaking either.

Whole Grains

Whole Wheat Flour: This flour is ground from the complete wheat berry and contains the wheat germ and the wheat bran. It is coarser and heavier than white flour, and does not rise as much. I purchase fresh wheat in bulk and grind it myself for the best-tasting bread; however, this may be more than most people can do. Grocery stores carry whole wheat flour, usually right alongside the white flour.

Graham Flour: In the early 20th century, Sylvester Graham publicly argued the merits of grains in the diet, wheat in particular. Graham flour is essentially equivalent to whole wheat flour, except that the milling process varies somewhat, with a slightly coarser grind and larger particles of bran throughout. This gives it a sweeter flavor than whole wheat flour. In recipes calling for graham flour, you may freely substitute whole wheat flour if graham flour is not available.

Semolina Flour: This is whole grain durum wheat with the bran layer removed. It can be used for breadmaking, particularly when used in combination with bread flour.

Bran: Bran is the outer covering of the kernel of wheat or oat. It is rich in fiber and is called for in small quantities in some recipes. Recently, much has been said about the benefits of oat bran. Both oat and wheat bran are available at most grocery stores.

Wheat Germ: This part of the wheat grain is readily available in grocery stores. Like bran, it is used sparingly in recipes. Wheat germ should be kept in the refrigerator after the container is opened.

Gluten Flour: Gluten is a protein found in the wheat berry. Gluten is necessary for rising to occur. When mixed with water, it forms an elastic substance that catches the gas bubbles formed by the leavening agent. Flours made from wheat, including whole wheat flour, white flour, and bread flour, contain plenty of gluten, but some whole grain flours do not. I have found that some gluten flour added to the mix when using a low-gluten flour will make for better rising and texture. Gluten flour can be purchased at any good health food store. A few recipes call for gluten flour, but most make it optional. Some people are allergic to gluten. Those individuals should stick to low-gluten flours, including rye and quinoa.

Rye Flour: This flour is very low in gluten content, so it will not rise when used by itself. Most of the recipes in this book call for a mixture of rye and another flour with a higher gluten content. This will let the bread rise.

Barley Flour: Barley flour lends a sweet taste and smooth texture to bread. Most recipes call for it in combination with white or wheat flour, since it has no gluten content. You will probably have to go to a health food store to find barley flour.

Buckwheat: Buckwheat is a strong-tasting flour for which some aficionados have acquired a real taste. In spite of its name, it is not made from wheat. Buckwheat is actually a grass, which yields groats, which can then be ground into flour. It is usually used in somewhat small quantities, but if you develop a liking for the strong flavor it presents, you can use it in combination with whole wheat flour. Called *kasha* in some parts of the world.

Cracked Wheat: As its name implies, this is part of the wheat berry. It is very hard and usually requires some soaking before use. It is widely available at health food stores and can often also be found in grocery stores.

7-Grain Cereal: This cereal has an appearance similar to cracked wheat, but consists of seven grains, including wheat, barley, corn, and oats. It is available at health food stores.

Oats: Use rolled oats (oatmeal) for your oat recipes. Just use the type available at the grocery store. When measuring rolled oats, pack them down into the measuring cup to get a full measure.

Oat Flour: This is flour ground specifically for bread from the oat groats. Since it has no gluten content, it has to be used in combination with a wheat flour of some kind.

Quinoa: This flour is imported from South America; it was a staple grain of the Incas in ancient times. It has one of the highest protein contents of any grain, and gives bread a somewhat nutty flavor.

Soy Flour: This flour is ground from soybeans; it is high in protein content at about 40–50%. It is very nutritious, but not flavorful, and is often used as an ingredient for enriching the nutritional value of bread.

Millet: This is a small, yellow, perfectly round grain. It can be used in bread whole, raw or cooked, or milled into flour.

Rice: Rice, a staple throughout the world, can be cooked and added to bread, or made into flour. The flour absorbs moisture more slowly than most flours, so it is well known among bakers as an excellent flour for dusting breads and pizza.

Liquids

Water is called for in most recipes. It should be used warm (between 100 and 110°F (37.8 to 43.3°C). I have found that hot tap water works fine. Don't heat the water any further, because water that is too hot can kill the yeast.

Milk: When milk is called for in a recipe, I use 1% or skim milk. In fact, the nutritional counts in the recipes in this book are calculated using values for 1% milk. If you do not have milk on hand, try using dry milk and adding the requisite amount of water to the recipe. Milk should usually be warmed to 100 to 110°F (37.8 to 43.3°C); the microwave works well for this at 45 seconds on high. Be careful not to overheat the milk, or you will kill the yeast.

Buttermilk: You can use buttermilk in its fresh form, or purchase buttermilk powder to mix it as needed. I do the latter, since I don't particularly like to drink buttermilk, and since recipes usually call for only small amounts. In most recipes, it is safe to substitute low-fat or skim milk for buttermilk. You may sacrifice some flavor, but it will be result in a lower fat content for your bread.

Cream: There are several types of cream available at most grocery stores: heavy cream, light cream, whipping cream, and half-and-half. Some recipes call for heavy or light cream, but I have found that whipping cream works fine in most cases where cream is called for. Note that *whipping cream* and *whipped cream* are different. Whipped cream has had sugar added and is already in whipped form. Whipping cream comes in a carton and pours like milk.

Eggs: Most of the recipes in this book have been formulated to call for whole eggs, rather than portions of eggs or egg whites only. However, if you are concerned about the cholesterol in eggs, you may freely substitute any commercially available egg substitute. Use ¼ cup (4 tablespoons) of egg substitute instead of each whole egg. You also may use powdered eggs, ¼ cup of mixed eggs instead of each whole egg.

Butter: Many of the recipes in this book call for butter. You may substitute margarine or vegetable oil in the same quantities for butter. Butter, however, will provide the most flavor. I keep my butter in the freezer because spoilage is the biggest problem with real butter. When I need butter, I remove it from the freezer, cut the required quantity from the cube, and replace the butter in the freezer. It takes only a few minutes for the portion of butter to get to room temperature,; then it can be placed in the bread pan. There is no need to melt butter or margarine before adding to the recipes, but it is best if the butter chunks are 1 tablespoon or smaller.

Olive Oil: I have used olive oil exclusively in these recipes, instead of calling for other oils. The taste is better and olive oil has no cholesterol. However, if you prefer another type of cooking oil, such as canola, corn oil, or any other vegetable oil, you may freely substitute. If you use olive oil, use a good grade of extra virgin olive oil.

Other Ingredients

Salt: Salt is a yeast inhibitor, and is necessary in most recipes. If you are on a salt-restricted diet, you can eliminate the salt from the recipes. You should know, however, that if you do so, the characteristics of the bread will change. The bread will rise differently; it may rise too much and then collapse. The resulting texture may also be different. Keep in mind that other ingredients often have salt content. If you are on a salt-restricted diet, check the nutritional values for each recipe to see if there are "hidden salts" in the recipe. Butter, for example, is one of the ingredients that has a sodium content. Avoid using salt substitutes as alternatives. They are chemically based and do not have the yeast inhibiting properties of real salt. They will do no good, and they may cause other chemical reactions that will change the properties of your bread.

Yeast: The recipes in this book call for yeast in teaspoons. I use active dry yeast, and I buy it in bulk. If kept in the refrigerator, it will last a long time. In fact, with my bread machine running, a supply of yeast doesn't last long at all. If you use cake yeast, you will need to make the conversion from teaspoons. If you purchase yeast in packets at the grocery store, one packet contains one scant tablespoon, or about 2¼ teaspoons of yeast. Do not use rapid rise yeast in these recipes.

Not all bread machines use the same amount of yeast in the large recipes. This is due to differences in cycle lengths and the yeast dispensing mechanisms available on a few machines. If a recipe does not rise enough, try adding an extra ½ teaspoon of yeast.

Yeast feeds on sugars and is inhibited by salts. It likes a warm environment, but too much heat will kill it. Most traditional bread recipes will require you to "proof" your yeast before using it. Proofing means mixing the yeast with sugar and warm (105 to 110°F, 40.6 to 43.3°C) water to allow it to become active before adding it to the recipe. Proofing is not necessary with bread machines; however, it is a good technique to use if you want to make sure your yeast is active (not too old). Yeast can be placed directly into the bread pan. When it touches liquid, it will begin to be active.

Sugars and Sweeteners: These are necessary in all bread recipes because they provide food for the yeast. Recipes in this book call for sugar (white, granulated), honey, syrup, molasses, or brown sugar. Molasses comes in various types, but I use blackstrap when baking. I have tried others, and haven't noticed any appreciable difference in the outcome, so use whatever molasses you happen to have on hand if a recipe calls for it. By the way, if the recipe calls for olive oil and honey or molasses, measure the olive oil first and don't rinse the spoon off. The honey or molasses will slide right out of the spoon into your pan!

Dough Enhancer: This product is difficult to find. Even health food stores may not carry it. You can find it at baking specialty stores or obtain it through mail order. Dough enhancer is a tofu (soybean) based powder that makes the dough smoother, and it is what commercial bakers often use to obtain the smooth-textured bread you buy at the store.

Spices, Nuts, and Seeds: These ingredients are called for in wide variety in recipes. I found most of the spices, seeds, and nuts called for in these recipes at the grocery store. If you cannot find them, you might try your health food store, which will usually stock some of the lesser known spices. Feel free to experiment with spices, adding more of spices you like and deleting those you do not. Often it is the blend of spices that makes the flavor, rather than any single spice, in those recipes calling for two or three different spices.

You will find that your spice cabinet enlarges as you bake more breads. Eventually, you will have a stock of almost any spice called for in a recipe. Preserving spices and seeds is not a problem, but preserving fresh nuts is. A few recipes call for fresh-chopped nuts. Use any type of nuts you enjoy, but keep in mind that nuts will go rancid if not used in a short period, so keep your supply of nuts fresh.

The Order of Ingredients

There are two ways to place ingredients in the baking pan: Dry ingredients first or wet ingredients first. Most machines call for wet ingredients first, so that order is used in this book. Actually, dry first will work in all machines, except when you want to use a timed bake function. In that case, you will not want to activate the yeast until the baking process starts, so wet ingredients will have to go first, with yeast last. The machines that recommend dry ingredients first call for yeast as the first ingredient, followed by the other dry ingredients and, finally, the liquids. If your machine calls for dry ingredients first, add the ingredients to the pan in reverse order from that listed here.

Preparation of Ingredients

Most bread recipes call for all ingredients to be at room temperature, except for liquids, which are sometimes called for at 105 to 110°F (40.6 to 43.3°C). I have experimented with this and have not had real problems adding refrigerated ingredients. Rather than worry too much about it, just try setting all of your ingredients out first and then adding them. Once you get to the refrigerated ingredients, they have usually approached room temperature anyway.

When warm water is called for, it should be in the 105 to 110°F (40.6 to 43.3°C) range. I used to use a thermometer to make sure that the water was the correct temperature; however, I soon gave up on that when I found that hot tap water usually approached that range. Hot tap water varies, however, so make sure that yours is not too hot (too hot presents a much bigger problem than too cold).

Milk can be measured and then left to reach room temperature, or you can use the microwave to warm it up. Just be sure that if you use the microwave, you don't overheat the milk, which is easy to do in the microwave. If you overheat it, let it sit until it cools to 110°F (43.3°C) or lower before adding it to the bread pan.

For measuring flour and dry ingredients, I use the dip-and-level method, rather than the spoon method. For the dip-and-level method, simply dip your measuring cup into the flour and level it with a knife or other flat edge.

Making Substitutions and Modifications

I would recommend that you try the recipes as given the first time. Then if you want to make substitutions or modifications, experiment all you want. I have found that the best way to experiment is to alter one item at a time. If you alter too many things at once and the recipe fails, you will not be able to determine the cause of the failure. However, if you only altered one ingredient, you will know that the alteration was the only variable that could have caused failure.

You can freely make the substitutions mentioned in the ingredients section, including margarine for butter, low-fat or skim milk for buttermilk, egg substitutes for whole eggs, and all-purpose flour for bread flour. Keep in mind, however, that these substitutions will alter the original recipe somewhat and results will be different.

Avoid the use of chemically based substitutes, such as sugar and salt substitutes. These chemically based products may taste the same in coffee or soft drinks, but they break down differently from sodium or sugar in baking environments and will not work properly with yeast breads. It is better simply to eliminate salt, for example, than to use a salt substitute. Yeast feeds fine on sugar, but doesn't have much of a taste for artificial sweeteners.

Once you have gained a feel for a recipe, and for your machine, feel free to experiment. Most of the recipes in this book were developed that way, and you can have a lot of fun trying new and wonderful ideas. It is best to begin with established recipes and make successive alterations until you arrive at the perfect bread. Be sure and keep a log of your changes and the results. That way you can learn as you go and won't repeat mistakes. It also helps to have a basic understanding of the principles of baking with yeast, and of the characteristics of the ingredients you are using.

Slicing Your Bread

When you get that loaf out of the machine, it smells wonderful. In fact, it has probably filled the whole house with the unmistakable odor of baking bread! You may want to dig in and eat the whole loaf right on the spot. Of course, you can do that. There is nothing better than fresh, hot bread. However, if your aim is to slice the bread and keep it for a few days, or use it for tomorrow's breakfast or lunch, then you will need to slice it more carefully.

Bread is best sliced after it has had a chance to cool completely. It then regains some of its stiffness and is much easier to handle. Slicing hot bread is a bit like trying to slice jello. As you cut, the bread gives, and it is difficult to get a good, straight slice.

For best results, remove your bread from the machine as soon as the "all done" alarm sounds. Place it on a cooling rack and let it cool completely (probably an hour or so). Although many machines now include cooling cycles, they cannot completely cool the bread, because the bread is still in the pan, where moisture and heat are trapped.

To slice the bread, use a serrated knife designed especially for slicing bread. Use a sawing motion and let the knife do the work. Putting too much downward pressure on the bread will smash it down and will give you uneven slices.

I inherited a meat slicer and don't use it for meat at all, but I have found it to be a wonderful bread slicer. I just set the thickness and the serrated blade cuts right through my cool loaf. If you have a slicer and your loaf is too big for it (the Welbilt loaves are too big for mine), cut the loaf in half lengthwise, making two half rounds. Then slice each half loaf with your slicer.

Nutritional Values

I am convinced that much of the consumer motivation behind the boom in bread machines sales is due to a desire to eat healthier foods. Whole grain breads are wonderful sources of nutrients, have no chemical preservatives, and taste great.

Each recipe is followed by the nutritional values. The values are per loaf, so to obtain a serving value, estimate how many slices you will make from the loaf and divide the value by the number of slices in the loaf. The nutritional values are estimates only, and should not be construed as anything else. They were derived by using *MasterCook* software package. Each of the ingredients in the recipes was calculated and totaled for each size of loaf. Below is an explanation of some of the main values used.

Calories are total calories for a loaf.

Protein is measured in grams. You will not find breads to be high in protein content, but when taken with other foods (meats or legumes like beans) that are high in protein, a healthy combination is made.

Carbohydrates are also measured in grams. Carbohydrates, especially from whole grain sources, provide a good ratio of nutrients to calories (the opposite of "empty calories") and should constitute 45 to 48% of our daily intake of calories.

Fat is listed as total fat and saturated fat. We should try to reduce the amount of fats in our diet, and saturated fats should be avoided as much as possible. Government recommendations are that we limit our total calories from fat to 30% of our daily intake of calories, and limit saturated fat calories to only 10%. I have computed the percentage of calories from fat for each recipe, in addition to giving you the amount of total fat and saturated fat in grams. These breads are very healthy from the standpoint of percentage of calories from fats.

Cholesterol content is measured in milligrams. Cholesterol is only found in animal fats.

Sodium is measured for each recipe (in milligrams); it can derive not only from the salt added to the recipe, but from the sodium content of some other recipe ingredients. If you are on a low-sodium diet, you can reduce the salt content of the loaf, with the limitations discussed previously.

Fiber is important to a growing number of health-conscious individuals. The fiber content of each recipe is measured in grams. Fiber takes several forms, and so the figure given is a total figure that includes both dietary and crude fiber. Most nutritionists would recommend at least 25 grams of fiber per day in your diet.

Recipe Testing

Your strategy for testing recipes should be to try the 1-pound loaf first, even if you have a 1½ or 2 pound capacity machine. This offers three advantages:

1. You can make sure you like the taste and texture of the bread, while using a small quantity of ingredients for the first test.

2. You can make sure the bread works well in your machine with fewer ingredients at risk.

3. You can make sure that your particular baking conditions will not produce an oversize loaf, with little risk of a mess if they do.

Once you have tested a bread, make alterations to suit your taste, baking conditions, and machine. For example, you can increase or reduce yeast amounts, liquidity, substitute seeds or nuts, or make other ingredient substitutions. I would highly recommend, however, that you try the recipe once as given before making your own modifications. That gives you a basis upon which to make your changes and a point of reference, as discussed earlier. After that, be creative.

THE HISTORY OF BREAD

It is unclear where the wheat plant originated. Historians know that it was cultivated in southwestern Asia as early as 15,000 BC. In 1948, archeologists from the University of Chicago unearthed an Iraqi village, dated at about 6,700 BC, and found the berries from several types of wheat.

Over the centuries, it probably became obvious to early people, mostly nomadic hunters and gatherers, that the wheat plant could be cultivated. These early farmers also discovered that wheat could be stored and used as both food and seed for the next crop.

Early man probably chewed wheat berries, rather than grinding and baking them. Later, he learned to grind the wheat into flour and use it to make an early form of hot cereal or porridge. Eventually, he learned to bake the dough. This early bread was not leavened, and was probably a densely textured flat bread.

Around 3,000 BC, the Egyptians discovered how to make leavened bread. As leavening was developed, originally with the use of sourdough starters, wheat remained the grain of choice, since it had the best properties and cellular structure for rising. Egyptian traders spread the idea to Greece and Rome, where hundreds of varieties of bread were developed.

In medieval Europe, baker's guilds were developed, as baking bread became both an occupation and an art form.

Commercial bread, as we know it, is a relatively recent product. As late as the 1940s, most bread eaten in America was homemade. Today, millions of loaves of bread are baked daily in completely automated bakeries, but the quality of the bread has been somewhat compromised in the process, due to the addition of preservatives to lengthen shelf life and other time-saving manufacturing devices.

Today, the best bread is still homemade. Bread machines were developed to give you the best of both worlds: convenience and homemade quality. You can choose the type of bread you want, control the ingredients, and eat it fresh from the oven (or bread machine).

WHITE BREADS

The recipes in this section are all variations of white bread. They are typically finely textured and high rising, and they go well with just about any other food. The breads range from slightly sweet to spicy to fruity. Experiment with the recipes by substituting the fruits, nuts, and spices of your choice.

Basic White Bread

This is the best basic white-bread recipe I have found for the bread machine. It is consistently good when baked in different machines and goes with about any meal. It also makes excellent toast.

1½-pound

1 teaspoon active dry yeast

3 tablespoons sugar

3 cups bread flour

1½ teaspoons salt

1½ tablespoons butter

4½ ounces warm milk

4½ ounces warm water

1-pound

½ teaspoon active dry yeast

2 tablespoons sugar

2 cups bread flour

1 teaspoon salt

1 tablespoon butter

3 ounces warm milk

3 ounces warm water

Note:

For Panasonic/National machines, use 2 teaspoons of yeast for the 1½-pound loaf.

NUTRITIONAL ANALYSIS			
	1½-POUND	1-POUND	
TOTAL CALORIES	1837	1234	
TOTAL PROTEIN	55	36	GRAMS
TOTAL CARBOHYDRATES	341	227	GRAMS
TOTAL FAT	26	17	GRAMS
TOTAL SATURATED FAT	12	8	GRAMS
TOTAL CHOLESTEROL	52	35	MILLIGRAMS
TOTAL SODIUM	3276	2184	MILLIGRAMS
TOTAL FIBRE	6	4	GRAMS
% CALORIES FROM FAT	13	13	

Challah Bread (Jewish Egg Bread)

A festive white bread, challah is rich with eggs, butter, and honey. You will find it much richer than basic white bread.

1½-pound

2½ teaspoons active dry yeast

1½ teaspoons poppy seeds

3 cups bread flour

1½ teaspoons salt

3 tablespoons honey

3 tablespoons butter

3 eggs

6 ounces warm water

1-pound

1½ teaspoons active dry yeast

1 teaspoon poppy seeds

2 cups bread flour

1 teaspoon salt

2 tablespoons honey

3 tablespoons butter

2 eggs

4 ounces warm water

Note:

For Panasonic/National machines, use 3½ teaspoons of yeast for the 1½-pound loaf.

NUTRITIONAL ANALYSIS			
	1½-POUND	1-POUND	
TOTAL CALORIES	2230	1486	
TOTAL PROTEIN	72	48	GRAMS
TOTAL CARBOHYDRATES	351	234	GRAMS
TOTAL FAT	58	39	GRAMS
TOTAL SATURATED FAT	27	18	GRAMS
TOTAL CHOLESTEROL	732	488	MILLIGRAMS
TOTAL SODIUM	3401	2267	MILLIGRAMS
TOTAL FIBRE	7	5	GRAMS
% CALORIES FROM FAT	24	24	

Zuñi Bread

This Southwest Indian bread combines the high-rising texture of white bread with the crunchiness of corn bread. It is excellent with a good, hot Southwestern chili. Note that all-purpose flour is used instead of bread flour in this recipe.

1½-pound

1½ teaspoons active dry yeast

2½ cups all-purpose flour

¾ cup yellow cornmeal

1 teaspoon salt

1½ tablespoons molasses

1½ tablespoons olive oil

1 cup warm water

1-pound

1 teaspoon active dry yeast

1¾ cups all-purpose flour

½ cup yellow cornmeal

½ teaspoon salt

1 tablespoon molasses

1 tablespoon olive oil

5½ ounces warm water

Notes:
1. For Panasonic/National machines, use 2½ teaspoons of yeast for the 1½-pound loaf.
2. For DAK/Welbilt machines, add 1 extra tablespoon of warm water in the 1½-pound recipe only.

NUTRITIONAL ANALYSIS			
	1½-POUND	1-POUND	
TOTAL CALORIES	1848	1273	
TOTAL PROTEIN	50	35	GRAMS
TOTAL CARBOHYDRATES	341	236	GRAMS
TOTAL FAT	29	20	GRAMS
TOTAL SATURATED FAT	4	3	GRAMS
TOTAL CHOLESTEROL	0	0	MILLIGRAMS
TOTAL SODIUM	2194	1107	MILLIGRAMS
TOTAL FIBRE	16	11	GRAMS
% CALORIES FROM FAT	14	14	

Sheepherder's Bread

This is a favorite of many of my testers, especially those who like French breads. The recipe is simple but tasty, like those used by sheepherders in days of old. Time this bread to be done right before dinner; then tear it apart, rather than slice it, while still hot. Note that all-purpose flour is used to give it an authentic texture.

1½-pound

1½ teaspoons active dry yeast

2 tablespoons sugar

3 cups all-purpose flour

1 teaspoon salt

2½ tablespoons butter

1 cup warm water

1-pound

1 teaspoon active dry yeast

4 teaspoons sugar

2 cups all-purpose flour

¼ teaspoon salt

1½ tablespoons butter

5½ ounces warm water

Note:

For Panasonic/National machines, use 2 teaspoons of yeast for the 1½-pound loaf.

NUTRITIONAL ANALYSIS			
	1½-POUND	1-POUND	
TOTAL CALORIES	1838	1208	
TOTAL PROTEIN	51	34	GRAMS
TOTAL CARBOHYDRATES	323	216	GRAMS
TOTAL FAT	36	22	GRAMS
TOTAL SATURATED FAT	19	11	GRAMS
TOTAL CHOLESTEROL	78	47	MILLIGRAMS
TOTAL SODIUM	2142	1073	MILLIGRAMS
TOTAL FIBRE	7	4	GRAMS
% CALORIES FROM FAT	17	16	

Ham-and-Cheese Bread

Real cheese and pieces of ham make this a tangy, tasty bread. It is very moist and rich. It's literally a sandwich in a loaf of bread.

1½-pound	1-pound
2 teaspoons active dry yeast	1½ teaspoons active dry yeast
3½ teaspoons sugar	2½ teaspoons sugar
¼ cup chopped ham pieces	3 tablespoons chopped ham pieces
½ cup grated Swiss cheese	¼ cup grated Swiss cheese
2½ tablespoons dehydrated minced onion	5 teaspoons dehydrated minced onion
¾ cup grated cheddar cheese	½ cup grated cheddar cheese
1½ teaspoons paprika	1 teaspoon paprika
2½ tablespoons grated Parmesan cheese	5 teaspoons grated Parmesan cheese
1 teaspoon dry mustard	½ teaspoon dry mustard
½ teaspoon salt	¼ teaspoon salt
2½ cups bread flour	1¾ cups bread flour
2½ tablespoons butter	5 teaspoons butter
7 ounces warm milk	4½ ounces warm milk

Notes:
1. For Panasonic/National machines, use 3 teaspoons of yeast for the 1½-pound loaf.
2. This bread has a high liquid content, so the top may fall during baking.
3. Use a light crust setting. The crust will be somewhat darker than usual, due to the fresh cheese in the recipe.

NUTRITIONAL ANALYSIS			
	1½-POUND	1-POUND	
TOTAL CALORIES	2354	1585	
TOTAL PROTEIN	97	64	GRAMS
TOTAL CARBOHYDRATES	290	202	GRAMS
TOTAL FAT	89	57	GRAMS
TOTAL SATURATED FAT	52	33	GRAMS
TOTAL CHOLESTEROL	237	150	MILLIGRAMS
TOTAL SODIUM	2698	2142	MILLIGRAMS
TOTAL FIBRE	7	5	GRAMS
% CALORIES FROM FAT	34	33	

Sour-Cream Bread

Somewhat tangy with poppy seeds, this bread doesn't rise as much as traditional white breads. However, it is excellent for cold-cuts sandwiches.

1½-pound

1 teaspoon active dry yeast

2 tablespoons sugar

3 cups bread flour

1 tablespoon poppy seeds

1½ teaspoons salt

1 cup sour cream

1½ ounces warm water

1-pound

½ teaspoon active dry yeast

4 teaspoons sugar

2 cups bread flour

2 teaspoons poppy seeds

1 teaspoon salt

¾ cup sour cream

1 tablespoon warm water

Notes:
1. For Panasonic/National machines, use 2 teaspoons of yeast for the 1½-pound loaf.
2. For DAK/Welbilt machines, use 2½ ounces of warm water in the 1½-pound loaf.

NUTRITIONAL ANALYSIS			
	1½-POUND	1-POUND	
TOTAL CALORIES	2122	1454	
TOTAL PROTEIN	59	40	GRAMS
TOTAL CARBOHYDRATES	335	224	GRAMS
TOTAL FAT	59	43	GRAMS
TOTAL SATURATED FAT	31	23	GRAMS
TOTAL CHOLESTEROL	102	77	MILLIGRAMS
TOTAL SODIUM	3331	2231	MILLIGRAMS
TOTAL FIBRE	7	5	GRAMS
% CALORIES FROM FAT	25	27	

Sally Lunn Bread

The origins of the name of this bread are unclear, but it is a rich variation on the white-bread theme with egg and extra sugar. It makes a rich sandwich bread and is excellent for toast. Sally Lunn is a high riser.

1½-pound

1 teaspoon active dry yeast

4 tablespoons sugar

3 cups bread flour

1 teaspoon salt

5 ounces warm milk

2 eggs

5½ tablespoons butter

½ cup warm water

1-pound

½ teaspoon active dry yeast

3 tablespoons sugar

2 cups bread flour

½ teaspoon salt

3½ ounces warm milk

1 egg

3½ tablespoons butter

1½ ounces warm water

Note:
For Panasonic/National machines, use 2 teaspoons of yeast for the 1½-pound loaf.

NUTRITIONAL ANALYSIS			
	1½-POUND	1-POUND	
TOTAL CALORIES	2440	1601	
TOTAL PROTEIN	68	43	GRAMS
TOTAL CARBOHYDRATES	355	241	GRAMS
TOTAL FAT	81	51	GRAMS
TOTAL SATURATED FAT	44	28	GRAMS
TOTAL CHOLESTEROL	603	326	MILLIGRAMS
TOTAL SODIUM	2348	1191	MILLIGRAMS
TOTAL FIBRE	6	4	GRAMS
% CALORIES FROM FAT	30	28	

Picnic Bread

Picnic bread is fun for cold-cuts sandwiches because it already contains relish! This bread has a sweet and spicy taste and slightly yellow color. It looks and tastes great.

1½-pound

1½ teaspoons active dry yeast

2 tablespoons sugar

3 cups bread flour

1½ teaspoons salt

¼ cup sweet pickle relish
    (drained)

1½ tablespoons butter

6½ ounces warm milk

3 tablespoons warm water

1-pound

1 teaspoon active dry yeast

1½ tablespoons sugar

2 cups bread flour

1 teaspoon salt

2 tablespoons sweet pickle relish
    (drained)

1 tablespoon butter

½ cup warm milk

2 tablespoons warm water

Note:

For Panasonic/National machines, use 2½ teaspoons of yeast for the 1½-pound loaf.

NUTRITIONAL ANALYSIS			
	1½-POUND	1-POUND	
TOTAL CALORIES	1904	1259	
TOTAL PROTEIN	58	38	GRAMS
TOTAL CARBOHYDRATES	353	234	GRAMS
TOTAL FAT	27	18	GRAMS
TOTAL SATURATED FAT	13	9	GRAMS
TOTAL CHOLESTEROL	55	36	MILLIGRAMS
TOTAL SODIUM	3735	2414	MILLIGRAMS
TOTAL FIBRE	7	4	GRAMS
% CALORIES FROM FAT	13	13	

Buttermilk & Honey Bread

This traditional farm bread is a good white-bread staple, making it excellent for sandwiches or toast.

1½-pound

1 teaspoon active dry yeast

3 cups bread flour

1½ teaspoons salt

½ teaspoon sugar

1½ tablespoons honey

1 tablespoon butter

¾ cup buttermilk

3 ounces warm water

1-pound

½ teaspoon active dry yeast

2 cups bread flour

1 teaspoon salt

½ teaspoon sugar

1 tablespoon honey

1 tablespoon butter

3 ounces buttermilk

3 ounces warm water

Note:

For machines with yeast dispensers, use 2 teaspoons of yeast for the 1½-pound loaf.

NUTRITIONAL ANALYSIS			
	1½-POUND	1-POUND	
TOTAL CALORIES	1777	1205	
TOTAL PROTEIN	58	37	GRAMS
TOTAL CARBOHYDRATES	336	223	GRAMS
TOTAL FAT	20	17	GRAMS
TOTAL SATURATED FAT	9	8	GRAMS
TOTAL CHOLESTEROL	47	39	MILLIGRAMS
TOTAL SODIUM	3323	2196	MILLIGRAMS
TOTAL FIBRE	6	4	GRAMS
% CALORIES FROM FAT	10	12	

Buttermilk Potato Bread

The potato and buttermilk make this a richer-than-normal white bread. It's excellent with soup.

1½-pound

1½ teaspoons active dry yeast

3 cups bread flour

1½ teaspoons salt

1 tablespoon sugar

3 tablespoons instant mashed-potato flakes or buds

5 ounces warm water

1 tablespoon butter

½ cup buttermilk

1-pound

1 teaspoon active dry yeast

2 cups bread flour

1 teaspoon salt

2 teaspoons sugar

2 tablespoons instant mashed-potato flakes or buds

3½ ounces warm water

½ tablespoon butter

⅓ cup buttermilk

Note:

For machines with yeast dispensers, use 3 teaspoons of yeast for the 1½-pound loaf.

NUTRITIONAL ANALYSIS			
	1½-POUND	1-POUND	
TOTAL CALORIES	1748	1183	
TOTAL PROTEIN	57	41	GRAMS
TOTAL CARBOHYDRATES	325	221	GRAMS
TOTAL FAT	22	13	GRAMS
TOTAL SATURATED FAT	9	5	GRAMS
TOTAL CHOLESTEROL	41	28	MILLIGRAMS
TOTAL SODIUM	3420	2325	MILLIGRAMS
TOTAL FIBRE	7	4	GRAMS
% CALORIES FROM FAT	11	10	

Herb Cheddar Bread

The spices and cheese in this bread give it a wonderful tangy taste and moist texture. It is especially good with soup or salad.

1½-pound	1-pound
1½ teaspoons active dry yeast	1 teaspoon active dry yeast
3 cups bread flour	2 cups + 2 tablespoons bread flour
1 teaspoon tarragon	½ teaspoon tarragon
1½ teaspoons chervil	1 teaspoon chervil
1½ teaspoons basil	1 teaspoon basil
1 teaspoon salt	½ teaspoon salt
1½ teaspoons sugar	1 teaspoon sugar
½ cup grated cheddar cheese	⅓ cup grated cheddar cheese
1½ tablespoons olive oil	1 tablespoon olive oil
7 ounces warm water	5 ounces warm water

Notes:

1. For machines with yeast dispensers, use 3 teaspoons of yeast for the 1½-pound loaf.
2. The dough ball will be somewhat dry at first, but this will change as the cheese is heated and melts. For low-power motors, the motor may labor with the large recipe. If this happens, add 2 extra tablespoons of warm water.

NUTRITIONAL ANALYSIS			
	1½-POUND	1-POUND	
TOTAL CALORIES	1925	1366	
TOTAL PROTEIN	65	46	GRAMS
TOTAL CARBOHYDRATES	306	221	GRAMS
TOTAL FAT	46	31	GRAMS
TOTAL SATURATED FAT	16	10	GRAMS
TOTAL CHOLESTEROL	60	39	MILLIGRAMS
TOTAL SODIUM	2490	1303	MILLIGRAMS
TOTAL FIBRE	7	5	GRAMS
% CALORIES FROM FAT	22	20	

Honey Seed Bread

This bread feature four popular seeds. Substitute other seeds, if you like.

1½-pound

1½ teaspoons active dry yeast

3 cups bread flour

½ tablespoon sesame seeds

½ tablespoon poppy seeds

½ tablespoon fennel seeds

1 tablespoon sunflower seeds

1½ teaspoons salt

½ teaspoon sugar

1 tablespoon honey

1 tablespoon butter

9 ounces warm milk

1-pound

1 teaspoon active dry yeast

2 cups bread flour

1 teaspoon sesame seeds

1 teaspoon poppy seeds

1 teaspoon fennel seeds

2 teaspoons sunflower seeds

1 teaspoon salt

½ teaspoon sugar

½ tablespoon honey

½ tablespoon butter

¾ cup warm milk

Notes:

1. For machines with yeast dispensers, use 3 teaspoons of yeast for the 1½-pound loaf.
2. For machines with low-power motors, add 2 tablespoons of warm milk to the 1½-pound recipe.
3. Seeds may be added at the mix cycle beep, if your machine is so equipped.

NUTRITIONAL ANALYSIS			
	1½-POUND	1-POUND	
TOTAL CALORIES	1932	1295	
TOTAL PROTEIN	65	44	GRAMS
TOTAL CARBOHYDRATES	338	225	GRAMS
TOTAL FAT	34	24	GRAMS
TOTAL SATURATED FAT	11	6	GRAMS
TOTAL CHOLESTEROL	42	23	MILLIGRAMS
TOTAL SODIUM	3354	2236	MILLIGRAMS
TOTAL FIBRE	8	5	GRAMS
% CALORIES FROM FAT	16	16	

Jalapeño Cheese Bread

For best results, use cheddar cheese that's made with jalapeño peppers. Such cheese is available in most supermarkets.

1½-pound

2 teaspoons active dry yeast

1¼ cup grated cheddar/jalapeño cheese

½ teaspoon cilantro (coriander)

3½ teaspoons sugar

½ teaspoon salt

1 teaspoon dry mustard

2½ tablespoons dried minced onion

2½ cups bread flour

7 ounces warm milk

2½ tablespoons butter

1-pound

1½ teaspoons active dry yeast

¾ cup grated cheddar/jalapeño cheese

½ teaspoon cilantro (coriander)

2½ teaspoons sugar

½ teaspoon salt

½ teaspoon dry mustard

1½ tablespoons dried minced onion

1⅔ cups bread flour

4½ ounces warm milk

1½ tablespoons butter

Note:
For machines with yeast dispensers, use 4 teaspoons of yeast for the 1½-pound loaf.

NUTRITIONAL ANALYSIS			
	1½-POUND	1-POUND	
TOTAL CALORIES	2262	1453	
TOTAL PROTEIN	87	56	GRAMS
TOTAL CARBOHYDRATES	287	191	GRAMS
TOTAL FAT	84	51	GRAMS
TOTAL SATURATED FAT	50	30	GRAMS
TOTAL CHOLESTEROL	235	141	MILLIGRAMS
TOTAL SODIUM	2062	1669	MILLIGRAMS
TOTAL FIBRE	6	4	GRAMS
% CALORIES FROM FAT	34	32	

Nut Bread

Nut bread is excellent with all kinds of cheese.

1½-pound

1½ teaspoons active dry yeast

2¼ cups + 2 tablespoons bread flour

½ cup chopped or ground nuts

½ cup brown sugar

½ cup warm milk

1 egg

½ teaspoon walnut or almond extract

½ teaspoon vanilla extract

2½ tablespoons butter

¼ cup warm water

1 teaspoon salt

1½ teaspoons cinnamon

1-pound

1 teaspoon active dry yeast

1½ cups + 2 tablespoons bread flour

⅓ cup chopped or ground nuts

⅓ cup brown sugar

2½ ounces warm milk

1 egg

½ teaspoon walnut or almond extract

½ teaspoon vanilla extract

1½ tablespoons butter

1½ ounces warm water

½ teaspoon salt

1 teaspoon cinnamon

Notes:
1. For machines with yeast dispensers, use 3 teaspoons of yeast for the 1½-pound loaf.
2. Measure the nuts whole before chopping or grinding them.

NUTRITIONAL ANALYSIS			
	1½-POUND	1-POUND	
TOTAL CALORIES	2365	1602	
TOTAL PROTEIN	60	42	GRAMS
TOTAL CARBOHYDRATES	362	244	GRAMS
TOTAL FAT	78	51	GRAMS
TOTAL SATURATED FAT	24	15	GRAMS
TOTAL CHOLESTEROL	296	263	MILLIGRAMS
TOTAL SODIUM	172	133	MILLIGRAMS
TOTAL FIBRE	8	6	GRAMS
% CALORIES FROM FAT	29	29	

Olive Bread

This bread has the flavor of olives and it has small olive pieces throughout the loaf.

1½-pound

1 teaspoon active dry yeast

5 tablespoons chopped black olives

3 cups + 1 tablespoon bread flour

1 teaspoon salt

2 tablespoons sugar

2 tablespoons olive oil

9 ounces warm water

1-pound

½ teaspoon active dry yeast

3½ tablespoons chopped black olives

2 cups bread flour

½ teaspoon salt

1½ tablespoons sugar

1 tablespoon olive oil

¾ cup warm water

Note:

For machines with yeast dispensers, use 2 teaspoons of yeast for the 1½-pound loaf.

NUTRITIONAL ANALYSIS			
	1½-POUND	1-POUND	
TOTAL CALORIES	1897	1212	
TOTAL PROTEIN	52	34	GRAMS
TOTAL CARBOHYDRATES	332	219	GRAMS
TOTAL FAT	38	21	GRAMS
TOTAL SATURATED FAT	5	3	GRAMS
TOTAL CHOLESTEROL	0	0	
SODIUM	2513	1332	MILLIGRAMS
TOTAL FIBRE	8	5	GRAMS
% CALORIES FROM FAT	18	16	

Potato Sesame Bread

The soft texture from the potato flakes combined with the nutty flavor of the sesame seeds make this an excellent breakfast bread.

1½-pound

1 teaspoon active dry yeast

2¾ cups bread flour

1 teaspoon parsley flakes

3 tablespoons sesame seeds

1 teaspoon salt

4 tablespoons instant mashed-potato flakes or buds

¼ cup instant dry milk

2 tablespoons sugar

½ cup buttermilk

2 eggs

2 tablespoons butter

5 ounces warm water

1-pound

½ teaspoon active dry yeast

1¾ cups + 2 tablespoons bread flour

½ teaspoon parsley flakes

2 tablespoons sesame seeds

½ teaspoon salt

3 tablespoons instant mashed-potato flakes or buds

3 tablespoons instant dry milk

1½ tablespoons sugar

2½ ounces buttermilk

1 egg

1½ tablespoons butter

3½ ounces warm water

Note:
For machines with yeast dispensers, use 2 teaspoons of yeast for the 1½-pound loaf.

NUTRITIONAL ANALYSIS			
	1½-POUND	1-POUND	
TOTAL CALORIES	2171	1473	
TOTAL PROTEIN	78	51	GRAMS
TOTAL CARBOHYDRATES	333	229	GRAMS
TOTAL FAT	57	38	GRAMS
TOTAL SATURATED FAT	21	14	GRAMS
TOTAL CHOLESTEROL	503	269	MILLIGRAMS
TOTAL SODIUM	2652	1414	MILLIGRAMS
TOTAL FIBRE	7	5	GRAMS
% CALORIES FROM FAT	24	23	

Raisin Walnut Bread

This white bread has whole-grain flavor. If you like it sweeter, try doubling the sugar in the recipe.

1½-pound

2 teaspoons active dry yeast

2¼ cups bread flour

¼ cup chopped walnuts

¼ cup golden raisins

⅓ cup whole-wheat flour

2 tablespoons oat bran

⅓ cup rye flour

1 teaspoon salt

1½ teaspoons sugar

½ teaspoon walnut extract

1 cup warm water

1-pound

1½ teaspoons active dry yeast

1½ cups bread flour

2 tablespoons chopped walnuts

2 tablespoons golden raisins

¼ cup whole-wheat flour

1½ tablespoons oat bran

¼ cup rye flour

½ teaspoon salt

1 teaspoon sugar

¼ teaspoon walnut extract

6½ ounces warm water

Note:

For machines with yeast dispensers, use 3½ teaspoons of yeast for the 1½-pound loaf.

NUTRITIONAL ANALYSIS			
	1½-POUND	1-POUND	
TOTAL CALORIES	1740	1137	
TOTAL PROTEIN	55	37	GRAMS
TOTAL CARBOHYDRATES	327	218	GRAMS
TOTAL FAT	26	15	GRAMS
TOTAL SATURATED FAT	3	2	GRAMS
TOTAL CHOLESTEROL	0	0	
TOTAL SODIUM	2148	1076	MILLIGRAMS
TOTAL FIBRE	20	14	GRAMS
% CALORIES FROM FAT	14	12	

Shredded-Wheat Nut Bread

The small amount of shredded-wheat cereal in this bread gives it a light but distinct wheat flavor, although it retains the texture and appearance of white bread.

1½-pound

1 teaspoon active dry yeast

3 cups bread flour

¼ cup chopped nuts

1 shredded-wheat biscuit

½ teaspoon salt

1 tablespoon molasses

½ tablespoon olive oil

¾ cup warm milk

¼ cup warm water

1-pound

½ teaspoon active dry yeast

2 cups bread flour

3 tablespoons chopped nuts

⅔ shredded-wheat biscuit

¼ teaspoon salt

½ tablespoon molasses

½ tablespoon olive oil

½ cup warm milk

1½ ounces warm water

Note:

For machines with yeast dispensers, use 2 teaspoons of yeast for the 1½ pound loaf.

NUTRITIONAL ANALYSIS			
	1½-POUND	1-POUND	
TOTAL CALORIES	1939	1323	
TOTAL PROTEIN	62	42	GRAMS
TOTAL CARBOHYDRATES	340	226	GRAMS
TOTAL FAT	35	27	GRAMS
TOTAL SATURATED FAT	5	4	GRAMS
TOTAL CHOLESTEROL	8	5	MILLIGRAMS
TOTAL SODIUM	1184	609	MILLIGRAMS
TOTAL FIBRE	8	5	GRAMS
% CALORIES FROM FAT	16	18	

Sunflower Bread

This nutritious bread has the aroma and flavor of sunflower seeds. The sunflower-seed oil, released during baking, permeates the bread, giving it a distinctively nutty taste.

1½-pound

1½ teaspoons active dry yeast

2½ cups bread flour

4 tablespoons sunflower seeds

1½ teaspoons salt

½ cup oat bran

1 tablespoon sugar

2 tablespoons molasses

2 tablespoons butter

½ cup warm milk

4½ ounces warm water

1-pound

1 teaspoon active dry yeast

1¾ cups bread flour

2½ tablespoons sunflower seeds

1 teaspoon salt

⅓ cup oat bran

2 teaspoons sugar

1½ tablespoons molasses

1 tablespoon butter

3 ounces warm milk

3 ounces warm water

Note:

For machines with yeast dispensers, use 3 teaspoons of yeast for the 1½-pound loaf.

NUTRITIONAL ANALYSIS			
	1½-POUND	1-POUND	
TOTAL CALORIES	1979	1310	
TOTAL PROTEIN	60	41	GRAMS
TOTAL CARBOHYDRATES	327	224	GRAMS
TOTAL FAT	49	28	GRAMS
TOTAL SATURATED FAT	18	10	GRAMS
TOTAL CHOLESTEROL	67	35	MILLIGRAMS
TOTAL SODIUM	3299	2207	MILLIGRAMS
TOTAL FIBRE	12	8	GRAMS
% CALORIES FROM FAT	22	20	

Walnut Bread

This bread has a great walnut flavor and crunch. It's excellent toasted with cheese.

1½-pound

2 teaspoons active dry yeast

2 cups bread flour

¾ cup chopped walnuts

1 teaspoon salt

3 tablespoons brown sugar

1 cup whole-wheat flour

½ teaspoon walnut extract

5 ounces warm milk

½ cup warm water

1-pound

1½ teaspoons active dry yeast

1⅓ cups bread flour

½ cup chopped walnuts

½ teaspoon salt

2 tablespoons brown sugar

⅔ cup whole-wheat flour

¼ teaspoon walnut extract

3 ounces warm milk

3 ounces warm water

Note:

For machines with yeast dispensers, use 3½ teaspoons of yeast for the 1½-pound loaf.

NUTRITIONAL ANALYSIS			
	1½-POUND	1-POUND	
TOTAL CALORIES	2205	1467	
TOTAL PROTEIN	69	46	GRAMS
TOTAL CARBOHYDRATES	351	234	GRAMS
TOTAL FAT	64	43	GRAMS
TOTAL SATURATED FAT	7	5	GRAMS
TOTAL CHOLESTEROL	6	4	MILLIGRAMS
TOTAL SODIUM	2237	1131	MILLIGRAMS
TOTAL FIBRE	24	16	GRAMS
% CALORIES FROM FAT	26	26	

Walnut Herb Bread

This bread has a spicy flavor in addition to the light walnut taste and crunch. You could substitute almonds, Brazil nuts, or pecans for walnuts.

1½-pound

1½ teaspoons active dry yeast

3 cups bread flour

¼ cup chopped walnuts

½ teaspoon dill weed

½ teaspoon oregano

½ teaspoon dried parsley flakes

½ teaspoon dried lemon peel

1½ teaspoons salt

1 tablespoon brown sugar

1½ tablespoons butter

9 ounces warm water

1-pound

1 teaspoon active dry yeast

2 cups bread flour

2 tablespoons chopped walnuts

¼ teaspoon dill weed

¼ teaspoon oregano

¼ teaspoon dried parsley flakes

¼ teaspoon dried lemon peel

1 teaspoon salt

2 teaspoons brown sugar

1 tablespoon butter

¾ cup warm water

Notes:

1. For machines with yeast dispensers, use 3 teaspoons of yeast for the 1½-pound loaf.
2. If salted nuts are used, reduce the salt by ½ teaspoon.

NUTRITIONAL ANALYSIS			
	1½-POUND	1-POUND	
TOTAL CALORIES	1893	1229	
TOTAL PROTEIN	55	36	GRAMS
TOTAL CARBOHYDRATES	319	212	GRAMS
TOTAL FAT	43	25	GRAMS
TOTAL SATURATED FAT	13	9	GRAMS
TOTAL CHOLESTEROL	47	31	MILLIGRAMS
TOTAL SODIUM	3215	2143	MILLIGRAMS
TOTAL FIBRE	8	5	GRAMS
% CALORIES FROM FAT	20	19	

Wheat-Germ Bread

The addition of nutritious wheat germ gives this traditional white bread a slightly nutty flavor.

1½-pound

1½ teaspoons active dry yeast

2¾ cups bread flour

½ cup wheat germ

2 teaspoons salt

3 tablespoons olive oil

2 tablespoons honey

1 cup warm water

1-pound

1 teaspoon active dry yeast

1¾ cups bread flour

¼ cup wheat germ

1½ teaspoons salt

2 tablespoons olive oil

1 tablespoon honey

5 ounces warm water

Note:

For machines with yeast dispensers, use 3 teaspoons of yeast for the 1½-pound loaf.

NUTRITIONAL ANALYSIS			
	1½-POUND	1-POUND	
TOTAL CALORIES	2057	1275	
TOTAL PROTEIN	65	39	GRAMS
TOTAL CARBOHYDRATES	340	207	GRAMS
TOTAL FAT	54	35	GRAMS
TOTAL SATURATED FAT	7	5	GRAMS
TOTAL CHOLESTEROL	0	0	
TOTAL SODIUM	4275	3205	MILLIGRAMS
TOTAL FIBRE	13	7	GRAMS
% CALORIES FROM FAT	24	25	

WHEAT BREADS

This section features breads that emphasize whole wheat, both in flavor and texture. The breads vary in the percentage of whole-wheat flour used, but each is unique in its distinctive wheat flavor combined with the flavors of other wonderful ingredients.

100% Wheat Bread

This recipe is one of the best I have tasted. It captures the essence of whole-grain bread with its rich wheat flavor and its somewhat crumbly texture. Spread honey on a toasted slice for an unbelievable taste treat.

1½-pound

4 teaspoons active dry yeast

3 tablespoons honey

3 cups whole-wheat flour

2 teaspoons salt

¼ cup + 2 tablespoons wheat gluten

1½ cups warm water

1-pound

2½ teaspoons active dry yeast

2 teaspoons honey

2 cups whole-wheat flour

1½ teaspoons salt

¼ cup wheat gluten

1 cup warm water

Notes:

1. For Panasonic/National machines, use 4 teaspoons of yeast for the 1½-pound loaf.
2. You will notice that the dough seems a little more liquid than usual. That is normal for this recipe, and the amount of liquid will yield a moist loaf. If the loaf collapses in your machine, cut back the liquid slightly (1 ounce or so) on the next try.

NUTRITIONAL ANALYSIS			
	1½-POUND	1-POUND	
TOTAL CALORIES	1729	1152	
TOTAL PROTEIN	98	65	GRAMS
TOTAL CARBOHYDRATES	340	226	GRAMS
TOTAL FAT	10	7	GRAMS
TOTAL SATURATED FAT	1	1	GRAMS
TOTAL CHOLESTEROL	0	0	MILLIGRAMS
TOTAL SODIUM	4275	3205	MILLIGRAMS
TOTAL FIBRE	50	33	GRAMS
% CALORIES FROM FAT	5	5	

Bran Bread

Here, oat bran combines with wheat to make a soft, light wheat bread that slices like white bread but has a unique wheat flavor.

1½-pound

2 teaspoons active dry yeast

1¼ cups bread flour

1¼ cups whole-wheat flour

¾ cup oat bran

1½ teaspoons salt

3 tablespoons brown sugar

3 tablespoons butter

9 ounces warm water

1-pound

1½ teaspoons active dry yeast

¾ cup + 2 tablespoons bread flour

¾ cup + 2 tablespoons whole-wheat flour

½ cup oat bran

1 teaspoon salt

2 tablespoons brown sugar

2 tablespoons butter

6 ounces warm water

Notes:

1. For machines with yeast dispensers, use 3½ teaspoons of yeast for the 1½-pound loaf.
2. For a variation, try using wheat bran instead of oat bran.

NUTRITIONAL ANALYSIS			
	1½-POUND	1-POUND	
TOTAL CALORIES	1802	1199	
TOTAL PROTEIN	56	37	GRAMS
TOTAL CARBOHYDRATES	312	208	GRAMS
TOTAL FAT	45	30	GRAMS
TOTAL SATURATED FAT	23	15	GRAMS
TOTAL CHOLESTEROL	93	62	MILLIGRAMS
TOTAL SODIUM	3222	2148	MILLIGRAMS
TOTAL FIBRE	32	21	GRAMS
% CALORIES FROM FAT	22	22	

Cashew Date Bread

This bread was created for cashew-nut lovers. The dates give the bread an exotic and sweet flavor that nicely complements that of the cashew nuts.

1½-pound	1-pound
1½ teaspoons active dry yeast	1 teaspoon active dry yeast
2 cups bread flour	1⅓ cups bread flour
¼ cup chopped dates	3 tablespoons chopped dates
¼ cup chopped raw cashew nuts	3 tablespoons chopped raw cashew nuts
½ cup whole-wheat flour	⅓ cup whole-wheat flour
½ teaspoon cinnamon	¼ teaspoon cinnamon
1 teaspoon salt	½ teaspoon salt
3 tablespoons rolled oats	2 tablespoons rolled oats
2 tablespoons butter	1½ tablespoons butter
3 tablespoons honey	2 tablespoons honey
3 ounces warm buttermilk	2 ounces warm buttermilk
¾ cup warm water	½ cup warm water

Notes:
1. For machines with yeast dispensers, use 3 teaspoons of yeast for the 1½-pound loaf.
2. If roasted, salted cashews are used, reduce the salt by ¼ teaspoon.

NUTRITIONAL ANALYSIS			
	1½-POUND	1-POUND	
TOTAL CALORIES	2004	1375	
TOTAL PROTEIN	54	36	GRAMS
TOTAL CARBOHYDRATES	346	233	GRAMS
TOTAL FAT	49	36	GRAMS
TOTAL SATURATED FAT	17	13	GRAMS
TOTAL CHOLESTEROL	70	52	MILLIGRAMS
TOTAL SODIUM	2204	1115	MILLIGRAMS
TOTAL FIBRE	18	12	GRAMS
% CALORIES FROM FAT	22	24	

Date Molasses Bread

Dates, molasses, and a high percentage of whole-wheat flour make this slightly sweet bread a favorite for toast.

1½-pound

2 teaspoons active dry yeast

½ cup bread flour

2½ cups whole-wheat flour

¾ cup chopped dates

½ teaspoon salt

1 tablespoon butter

½ cup warm milk

2 tablespoons molasses

5 ounces warm water

1-pound

1½ teaspoons active dry yeast

⅓ cup bread flour

1⅔ cups whole-wheat flour

½ cup chopped dates

½ teaspoon salt

½ tablespoon butter

3 ounces warm milk

1½ tablespoons molasses

3½ ounces warm water

Notes:
1. For machines with yeast dispensers, use 4 teaspoons of yeast for the 1½-pound loaf.
2. If your machine is equipped with a whole-grain cycle, use it for this bread.
3. You may add the dates at the mix-cycle beep, if your machine is so equipped.

NUTRITIONAL ANALYSIS			
	1½-POUND	1-POUND	
TOTAL CALORIES	1918	1277	
TOTAL PROTEIN	58	39	GRAMS
TOTAL CARBOHYDRATES	401	270	GRAMS
TOTAL FAT	20	12	GRAMS
TOTAL SATURATED FAT	9	5	GRAMS
TOTAL CHOLESTEROL	36	19	MILLIGRAMS
TOTAL SODIUM	1169	1142	MILLIGRAMS
TOTAL FIBRE	46	31	GRAMS
% CALORIES FROM FAT	9	8	

Farmer's Bread

This is a traditional, crumbly-textured whole-wheat bread. Dough conditioner (optional) can be added to give the bread a less crumbly texture, if desired.

1½-pound

1½ teaspoons active dry yeast

1 cup bread flour

½ cup seedless raisins

1 tablespoon dough conditioner (optional)

2 cups whole-wheat flour

1 teaspoon salt

1½ tablespoons brown sugar

1½ tablespoons butter

9 ounces warm milk

1-pound

1 teaspoon active dry yeast

¾ cup bread flour

⅓ cup seedless raisins

2 teaspoons dough conditioner (optional)

1¼ cups whole-wheat flour

½ teaspoon salt

1 tablespoon brown sugar

1 tablespoon butter

¾ cup warm milk

Notes:

1. For machines with yeast dispensers, use 3 teaspoons of yeast for the 1½-pound loaf.
2. If your machine is equipped with a whole-grain cycle, use it for this bread.

NUTRITIONAL ANALYSIS			
	1½-POUND	1-POUND	
TOTAL CALORIES	1878	1258	
TOTAL PROTEIN	62	41	GRAMS
TOTAL CARBOHYDRATES	365	244	GRAMS
TOTAL FAT	27	18	GRAMS
TOTAL SATURATED FAT	14	9	GRAMS
TOTAL CHOLESTEROL	58	39	MILLIGRAMS
TOTAL SODIUM	2293	1173	MILLIGRAMS
TOTAL FIBRE	37	23	GRAMS
% CALORIES FROM FAT	13	13	

Graham Bread

Graham flour's special milling process gives it taste that's slightly sweeter than regular whole-wheat flour. That sweetness is evident in this light wheat bread.

1½-pound	1-pound
1 teaspoon active dry yeast	½ teaspoon active dry yeast
2¼ cups + 3 tablespoons bread flour	1½ cups + 2 tablespoons bread flour
¾ cup graham flour	½ cup graham flour
1 teaspoon salt	½ teaspoon salt
⅓ cup dry milk	¼ cup dry milk
3 tablespoons brown sugar	2 tablespoons brown sugar
1 egg	1 egg
1½ tablespoons molasses	1 tablespoon molasses
1½ tablespoons butter	1 tablespoon butter
1 cup warm water	5 ounces warm water

Notes:

1. For machines with yeast dispensers, use 2 teaspoons of yeast for the 1½-pound loaf.
2. You may substitute whole-wheat flour for graham flour, if graham flour isn't available.

NUTRITIONAL ANALYSIS			
	1½-POUND	1-POUND	
TOTAL CALORIES	2094	1430	
TOTAL PROTEIN	70	50	GRAMS
TOTAL CARBOHYDRATES	386	259	GRAMS
TOTAL FAT	30	21	GRAMS
TOTAL SATURATED FAT	13	9	GRAMS
TOTAL CHOLESTEROL	265	248	MILLIGRAMS
TOTAL SODIUM	2403	1282	MILLIGRAMS
TOTAL FIBRE	17	11	GRAMS
% CALORIES FROM FAT	13	14	

Honey Wheat Bread

This traditional light wheat bread has the texture of white bread and a mild wheat taste.

1½-pound	1-pound
1½ teaspoons active dry yeast	1 teaspoon active dry yeast
½ teaspoon sugar	½ teaspoon sugar
2 cups bread flour	1¼ cups bread flour
1½ teaspoons salt	1 teaspoon salt
1¼ cups whole-wheat flour	¾ cup whole-wheat flour
1 egg	1 egg
1½ tablespoons butter	1 tablespoon butter
4 tablespoons honey	2 tablespoons honey
½ cup warm milk	¼ cup warm milk
¼ cup warm water	¼ cup warm water

Note:
For machines with yeast dispensers, use 3 teaspoons of yeast for the 1½-pound loaf.

NUTRITIONAL ANALYSIS			
	1½-POUND	1-POUND	
TOTAL CALORIES	2033	1259	
TOTAL PROTEIN	65	42	GRAMS
TOTAL CARBOHYDRATES	381	228	GRAMS
TOTAL FAT	31	22	GRAMS
TOTAL SATURATED FAT	14	10	GRAMS
TOTAL CHOLESTEROL	265	247	MILLIGRAMS
TOTAL SODIUM	3331	2231	MILLIGRAMS
TOTAL FIBRE	23	14	GRAMS
% CALORIES FROM FAT	14	15	

Sesame Wheat Bread

This light wheat bread has a nutty sesame flavor. Try varying the amount of sesame seeds to suit your taste.

1½-pound

2 teaspoons active dry yeast

2¼ cups bread flour

¾ cup whole-wheat flour

1 tablespoon sesame seeds

1½ teaspoons salt

1 tablespoon brown sugar

2 tablespoons butter

3 ounces warm milk

¾ cup warm water

1-pound

1½ teaspoon active dry yeast

1½ cups bread flour

½ cup whole-wheat flour

2 teaspoons sesame seeds

1 teaspoon salt

2 teaspoons brown sugar

1½ tablespoons butter

¼ cup warm milk

½ cup warm water

Note:

For machines with yeast dispensers, use 3½ teaspoons of yeast for the 1½-pound loaf.

NUTRITIONAL ANALYSIS			
	1½-POUND	1-POUND	
TOTAL CALORIES	1774	1201	
TOTAL PROTEIN	56	38	GRAMS
TOTAL CARBOHYDRATES	311	207	GRAMS
TOTAL FAT	35	25	GRAMS
TOTAL SATURATED FAT	16	12	GRAMS
TOTAL CHOLESTEROL	66	49	MILLIGRAMS
TOTAL SODIUM	3259	2173	MILLIGRAMS
TOTAL FIBRE	17	11	GRAMS
% CALORIES FROM FAT	18	19	

Sunflower Potato Bread

The mixture of potato flakes, sunflower seeds, and wheat gives this bread its hearty, whole-grain flavor.

1½-pound

2 teaspoons active dry yeast

3 tablespoons brown sugar

2 cups bread flour

3 tablespoons sunflower seeds

1 cup whole-wheat flour

1½ teaspoons salt

½ cup instant mashed-potato flakes or buds

3 tablespoons butter

1¼ cups warm water

1-pound

1½ teaspoons active dry yeast

2 tablespoons brown sugar

1⅓ cups bread flour

2 tablespoons sunflower seeds

⅔ cup whole-wheat flour

1 teaspoon salt

⅓ cup instant mashed-potato flakes or buds

2 tablespoons butter

7 ounces warm water

Note:

For machines with yeast dispensers, use 3½ teaspoons of yeast for the 1½-pound loaf.

NUTRITIONAL ANALYSIS			
	1½-POUND	1-POUND	
TOTAL CALORIES	2134	1422	
TOTAL PROTEIN	59	40	GRAMS
TOTAL CARBOHYDRATES	350	234	GRAMS
TOTAL FAT	59	39	GRAMS
TOTAL SATURATED FAT	24	16	GRAMS
TOTAL CHOLESTEROL	93	62	MILLIGRAMS
TOTAL SODIUM	3581	2385	MILLIGRAMS
TOTAL FIBRE	20	14	GRAMS
% CALORIES FROM FAT	25	25	

Whole-Wheat & Buckwheat Bread

This bread doesn't rise much, usually making a dense, flat loaf. If you like buckwheat, this is an excellent, densely textured bread.

1½-pound	1-pound
2½ teaspoons active dry yeast	2 teaspoons active dry yeast
1 cup buckwheat flour	⅔ cup buckwheat flour
2 cups whole-wheat flour	1⅓ cups whole-wheat flour
1½ tablespoons wheat gluten (optional)	1 tablespoon wheat gluten (optional)
2 teaspoons salt	1 teaspoon salt
1 tablespoon brown sugar	2 teaspoons brown sugar
2 tablespoons butter	1½ tablespoons butter
1½ tablespoons molasses	1 tablespoon molasses
¼ cup warm water	1½ ounces warm water
¾ cup warm milk	½ cup warm milk

Notes:
1. For machines with yeast dispensers, use 4½ teaspoons of yeast for the 1½-pound loaf.
2. For machines with low-power motors, add 2 tablespoons of warm water for the 1½-pound loaf.
3. If your machine is equipped with a whole-grain cycle, use it for this bread.

NUTRITIONAL ANALYSIS			
	1½-POUND	1-POUND	
TOTAL CALORIES	1651	1120	
TOTAL PROTEIN	57	38	GRAMS
TOTAL CARBOHYDRATES	304	203	GRAMS
TOTAL FAT	33	24	GRAMS
TOTAL SATURATED FAT	17	13	GRAMS
TOTAL CHOLESTEROL	70	52	MILLIGRAMS
TOTAL SODIUM	4390	2217	MILLIGRAMS
TOTAL FIBRE	31	21	GRAMS
% CALORIES FROM FAT	18	19	

Whole-Wheat Buttermilk Raisin Bread

This coarsely textured wheat bread has a slightly sweet taste. Add additional raisins, if you like.

1½-pound	**1-pound**
2 teaspoons active dry yeast	1½ teaspoons active dry yeast
½ cup bread flour	½ cup bread flour
2½ cups whole-wheat flour	1½ cups whole-wheat flour
6 tablespoons raisins	¼ cup raisins
½ teaspoon baking soda	¼ teaspoon baking soda
1½ teaspoons salt	1 teaspoon salt
2½ tablespoons butter	1½ tablespoons butter
5 ounces buttermilk	½ cup buttermilk
2 tablespoons honey	1½ tablespoons honey
¼ cup warm water	2 tablespoons warm water

Notes:
1. For machines with yeast dispensers, use 3½ teaspoons of yeast for the 1½-pound loaf.
2. If your machine is equipped with a whole-grain cycle, use it for this bread.

NUTRITIONAL ANALYSIS			
	1½-POUND	1-POUND	
TOTAL CALORIES	1884	1275	
TOTAL PROTEIN	60	41	GRAMS
TOTAL CARBOHYDRATES	353	242	GRAMS
TOTAL FAT	37	23	GRAMS
TOTAL SATURATED FAT	20	12	GRAMS
TOTAL CHOLESTEROL	90	57	GRAMS
TOTAL SODIUM	3310	2220	MILLIGRAMS
TOTAL FIBRE	42	26	GRAMS
% CALORIES FROM FAT	18	16	

Whole-Wheat Cranberry Bread

Tart cranberries give this 100 percent–wheat bread a tangy flavor. It has a crumbly whole-wheat texture, which makes it excellent for toast.

1½-pound

2 teaspoons active dry yeast

3½ cups whole-wheat flour

½ cup whole cranberries

½ cup brown sugar

1½ teaspoons salt

3 tablespoons molasses

2 tablespoons butter

¾ cup warm water

1-pound

1½ teaspoons active dry yeast

2¼ cups + 2 tablespoons whole-wheat flour

⅓ cup whole cranberries

⅓ cup brown sugar

1 teaspoon salt

2 tablespoons molasses

1½ tablespoons butter

½ cup warm water

Notes:
1. For machines with yeast dispensers, use 3½ teaspoons of yeast for the 1½-pound loaf.
2. If your machine is equipped with a whole-grain cycle, use it for this bread.

NUTRITIONAL ANALYSIS			
	1½-POUND	1-POUND	
TOTAL CALORIES	2317	1576	
TOTAL PROTEIN	60	41	GRAMS
TOTAL CARBOHYDRATES	477	321	GRAMS
TOTAL FAT	31	22	GRAMS
TOTAL SATURATED FAT	16	12	GRAMS
TOTAL CHOLESTEROL	62	47	MILLIGRAMS
TOTAL SODIUM	3303	2202	MILLIGRAMS
TOTAL FIBRE	54	36	GRAMS
% CALORIES FROM FAT	12	13	

Whole-Wheat Egg Bread

This 100-percent wheat bread has a soft texture due to the eggs. Using maple syrup as a sweetener takes the edge off the sometimes slightly bitter taste of the whole wheat.

1½-pound

3 teaspoons active dry yeast

1 teaspoon sugar

3¼ cups whole-wheat flour

2 teaspoons salt

3 eggs

4 tablespoons olive oil

4 tablespoons maple syrup

3 ounces warm water

1-pound

2 teaspoons active dry yeast

½ teaspoon sugar

2¼ cups whole-wheat flour

1 teaspoon salt

2 eggs

2½ tablespoons olive oil

2½ tablespoons maple syrup

¼ cup warm water

Notes:

1. For machines with yeast dispensers, use 5½ teaspoons of yeast for the 1½-pound loaf.
2. If your machine is equipped with a whole-grain cycle, use it for this bread.
3. Because eggs vary in their effect on the consistency of the dough, be sure to watch the dough as it mixes. If it seems too runny, add flour, one tablespoon at a time, until the consistency is about right.

NUTRITIONAL ANALYSIS			
	1½-POUND	1-POUND	
TOTAL CALORIES	2260	1510	
TOTAL PROTEIN	75	52	GRAMS
TOTAL CARBOHYDRATES	344	233	GRAMS
TOTAL FAT	76	49	GRAMS
TOTAL SATURATED FAT	13	9	GRAMS
TOTAL CHOLESTEROL	639	426	MILLIGRAMS
TOTAL SODIUM	4500	2288	MILLIGRAMS
TOTAL FIBRE	50	35	GRAMS
% CALORIES FROM FAT	30	29	

Whole-Wheat Potato Bread

If you like soft-textured whole-wheat bread, try this. The potato flakes soften the bread and give it a spongy texture.

1½-pound

2 teaspoons active dry yeast

2¼ cups whole-wheat flour

1 teaspoon cardamom

3 tablespoons nonfat dry milk

2 teaspoons salt

5 tablespoons instant mashed-potato flakes or buds

5 tablespoons brown sugar

1 egg

4 tablespoons butter

7 ounces warm water

1-pound

1½ teaspoons active dry yeast

1¾ cups whole-wheat flour

½ teaspoon cardamom

2 tablespoons nonfat dry milk

1½ teaspoons salt

3½ tablespoons instant mashed-potato flakes or buds

3½ tablespoons brown sugar

1 egg

2½ tablespoons butter

5 ounces warm water

Notes:
1. For machines with yeast dispensers, use 3½ teaspoons of yeast for the 1½-pound loaf.
2. If your machine is equipped with a whole-grain cycle, use it for this bread.

NUTRITIONAL ANALYSIS			
	1½-POUND	1-POUND	
TOTAL CALORIES	1802	1324	
TOTAL PROTEIN	53	42	GRAMS
TOTAL CARBOHYDRATES	284	214	GRAMS
TOTAL FAT	60	40	GRAMS
TOTAL SATURATED FAT	31	20	GRAMS
TOTAL CHOLESTEROL	340	293	MILLIGRAMS
TOTALSODIUM	4674	3501	MILLIGRAMS
TOTAL FIBRE	35	27	GRAMS
% CALORIES FROM FAT	30	27	

Whole-Wheat Sally Lunn Bread

Because of its sweet flavor and whole-grain richness, this was my tasters' favorite 100-percent whole-wheat bread.

1½-pound	1-pound
2 teaspoons active dry yeast	1½ teaspoons active dry yeast
¼ teaspoon cream of tartar	¼ teaspoon cream of tartar
1 teaspoon cardamom	½ teaspoon cardamom
3¼ cups whole-wheat flour	2 cups + 2 tablespoons whole-wheat flour
1 teaspoon salt	½ teaspoon salt
½ cup + 1 tablespoon brown sugar	6 tablespoons brown sugar
2 eggs	1 egg
4 tablespoons butter	2½ tablespoons butter
7 ounces warm milk	5 ounces warm milk

Notes:

1. For machines with yeast dispensers, use 3½ teaspoons of yeast for the 1½-pound loaf.
2. If your machine is equipped with a whole-grain cycle, use it for this bread.

NUTRITIONAL ANALYSIS			
	1½-POUND	1-POUND	
TOTAL CALORIES	2435	1570	
TOTAL PROTEIN	75	48	GRAMS
TOTAL CARBOHYDRATES	416	274	GRAMS
TOTAL FAT	65	40	GRAMS
TOTAL SATURATED FAT	34	21	GRAMS
TOTAL CHOLESTEROL	559	297	MILLIGRAMS
TOTAL SODIUM	2411	1236	MILLIGRAMS
TOTAL FIBRE	50	33	GRAMS
% CALORIES FROM FAT	24	23	

Whole-Wheat Sourdough Bread

If you like both sourdough bread and wheat bread, try this. Sourdough adds a pungent flavor to this wheat bread. It's excellent topped with butter and honey.

1½-pound

1½ teaspoons active dry yeast

1 cup bread flour

1 teaspoon salt

2 cups whole-wheat flour

¾ cup sourdough starter

1 cup warm water

2 tablespoons honey

1-pound

1 teaspoon active dry yeast

½ cup bread flour

½ teaspoon salt

1⅓ cups whole-wheat flour

½ cup sourdough starter

5 ounces warm water

1½ tablespoons honey

Notes:
1. For machines with yeast dispensers, use 3 teaspoons of yeast for the 1½-pound loaf.
2. If you don't have sourdough starter, you can make your own. See pages 31–33.
3. Because sourdough starter varies in consistency, check the dough when mixing. If it seems too runny, add flour, one tablespoon at a time. If it seems too stiff, add warm water, one tablespoon at a time.

NUTRITIONAL ANALYSIS			
	1½-POUND	1-POUND	
TOTAL CALORIES	1811	1217	
TOTAL PROTEIN	63	42	GRAMS
TOTAL CARBOHYDRATES	382	257	GRAMS
TOTAL FAT	9	6	GRAMS
TOTAL SATURATED FAT	1	1	GRAM
TOTAL CHOLESTEROL	0	0	MILLIGRAMS
TOTAL SODIUM	2139	1071	MILLIGRAMS
TOTAL FIBRE	34	23	GRAMS
% CALORIES FROM FAT	4	4	

Whole-Wheat Three-Seed Bread

The three seeds (poppy, sunflower, and sesame) give a nutty flavor to this crunchy wheat-and-oatmeal bread. It's great for appetizer sandwiches. If you like seeds, you'll love this bread.

1½-pound

2 teaspoons active dry yeast

2 teaspoons gluten (optional)

2 tablespoons sunflower seeds

2 tablespoons sesame seeds

2 tablespoons poppy seeds

½ cup rolled oats

1 teaspoon salt

2 cups whole-wheat flour

3 tablespoons olive oil

2 tablespoons honey

1 cup warm water

1-pound

1½ teaspoons active dry yeast

1½ teaspoons gluten (optional)

4 teaspoons sunflower seeds

4 teaspoons sesame seeds

4 teaspoons poppy seeds

¼ cup rolled oats

½ teaspoon salt

1½ cups whole-wheat flour

2 tablespoons olive oil

4 teaspoons honey

5½ ounces warm water

Notes:

1. For Panasonic/National machines, use 3 teaspoons of yeast for the 1½-pound loaf.
2. Note that this bread has a slightly higher liquid content than other recipes. If you would like a stiffer, drier bread, add 2 extra tablespoons of whole-wheat flour.

NUTRITIONAL ANALYSIS			
	1½-POUND	1-POUND	
TOTAL CALORIES	1748	1208	
TOTAL PROTEIN	51	36	GRAMS
TOTAL CARBOHYDRATES	247	175	GRAMS
TOTAL FAT	72	48	GRAMS
TOTAL SATURATED FAT	9	6	GRAMS
TOTAL CHOLESTEROL	0	0	MILLIGRAMS
TOTAL SODIUM	2147	1076	MILLIGRAMS
TOTAL FIBRE	37	27	GRAMS
% CALORIES FROM FAT	37	36	

Whole-Wheat Bagel Bread

If you don't feel like making bagels but want the texture of bagels with the low-fat nutritional benefits, try this bread. It tastes like a bagel and is especially good sliced and toasted.

1½-pound

1½ teaspoons active dry yeast

1½ teaspoons gluten

3 cups whole-wheat flour

2 teaspoons salt

3 tablespoons honey

1 cup warm water

1-pound

1 teaspoon active dry yeast

1 teaspoons gluten

2 cups whole-wheat flour

1½ teaspoons salt

2 tablespoons honey

5½ ounces warm water

Note:
For Panasonic/National machines, use 3 teaspoons of yeast for the 1½-pound loaf.

NUTRITIONAL ANALYSIS			
	1½-POUND	1-POUND	
TOTAL CALORIES	1437	1030	
TOTAL PROTEIN	54	38	GRAMS
TOTAL CARBOHYDRATES	313	226	GRAMS
TOTAL FAT	7	5	GRAMS
TOTAL SATURATED FAT	1	1	GRAMS
TOTAL CHOLESTEROL	0	0	MILLIGRAMS
TOTAL SODIUM	4269	3202	MILLIGRAMS
TOTAL FIBRE	46	31	GRAMS
% CALORIES FROM FAT	4	4	

RYE BREADS

The distinctive taste of rye bread is loved the world over. Featured in this section are interesting variations on "standard" rye breads. As you bake rye breads in your bread machine, remember that the dough ball will usually be somewhat stiff and that rye breads don't rise much, giving them their uniquely dense texture.

German Rye Bread

If you like rye bread, you will love this authentic German country rye. Like all ryes, it has a dense texture and the distinctive taste of rye and caraway.

1½-pound

1 tablespoon active dry yeast

1 tablespoon caraway seeds

2¼ cups bread flour

1½ teaspoons salt

2½ tablespoons unsweetened cocoa

1½ cups rye flour

1¼ cups warm water

1½ tablespoons butter

2½ tablespoons molasses

1-pound

2 teaspoons active dry yeast

2 teaspoons caraway seeds

1½ cups bread flour

1 teaspoon salt

5 teaspoons unsweetened cocoa

1 cup rye flour

7 ounces warm water

1 tablespoon butter

5 teaspoons molasses

Note:

For Panasonic/National machines, use 3½ teaspoons of yeast for the 1½-pound loaf.

NUTRITIONAL ANALYSIS			
	1½-POUND	1-POUND	
TOTAL CALORIES	2136	1423	
TOTAL PROTEIN	72	48	GRAMS
TOTAL CARBOHYDRATES	403	269	GRAMS
TOTAL FAT	30	20	GRAMS
TOTAL SATURATED FAT	12	8	GRAMS
TOTAL CHOLESTEROL	47	31	MILLIGRAMS
TOTAL SODIUM	3250	2167	MILLIGRAMS
TOTAL FIBRE	10	6	GRAMS
% CALORIES FROM FAT	13	13	

Buckwheat Rye Bread

Due to the small amount of wheat flour used, this bread doesn't rise much. The result, however, is a bread with a dense texture and strong buckwheat flavor that will please buckwheat lovers.

1½-pound

2 teaspoons active dry yeast

1½ tablespoons gluten powder

1 tablespoon brown sugar

1½ cups rye flour

¼ teaspoon ground cloves

1 cup whole-wheat flour

½ cup buckwheat flour

1 teaspoon salt

3 tablespoons molasses

2 tablespoons butter

1 cup + 2 tablespoons warm water

1-pound

1½ teaspoons active dry yeast

1 tablespoon gluten powder

½ tablespoon brown sugar

1 cup rye flour

⅛ teaspoon ground cloves

⅔ cup whole-wheat flour

⅓ cup buckwheat flour

½ teaspoon salt

2 tablespoons molasses

1 tablespoon butter

¾ cup warm water

Notes:

1. For machines with yeast dispensers, use 4 teaspoons of yeast for the 1½-pound loaf.
2. If your machine is equipped with a whole-grain cycle, use it for this bread.

NUTRITIONAL ANALYSIS			
	1½-POUND	1-POUND	
TOTAL CALORIES	1670	1072	
TOTAL PROTEIN	52	35	GRAMS
TOTAL CARBOHYDRATES	312	206	GRAMS
TOTAL FAT	31	17	GRAMS
TOTAL SATURATED FAT	15	8	GRAMS
TOTAL CHOLESTEROL	62	31	MILLIGRAMS
TOTAL SODIUM	2192	1105	MILLIGRAMS
TOTAL FIBRE	39	26	GRAMS
% CALORIES FROM FAT	16	14	

Dijon Rye Bread

This mild rye has a tangy flavor. It's densely textured and doesn't rise much, but it's a great bread for sandwiches. Dijon mustard is made from white wine, vinegar, spices, and ground mustard seed, and it complements the rye flavor quite well.

1½-pound

1½ teaspoons active dry yeast

1 tablespoon gluten powder

2 teaspoons sugar

2¼ cups bread flour

½ cup rye flour

4½ tablespoons oat bran

1½ teaspoons ground caraway seeds

1½ teaspoons salt

4½ tablespoons Dijon mustard

2½ tablespoons molasses

2 tablespoons olive oil

7 ounces warm water

1-pound

1 teaspoon active dry yeast

2 teaspoons gluten powder

1½ teaspoons sugar

1½ cups bread flour

⅓ cup rye flour

3 tablespoons oat bran

1 teaspoon ground caraway seeds

1 teaspoon salt

3 tablespoons Dijon mustard

1½ tablespoons molasses

1½ tablespoons olive oil

4½ ounces warm water

Notes:

1. For machines with yeast dispensers, use 3 teaspoons of yeast for the 1½-pound loaf.
2. For machines with low-power motors, add 2 tablespoons of warm water for the 1½-pound loaf.
3. If your machine is equipped with a whole-grain cycle, use it for this bread.

NUTRITIONAL ANALYSIS			
	1½-POUND	1-POUND	
TOTAL CALORIES	1862	1252	
TOTAL PROTEIN	56	37	GRAMS
TOTAL CARBOHYDRATES	328	216	GRAMS
TOTAL FAT	36	26	GRAMS
TOTAL SATURATED FAT	5	3	GRAMS
TOTAL CHOLESTEROL	0	0	
TOTAL SODIUM	3245	2161	MILLIGRAMS
TOTAL FIBRE	17	11	GRAMS
% CALORIES FROM FAT	17	19	

Dill Rye Bread

This light rye has a spicy flavor. It's excellent as a sandwich bread.

1½-pound

1½ teaspoons active dry yeast

1½ tablespoons brown sugar

½ teaspoon caraway seeds

½ tablespoon dill seeds

2¼ cups bread flour

1 teaspoon salt

½ tablespoon dill weed

4 tablespoons nonfat dry milk

¾ cup rye flour

1½ tablespoons butter

9 ounces warm water

1-pound

1 teaspoon active dry yeast

1 tablespoon brown sugar

½ teaspoon caraway seeds

1 teaspoon dill seeds

1½ cups bread flour

½ teaspoon salt

1 teaspoon dill weed

2½ tablespoons nonfat dry milk

½ cup rye flour

1 tablespoon butter

¾ cup warm water

Notes:

For machines with yeast dispensers, use 3 teaspoons of yeast for the 1½-pound loaf.

NUTRITIONAL ANALYSIS			
	1½-POUND	1-POUND	
TOTAL CALORIES	1720	1144	
TOTAL PROTEIN	55	36	GRAMS
TOTAL CARBOHYDRATES	319	213	GRAMS
TOTAL FAT	25	16	GRAMS
TOTAL SATURATED FAT	12	8	GRAMS
TOTAL CHOLESTEROL	51	34	MILLIGRAMS
TOTAL SODIUM	2276	1157	MILLIGRAMS
TOTAL FIBRE	17	12	GRAMS
% CALORIES FROM FAT	13	13	

Oat Rye Bread

This bread has a soft, but dense, texture and a mild rye flavor. The loaf won't rise much and will stay fairly small.

1½-pound

2 teaspoons active dry yeast

1¼ cups bread flour

1½ teaspoons ground caraway seeds

1½ cups rye flour

¼ cup oat flour

1 teaspoon salt

1 egg

1½ tablespoons butter

1½ tablespoons molasses

6½ ounces warm water

2 teaspoons dough enhancer (optional)

1-pound

1½ teaspoons active dry yeast

¾ cup bread flour

1 teaspoon ground caraway seeds

1 cup rye flour

¼ cup oat flour

½ teaspoon salt

1 egg

1 tablespoon butter

1 tablespoon molases

½ cup warm water

½ tablespoon dough enhancer (optional)

Notes:

1. For machines with yeast dispensers, use 4 teaspoons of yeast for the 1½-pound loaf.
2. If your machine is equipped with a whole-grain cycle, use it for this bread.

NUTRITIONAL ANALYSIS			
	1½-POUND	1-POUND	
TOTAL CALORIES	1600	1085	
TOTAL PROTEIN	48	34	GRAMS
TOTAL CARBOHYDRATES	289	192	GRAMS
TOTAL FAT	29	21	GRAMS
TOTAL SATURATED FAT	13	9	GRAMS
TOTAL CHOLESTEROL	260	244	MILLIGRAMS
TOTAL SODIUM	2229	1152	MILLIGRAMS
TOTAL FIBRE	30	21	GRAMS
% CALORIES FROM FAT	16	17	

Swedish Rye Bread

Fennel seeds and orange juice give this traditional rye bread its distinctive flavor.

1½-pound

1½ teaspoons active dry yeast

2 teaspoons fennel seeds

½ teaspoon sugar

2 cups bread flour

1 cup rye flour

1½ teaspoon salt

1 tablespoon olive oil

4 tablespoons molasses

3 ounces orange juice

3 ounces warm milk

2 tablespoons warm water

1-pound

1 teaspoon active dry yeast

1 teaspoon fennel seeds

½ teaspoon sugar

1⅓ cups bread flour

⅔ cup rye flour

1 teaspoon salt

½ tablespoon olive oil

2½ tablespoons molasses

2 ounces orange juice

2 ounces warm milk

1½ tablespoons warm water

Notes:
1. For machines with yeast dispensers, use 3 teaspoons of yeast for the 1½-pound loaf.
2. For machines with low-power motors, add 2 tablespoons of warm water for the 1½-pound loaf.

NUTRITIONAL ANALYSIS			
	1½-POUND	1-POUND	
TOTAL CALORIES	1808	1178	
TOTAL PROTEIN	48	32	GRAMS
TOTAL CARBOHYDRATES	352	233	GRAMS
TOTAL FAT	21	12	GRAMS
TOTAL SATURATED FAT	3	2	GRAMS
TOTAL CHOLESTEROL	4	3	MILLIGRAMS
TOTAL SODIUM	3313	2206	MILLIGRAMS
TOTAL FIBRE	20	13	GRAMS
% CALORIES FROM FAT	11	9	

Corn Rye Bread

A must for rye lovers. Corn Rye is a wonderful, light variation of rye bread with the crunchiness of corn and the flavor of rye, wheat, and caraway.

1½-pound	1-pound
1½ teaspoons active dry yeast	1 teaspoon active dry yeast
1 teaspoon dough enhancer (optional)	½ teaspoon dough enhancer (optional)
2 teaspoons caraway seeds	1½ teaspoons caraway seeds
2½ tablespoons sesame seeds	5 teaspoons sesame seeds
¼ cup rye flour	2 tablespoons rye flour
¼ cup cornmeal	2 tablespoons cornmeal
2½ cups whole-wheat flour	1¾ cups whole-wheat flour
½ teaspoon salt	¼ teaspoon salt
2 teaspoons olive oil	1½ teaspoons olive oil
2 teaspoons molasses	1½ teaspoons molasses
1 cup warm water	¾ cup warm water

Notes:
1. For Panasonic/National machines, use 2½ teaspoons of yeast for the 1½-pound loaf.
2. For DAK/Welbilt machines, add 2 tablespoons of warm water to the 1½-pound recipe.

NUTRITIONAL ANALYSIS			
	1½-POUND	1-POUND	
TOTAL CALORIES	1506	1013	
TOTAL PROTEIN	54	36	GRAMS
TOTAL CARBOHYDRATES	281	188	GRAMS
TOTAL FAT	28	20	GRAMS
TOTAL SATURATED FAT	4	3	GRAMS
TOTAL CHOLESTEROL	0	0	MILLIGRAMS
TOTAL SODIUM	1094	551	MILLIGRAMS
TOTAL FIBRE	44	30	GRAMS
% CALORIES FROM FAT	17	17	

Russian Black Bread

This is a complete meal in a loaf. In fact, the story goes that during the siege of Leningrad, Russian black bread was all the Russians had to eat. It is nutritious and a must-try for rye lovers.

1½-pound

2 teaspoons active dry yeast

¼ teaspoon ground fennel seed

1 teaspoon dried onion

2 teaspoons ground caraway

¾ cup All-Bran cereal

1 teaspoon salt

½ teaspoon sugar

1 cup bread flour

1¼ cups rye flour

2 tablespoons butter

1½ tablespoons unsweetened cocoa

¼ cup molasses

1 tablespoon vinegar

¾ cup warm water

1-pound

1½ teaspoon active dry yeast

¼ teaspoon ground fennel seed

½ teaspoon dried onion

1½ teaspoons ground caraway

½ cup All-Bran cereal

½ teaspoon salt

½ teaspoon sugar

¾ cup bread flour

¾ cup rye flour

1½ tablespoons butter

1 tablespoon unsweetened cocoa

2½ tablespoons molasses

2 teaspoons vinegar

½ cup warm water

Note:
For Panasonic/National machines, use 3½ teaspoons of yeast for the 1½-pound loaf.

NUTRITIONAL ANALYSIS			
	1½-POUND	1-POUND	
TOTAL CALORIES	1688	1146	
TOTAL PROTEIN	53	36	GRAMS
TOTAL CARBOHYDRATES	326	218	GRAMS
TOTAL FAT	34	24	GRAMS
TOTAL SATURATED FAT	15	11	GRAMS
TOTAL CHOLESTEROL	62	47	MILLIGRAMS
TOTAL SODIUM	2788	1502	MILLIGRAMS
TOTAL FIBRE	29	19	GRAMS
% CALORIES FROM FAT	18	19	

Onion Rye Bread

The taste of toasted onion combined with rye made this bread the favorite of my rye-loving bread testers. It makes an excellent bread for a ham-and-cheese sandwich.

1½-pound	1-pound
1½ teaspoons active dry yeast	1 teaspoon active dry yeast
1 teaspoon caraway seeds	1 teaspoon caraway seeds
1 cup bread flour	¾ cup bread flour
3 tablespoons onion soup mix	2 tablespoons onion soup mix
1 cup rye flour	¾ cup rye flour
1 cup whole-wheat flour	½ cup whole-wheat flour
1 tablespoon butter	1 tablespoon butter
2 tablespoons milk	4 teaspoons milk
1 tablespoon olive oil	2 teaspoons olive oil
1 tablespoon vinegar	2 teaspoons vinegar
2 teaspoons molasses	1½ teaspoons molasses
7 ounces warm water	4½ ounces warm water

Note:

For Panasonic/National machines, use 3 teaspoons of yeast for the 1½-pound loaf.

NUTRITIONAL ANALYSIS			
	1½-POUND	1-POUND	
TOTAL CALORIES	1696	1178	
TOTAL PROTEIN	57	38	GRAMS
TOTAL CARBOHYDRATES	307	207	GRAMS
TOTAL FAT	34	27	GRAMS
TOTAL SATURATED FAT	10	9	GRAMS
TOTAL CHOLESTEROL	32	32	MILLIGRAMS
TOTAL SODIUM	2877	1920	MILLIGRAMS
TOTAL FIBRE	20	11	GRAMS
% CALORIES FROM FAT	18	21	

Pumpernickel Bread

The traditional taste of pumpernickel is a favorite of rye-bread lovers. With its dense rye texture, this bread is excellent when sliced thin for deli-type sandwiches.

1½-pound	1-pound
2½ teaspoons active dry yeast	2 teaspoons active dry yeast
1½ cups bread flour	1 cup bread flour
1½ cups rye flour	1 cup rye flour
1½ teaspoons salt	1 teaspoon salt
1 tablespoon caraway seed	2 teaspoons caraway seed
1 tablespoon butter	1 tablespoon butter
2 tablespoons molasses	2½ tablespoons molasses
6½ ounces warm water	4½ ounces warm water

Notes:
1. For Panasonic/National machines, use 4 teaspoons of yeast for the 1½-pound loaf.
2. For DAK/Welbilt machines, use 7½ ounces of warm water in the 1½-pound loaf.

NUTRITIONAL ANALYSIS			
	1½-POUND	1-POUND	
TOTAL CALORIES	1744	1188	
TOTAL PROTEIN	55	37	GRAMS
TOTAL CARBOHYDRATES	343	226	GRAMS
TOTAL FAT	21	18	GRAMS
TOTAL SATURATED FAT	8	8	GRAMS
TOTAL CHOLESTEROL	31	31	MILLIGRAMS
TOTAL SODIUM	3268	2177	MILLIGRAMS
TOTAL FIBRE	8	5	GRAMS
% CALORIES FROM FAT	11	14	

CORN BREADS

The three recipes in this section feature the staple grain of the Western Hemisphere: corn. Each of these recipes is a different variation of the use of corn in yeast bread, and you'll find each to be delightful in its own way.

Cornmeal Honey Bread

This simple bread has a white-bread look with a corn-bread crunch.

1½-pound	1-pound
1½ teaspoons active dry yeast	1 teaspoon active dry yeast
3 cups bread flour	2 cups bread flour
½ cup cornmeal	⅓ cup cornmeal
1½ teaspoons salt	1 teaspoon salt
3 tablespoons honey	2 tablespoons honey
1 tablespoon butter	½ tablespoon butter
¾ cup warm buttermilk	½ cup warm buttermilk
3 ounces warm water	¼ cup warm water

Note:
For machines with yeast dispensers, use 3 teaspoons of yeast for the 1½-pound loaf.

NUTRITIONAL ANALYSIS			
	1½-POUND	1-POUND	
TOTAL COLORIES	2084	1371	
TOTAL PROTEIN	63	42	GRAMS
TOTAL CARBOHYDRATES	405	270	GRAMS
TOTAL FAT	22	13	GRAMS
TOTAL SATURATED FAT	9	5	GRAMS
TOTAL CHOLESTEROL	47	26	MILLIGRAMS
TOTAL SODIUM	3345	2230	MILLIGRAMS
TOTAL FIBRE	13	9	GRAMS
% CALORIES FROM FAT	9	8	

Southwestern Pumpkin Bread

Pumpkin, a staple vegetable in Latin America, is good with Mexican food, such as refried beans, or Southwestern fare. Both the pumpkin and the corn give this bread a rich yellow color.

1½-pound	1-pound
1½ teaspoons active dry yeast	1 teaspoon active dry yeast
3 cups bread flour	2 cups bread flour
¼ cup cornmeal	2 tablespoons cornmeal
1½ teaspoons salt	1 teaspoon salt
¼ cup brown sugar	2 tablespoons brown sugar
½ cup canned pumpkin	⅓ cup canned pumpkin
1 egg	1 egg
5 ounces warm water	2½ ounces warm water

Note:

For machines with yeast dispensers, use 3 teaspoons of yeast for the 1½-pound loaf.

NUTRITIONAL ANALYSIS			
	1½-POUND	1-POUND	
TOTAL CALORIES	1920	1252	
TOTAL PROTEIN	60	42	GRAMS
TOTAL CARBOHYDRATES	386	245	GRAMS
TOTAL FAT	13	10	GRAMS
TOTAL SATURATED FAT	3	2	GRAMS
TOTAL CHOLESTEROL	213	213	MILLIGRAMS
TOTAL SODIUM	3296	2214	MILLIGRAMS
TOTAL FIBRE	10	6	GRAMS
% CALORIES FROM FAT	6	7	

White Corn Bread

This crunchy bread has a great look and texture. Try it with soup.

1½-pound

1½ teaspoons active dry yeast

¼ cup brown sugar

2¼ cups + 2 tablespoons bread flour

2 teaspoons salt

1 cup white cornmeal

2 eggs

2 tablespoons butter

7 ounces warm milk

1-pound

1 teaspoon active dry yeast

3 tablespoons brown sugar

1½ cups + 2 tablespoons bread flour

1½ teaspoons salt

⅔ cup white cornmeal

1 egg

1½ tablespoons butter

5 ounces warm milk

Notes:
1. For machines with yeast dispensers, use 3 teaspoons of yeast for the 1½-pound loaf.
2. Yellow cornmeal may be substituted for white cornmeal.

NUTRITIONAL ANALYSIS			
	1½-POUND	1-POUND	
TOTAL CALORIES	2519	1549	
TOTAL PROTEIN	78	46	GRAMS
TOTAL CARBOHYDRATES	446	273	GRAMS
TOTAL FAT	46	31	GRAMS
TOTAL SATURATED FAT	20	14	GRAMS
TOTAL CHOLESTEROL	497	266	MILLIGRAMS
TOTAL SODIUM	4566	3385	MILLIGRAMS
TOTAL FIBRE	20	13	GRAMS
% CALORIES FROM FAT	17	18	

OAT BREADS

The breads in this section all include rolled oats in their recipes. Rolled oats (oatmeal) give the bread a soft, spongy texture and good, rich flavor, not to mention additional nutritional benefits. Oatmeal lovers will find that the variety of other ingredients used in the recipes complements the oat flavor and texture, producing some interesting breads.

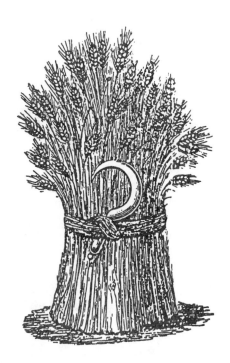

Oatmeal-Sesame Bread

I keep getting repeat requests for this one. It has the spongy texture of oatmeal bread with the nutty taste of sesame seeds. It's a great sandwich bread.

1½-pound

1½ teaspoons active dry yeast

2¾ cups bread flour

1 teaspoon salt

4 tablespoons brown sugar

8 tablespoons sesame seeds

6 tablespoons rolled oats

2 tablespoons butter

9 ounces warm water

1-pound

1 teaspoon active dry yeast

1¾ cups bread flour

½ teaspoon salt

2½ tablespoons brown sugar

5 tablespoons sesame seeds

¼ cup rolled oats

1½ tablespoons butter

¾ cup warm water

Note:

For Panasonic/National machines, use 3 teaspoons of yeast for the 1½-pound loaf.

NUTRITIONAL ANALYSIS			
	1½-POUND	1-POUND	
TOTAL CALORIES	2308	1489	
TOTAL PROTEIN	64	41	GRAMS
TOTAL CARBOHYDRATES	365	232	GRAMS
TOTAL FAT	67	45	GRAMS
TOTAL SATURATED FAT	20	14	GRAMS
TOTAL CHOLESTEROL	62	47	MILLIGRAMS
TOTAL SODIUM	2167	1088	MILLIGRAMS
TOTAL FIBRE	12	8	GRAMS
% CALORIES FROM FAT	26	27	

Nebraska Oatmeal Bread

This traditional oatmeal bread is easy to make, uses basic ingredients, and is tasty and nutritious. The loaf is fairly densely textured.

1½-pound

1½ teaspoons active dry yeast

2½ tablespoons brown sugar

2 cups bread flour

1½ teaspoons salt

1 cup rolled oats

1 tablespoon butter

1 cup warm milk

¼ cup warm water

1-pound

1 teaspoon active dry yeast

1½ tablespoons brown sugar

1⅓ cups bread flour

1 teaspoon salt

⅔ cup rolled oats

1 tablespoon butter

5 ounces warm milk

2 tablespoons warm water

Notes:
1. For machines with yeast dispensers, use 3 teaspoons of yeast for the 1½-pound loaf.
2. For a light-texture loaf, add an extra ½ teaspoon of yeast and an extra tablespoon of warm water for the 1½-pound recipe. Add ¼ teaspoon of yeast and ½ tablespoon of water for the 1-pound loaf.

NUTRITIONAL ANALYSIS			
	1½-POUND	1-POUND	
TOTAL CALORIES	1641	1114	
TOTAL PROTEIN	55	37	GRAMS
TOTAL CARBOHYDRATES	299	197	GRAMS
TOTAL FAT	24	20	GRAMS
TOTAL SATURATED FAT	10	9	GRAMS
TOTAL CHOLESTEROL	41	37	MILLIGRAMS
TOTAL SODIUM	3341	2222	MILLIGRAMS
TOTAL FIBRE	13	9	GRAMS
% CALORIES FROM FAT	13	16	

Pistachio Oatmeal Bread

The distinctive flavor of pistachio nuts permeates this loaf. To get the best distribution of the pistachio oil in the dough, add the nuts at the beginning rather than at the mix-cycle beep.

1½-pound

1½ teaspoons active dry yeast

¾ cup rolled oats

2½ cups bread flour

1 teaspoon salt

1 teaspoon sugar

1½ tablespoons butter

3 tablespoons honey

¾ cup warm milk

3 ounces warm water

⅓ cup chopped pistachio nuts

1-pound

1 teaspoon active dry yeast

½ cup rolled oats

1⅔ cups bread flour

½ teaspoon salt

½ teaspoon sugar

1 tablespoon butter

2 tablespoons honey

½ cup warm milk

¼ cup warm water

¼ cup chopped pistachio nuts

Note:

For machines with yeast dispensers, use 3 teaspoons of yeast for the 1½-pound loaf.

NUTRITIONAL ANALYSIS			
	1½-POUND	1-POUND	
TOTAL CALORIES	2157	1460	
TOTAL PROTEIN	64	43	GRAMS
TOTAL CARBOHYDRATES	359	239	GRAMS
TOTAL FAT	53	38	GRAMS
TOTAL SATURATED FAT	15	11	GRAMS
TOTAL CHOLESTEROL	54	36	MILLIGRAMS
TOTAL SODIUM	2239	1138	MILLIGRAMS
TOTAL FIBRE	14	9	GRAMS
% CALORIES FROM FAT	22	23	

Soy Oatmeal Bread

The addition of soy flour to this oatmeal bread boosts the nutritional level of the bread, particularly the protein content. This is a good low-fat bread.

1½-pound

1 teaspoon active dry yeast

⅓ cup soy flour

1¾ cups bread flour

1¼ cups rolled oats

½ teaspoon salt

1½ tablespoons butter

5 tablespoons molasses

7 ounces warm water

1-pound

½ teaspoon active dry yeast

¼ cup soy flour

1¼ cups bread flour

¾ cup rolled oats

¼ teaspoon salt

1 tablespoon butter

3 tablespoons molasses

5 ounces warm water

Note:

For machines with yeast dispensers, use 2 teaspoons of yeast for the 1½-pound loaf and 1 teaspoon for the 1-pound loaf.

NUTRITIONAL ANALYSIS			
	1½-POUND	1-POUND	
TOTAL CALORIES	1821	1218	
TOTAL PROTEIN	62	43	GRAMS
TOTAL CARBOHYDRATES	325	217	GRAMS
TOTAL FAT	28	18	GRAMS
TOTAL SATURATED FAT	12	8	GRAMS
TOTAL CHOLESTEROL	47	31	MILLIGRAMS
TOTAL SODIUM	1158	589	MILLIGRAMS
TOTAL FIBRE	16	10	GRAMS
% CALORIES FROM FAT	14	14	

Sunflower Oatmeal Bread

The sunflower seeds secrete an oil that mixes throughout the dough and gives this bread a fine, nutty flavor. It's excellent for breakfast toast.

1½-pound	1-pound
1½ teaspoons active dry yeast	1 teaspoon active dry yeast
2¼ cups bread flour	1½ cups bread flour
¼ cup sunflower seeds	2 tablespoons sunflower seeds
1 teaspoon salt	½ teaspoon salt
¼ cup rolled oats	2 tablespoons rolled oats
½ cup whole-wheat flour	½ cup whole-wheat flour
½ teaspoon sugar	½ teaspoon sugar
1 egg	1 egg
1 tablespoon butter	1 tablespoon butter
1 tablespoon molasses	½ tablespoon molasses
1½ tablespoons honey	1 tablespoon honey
3 ounces warm buttermilk	¼ cup warm buttermilk
½ cup warm water	3 ounces warm water

Notes:
1. For machines with yeast dispensers, use 3 teaspoons of yeast for the 1½-pound loaf.
2. Sunflower seeds may be added at the mix-cycle beep, if your machine is so equipped.

NUTRITIONAL ANALYSIS			
	1½-POUND	1-POUND	
TOTAL CALORIES	1969	1387	
TOTAL PROTEIN	66	48	GRAMS
TOTAL CARBOHYDRATES	336	233	GRAMS
TOTAL FAT	41	30	GRAMS
TOTAL SATURATED FAT	12	11	GRAMS
TOTAL CHOLESTEROL	252	249	MILLIGRAMS
TOTAL SODIUM	2278	1182	MILLIGRAMS
TOTAL FIBRE	15	12	GRAMS
% CALORIES FROM FAT	19	20	

WHOLE-GRAIN BREADS

The breads in this section are characterized by the use of whole-grain flours of all types. These tasty breads are among the most nutritious you can bake. If you purchased your bread machine to make healthful breads, take a close look at the recipes in this section.

Seven-Grain Bread

This bread is one of my family's favorites because of its crunchy texture and 100-percent wheat flavor. The addition of the dough enhancer will give the bread a smoother texture, but it is excellent either way.

1½-pound

3 teaspoons active dry yeast

1 tablespoon dough enhancer (optional)

3 cups whole-wheat flour

2 eggs

1 teaspoon salt

½ cup seven-grain cereal

4 tablespoons honey

3 tablespoons olive oil

1 cup warm water

1-pound

2 teaspoons active dry yeast

2 teaspoons dough enhancer (optional)

2 cups whole-wheat flour

1 egg

½ teaspoon salt

5 tablespoons seven-grain cereal

3 tablespoons honey

2 tablespoons olive oil

5 ounces warm water

Note:

Soak the seven-grain cereal in the water for 30-60 minutes before adding to recipe.

NUTRITIONAL ANALYSIS			
	1½-POUND	1-POUND	
TOTAL CALORIES	2149	1421	
TOTAL PROTEIN	71	45	GRAMS
TOTAL CARBOHYDRATES	356	242	GRAMS
TOTAL FAT	59	38	GRAMS
TOTAL SATURATED FAT	10	6	GRAMS
TOTAL CHOLESTEROL	426	213	MILLIGRAMS
TOTAL SODIUM	2265	1134	MILLIGRAMS
TOTAL FIBRE	53	35	GRAMS
% CALORIES FROM FAT	25	24	

Tri-Grain Bread

A hearty combination of barley, oats, and wheat makes this bread an excellent choice for breakfast toast or sandwiches. It has a strong grain flavor and is a whole-grain lover's delight.

1½-pound

1 tablespoon active dry yeast

1 tablespoon dough enhancer
  (optional)

1½ teaspoons gluten (optional)

2¼ cups bread flour

4½ tablespoons oat flour

¼ cup barley flour

5 tablespoons wheat germ

1½ teaspoons salt

3 teaspoons brown sugar

2 tablespoons butter

1 cup warm water

1-pound

2 teaspoons active dry yeast

2 teaspoons dough enhancer
  (optional)

1 teaspoon gluten (optional)

1½ cups bread flour

3 tablespoons oat flour

5 teaspoons barley flour

3 tablespoons wheat germ

1 teaspoon salt

2 teaspoons brown sugar

1½ tablespoons butter

5 ounces warm water

Notes:
1. For Panasonic/National machines, use 3½ teaspoons of yeast for the 1½-pound loaf.
2. For DAK/Welbilt machines, add 2 extra tablespoons of water for the 1½-pound loaf.

NUTRITIONAL ANALYSIS			
	1½-POUND	1-POUND	
TOTAL CALORIES	1728	1203	
TOTAL PROTEIN	59	38	GRAMS
TOTAL CARBOHYDRATES	302	213	GRAMS
TOTAL FAT	34	24	GRAMS
TOTAL SATURATED FAT	15	11	GRAMS
TOTAL CHOLESTEROL	62	47	MILLIGRAMS
TOTAL SODIUM	3216	2149	MILLIGRAMS
TOTAL FIBRE	18	11	GRAMS
% CALORIES FROM FAT	18	18	

Quinoa Bread

The nutty flavor of quinoa flour is evident in this high-protein loaf. Quinoa is the grain of the ancient Incas and has been a staple in South America for centuries. It has one of the highest protein contents of any of the grains.

1½-pound

1½ teaspoons active dry yeast

1½ tablespoons dry milk

3 tablespoons sugar

1½ teaspoons salt

½ cup quinoa flour

½ cup whole-wheat flour

2 cups bread flour

1½ tablespoons butter

9 ounces warm water

1-pound

1 teaspoon active dry yeast

1 tablespoon dry milk

2 tablespoons sugar

1 teaspoon salt

¼ cup quinoa flour

¼ cup whole-wheat flour

1½ cups bread flour

1 tablespoon butter

¾ cup warm water

Note:

For Panasonic/National machines, use 2 teaspoons of yeast for the 1½-pound loaf.

NUTRITIONAL ANALYSIS			
	1½-POUND	1-POUND	
TOTAL CALORIES	1841	1223	
TOTAL PROTEIN	57	37	GRAMS
TOTAL CARBOHYDRATES	342	228	GRAMS
TOTAL FAT	28	18	GRAMS
TOTAL SATURATED FAT	12	8	GRAMS
TOTAL CHOLESTEROL	48	32	MILLIGRAMS
TOTAL SODIUM	3253	2169	MILLIGRAMS
TOTAL FIBRE	12	7	GRAMS
% CALORIES FROM FAT	14	13	

Buckwheat-Barley Bread

This bread features the distinctive tastes of barley and buckwheat. It is a light whole-grain bread with a texture approaching that of white bread. Try making a tuna sandwich with it or having it with chicken soup.

1½-pound

1½ teaspoons active dry yeast

1 tablespoon dough enhancer
(optional)

¾ cup buckwheat flour

1½ tablespoons dry milk

3 tablespoons sugar

1½ teaspoons salt

¾ cup barley flour

1½ cups + 3 tablespoons bread flour

1½ tablespoons butter

9 ounces warm water

1-pound

1 teaspoon active dry yeast

2 teaspoons dough enhancer
(optional)

½ cup buckwheat flour

1 tablespoon dry milk

2 tablespoons sugar

1 teaspoon salt

½ cup barley flour

1 cup + 2 tablespoons bread flour

1 tablespoon butter

¾ cup warm water

Note:
For Panasonic/National machines, use 2 teaspoons of yeast for the 1½-pound loaf.

NUTRITIONAL ANALYSIS			
	1½-POUND	1-POUND	
TOTAL CALORIES	1766	1227	
TOTAL PROTEIN	54	37	GRAMS
TOTAL CARBOHYDRATES	325	229	GRAMS
TOTAL FAT	25	17	GRAMS
TOTAL SATURATED FAT	12	8	GRAMS
TOTAL CHOLESTEROL	48	32	MILLIGRAMS
TOTAL SODIUM	3253	2169	MILLIGRAMS
TOTAL FIBRE	15	10	GRAMS
% CALORIES FROM FAT	13	12	

Grape-Nuts Bread

Take one of your favorite breakfast cereals and make bread with it. It comes out with a wonderful nutty taste and great crunchy texture. Have it for breakfast along with your bowl of Grape-Nuts.

1½-pound	1-pound
1½ teaspoons active dry yeast	1 teaspoon active dry yeast
1 tablespoon dough enhancer (optional)	2 teaspoons dough enhancer (optional)
½ cup Grape-Nuts cereal	¼ cup Grape-Nuts cereal
1½ tablespoons dry milk	1 tablespoon dry milk
3 tablespoons sugar	2 tablespoons sugar
1½ teaspoons salt	1 teaspoon salt
1¼ cups whole-wheat flour	¾ cup whole-wheat flour
1½ cups bread flour	1 cup bread flour
1½ tablespoons butter	1 tablespoon butter
9 ounces warm water	¾ cup warm water

Note:

For Panasonic/National machines, use 2 teaspoons of yeast for the 1½-pound loaf.

NUTRITIONAL ANALYSIS			
	1½-POUND	1-POUND	
TOTAL CALORIES	1800	1130	
TOTAL PROTEIN	56	35	GRAMS
TOTAL CARBOHYDRATES	345	215	GRAMS
TOTAL FAT	24	15	GRAMS
TOTAL SATURATED FAT	12	8	GRAMS
TOTAL CHOLESTEROL	48	32	MILLIGRAMS
TOTAL SODIUM	3593	2338	MILLIGRAMS
TOTAL FIBRE	28	17	GRAMS
% CALORIES FROM FAT	12	12	

Sunflower-Nut Bread

This recipe combines sunflower seeds, nuts, whole wheat, and rolled oats, making a tangy-flavored light-textured bread. For extra crunchiness, add the seeds and nuts after the first rise instead of with the rest of the ingredients

1½-pound

2 teaspoons active dry yeast

2 tablespoons sunflower seeds

2 tablespoons chopped nuts

½ cup rolled oats

½ cup whole-wheat flour

1 teaspoon salt

1 tablespoon brown sugar

2 cups bread flour

4 teaspoons olive oil

½ cup warm water

1½ tablespoons butter

5 ounces warm milk

1-pound

1½ teaspoons active dry yeast

4 teaspoons sunflower seeds

4 teaspoons chopped nuts

½ cup rolled oats

½ cup whole-wheat flour

½ teaspoon salt

2 teaspoon brown sugar

1½ cups bread flour

1 tablespoon olive oil

3 ounces warm water

1 tablespoon butter

3½ ounces warm milk

Notes:
1. For Panasonic/National machines, use 3½ teaspoons of yeast for the 1½-pound loaf.
2. For DAK/Welbilt machines, use 5 ounces of warm water for the 1½-pound loaf.

NUTRITIONAL ANALYSIS			
	1½-POUND	1-POUND	
TOTAL CALORIES	1975	1412	
TOTAL PROTEIN	60	44	GRAMS
TOTAL CARBOHYDRATES	298	215	GRAMS
TOTAL FAT	62	44	GRAMS
TOTAL SATURATED FAT	17	12	GRAMS
TOTAL CHOLESTEROL	53	35	MILLIGRAMS
TOTAL SODIUM	2225	1131	MILLIGRAMS
TOTAL FIBRE	18	15	GRAMS
% CALORIES FROM FAT	28	28	

Barley Bread

If you like the sweet taste of barley, you'll enjoy this bread's distinctive barley flavor. It is a light-colored bread, with good texture and a whole-grain taste, punctuated by a light sesame flavor.

1½-pound

1½ teaspoons active dry yeast

1 tablespoon dough enhancer (optional)

2 teaspoons sesame seeds

1½ tablespoons dry milk

3 tablespoons sugar

1½ teaspoons salt

1 cup barley flour

2 cups bread flour

1½ tablespoons butter

9 ounces warm water

1-pound

1 teaspoon active dry yeast

2 teaspoons dough enhancer (optional)

1½ teaspoons sesame seeds

1 tablespoon dry milk

2 tablespoons sugar

1 teaspoon salt

¾ cup barley flour

1¼ cups bread flour

1 tablespoon butter

¾ cup warm water

Notes:

1. For Panasonic/National machines, use 3 teaspoons of yeast for the 1½-pound loaf.
2. For DAK/Welbilt machines, use 10 ounces of warm water for the 1½-pound loaf.

NUTRITIONAL ANALYSIS			
	1½-POUND	1-POUND	
TOTAL CALORIES	1754	1173	
TOTAL PROTEIN	53	35	GRAMS
TOTAL CARBOHYDRATES	312	206	GRAMS
TOTAL FAT	27	19	GRAMS
TOTAL SATURATED FAT	12	8	GRAMS
TOTAL CHOLESTEROL	48	32	MILLIGRAMS
TOTAL SODIUM	3255	2170	MILLIGRAMS
TOTAL FIBRE	19	14	GRAMS
% CALORIES FROM FAT	14	15	

Buckwheat Bread

This is the bread for buckwheat lovers. Because of its strong buckwheat flavor and texture, it is excellent with vegetable soups or for morning toast.

1½-pound

1½ teaspoons active dry yeast

1 tablespoon dough enhancer
   (optional)

1½ tablespoons dry milk

2 tablespoons sugar

1¾ cups + 2 tablespoons bread flour

1½ teaspoons salt

1 tablespoon wheat or oat bran

¼ cup wheat germ

1¼ cup buckwheat flour

1½ tablespoons butter

9 ounces warm water

1-pound

1 teaspoon active dry yeast

2 teaspoons dough enhancer
   (optional)

1 tablespoon dry milk

2 tablespoons sugar

1¼ cups bread flour

1 teaspoon salt

2 teaspoons wheat or oat bran

2 tablespoons wheat germ

¾ cup buckwheat flour

1 tablespoon butter

¾ cup warm water

Notes:

1. For Panasonic/National machines, use 3 teaspoons of yeast for the 1½-pound loaf.
2. For DAK/Welbilt machines, use 10 ounces of warm water in the 1½-pound loaf.

NUTRITIONAL ANALYSIS			
	1½-POUND	1-POUND	
TOTAL CALORIES	1881	1207	
TOTAL PROTEIN	65	41	GRAMS
TOTAL CARBOHYDRATES	353	226	GRAMS
TOTAL FAT	30	19	GRAMS
TOTAL SATURATED FAT	13	8	GRAMS
TOTAL CHOLESTEROL	48	32	MILLIGRAMS
TOTAL SODIUM	3254	2170	MILLIGRAMS
TOTAL FIBRE	8	5	GRAMS
% CALORIES FROM FAT	14	14	

Oat-Bran Bread

In addition to its good flavor, oat bran has been proven to be one of the healthiest of bread ingredients. This bread is a fine addition to any breakfast table.

1½-pound

1½ teaspoons active dry yeast

2 tablespoons dry milk

4 tablespoons sugar

½ cup oat bran

1 cup oat flour

1½ teaspoons salt

1½ cups bread flour

1½ tablespoons butter

9 ounces warm water

1-pound

1 teaspoon active dry yeast

1½ tablespoons dry milk

2½ tablespoons sugar

¼ cup oat bran

¾ cup oat flour

1 teaspoon salt

1 cup bread flour

1 tablespoon butter

¾ cup warm water

Notes:
1. For Panasonic/National machines, use 3 teaspoons of yeast for the 1½-pound loaf.
2. For DAK/Welbilt machines, use 10 ounces of warm water for the 1½-pound loaf.

NUTRITIONAL ANALYSIS			
	1½-POUND	1-POUND	
TOTAL CALORIES	1666	1117	
TOTAL PROTEIN	53	35	GRAMS
TOTAL CARBOHYDRATES	315	211	GRAMS
TOTAL FAT	26	17	GRAMS
TOTAL SATURATED FAT	11	8	GRAMS
TOTAL CHOLESTEROL	49	33	MILLIGRAMS
TOTAL SODIUM	3270	2185	MILLIGRAMS
TOTAL FIBRE	27	18	GRAMS
% CALORIES FROM FAT	14	14	

Multi-Grain Bread

This bread combines five types of whole-grain flours for a grain lover's delight. All of these grains together create a unique loaf with a distinctive, but elusive flavor.

1½-pound

3 teaspoons active dry yeast

1 tablespoon dough enhancer
  (optional)

1½ teaspoons gluten

¼ cup buckwheat flour

¼ cup whole-wheat flour

2 cups bread flour

¼ cup oat flour

¼ cup barley flour

3 tablespoons oat bran

2 tablespoons wheat germ

1 teaspoon salt

1 tablespoon brown sugar

2 tablespoons butter

9 ounces warm water

1-pound

2 teaspoons active dry yeast

2 teaspoons dough enhancer
  (optional)

1 teaspoon gluten

2 tablespoons buckwheat flour

2 tablespoons whole-wheat flour

1½ cups bread flour

2 tablespoons oat flour

2 tablespoons barley flour

2 tablespoons oat bran

4 teaspoons wheat germ

½ teaspoon salt

2 teaspoons brown sugar

1½ tablespoons butter

¾ cup warm water

Notes:
1. For Panasonic/National machines, use 3½ teaspoons of yeast for the 1½-pound loaf.
2. For DAK/Welbilt machines, use 10 ounces of warm water in the 1½-pound loaf.

NUTRITIONAL ANALYSIS			
	1½-POUND	1-POUND	
TOTAL CALORIES	1772	1227	
TOTAL PROTEIN	61	42	GRAMS
TOTAL CARBOHYDRATES	313	214	GRAMS
TOTAL FAT	33	24	GRAMS
TOTAL SATURATED FAT	15	11	GRAMS
TOTAL CHOLESTEROL	62	47	MILLIGRAMS
TOTAL SODIUM	2149	1078	MILLIGRAMS
TOTAL FIBRE	20	12	GRAMS
% CALORIES FROM FAT	17	18	

Barley Three-Seed Bread

The combination of barley, poppy seeds, sesame seeds, and sunflower seeds makes this bread unique, both in flavor and texture. It's excellent with salads.

1½-pound	1-pound
1½ teaspoons active dry yeast	1 teaspoon active dry yeast
3 tablespoons sugar	2 tablespoons sugar
2 cups bread flour	1⅓ cups bread flour
1 teaspoon poppy seeds	½ teaspoon poppy seeds
2 teaspoons sunflower seeds	1½ teaspoons sunflower seeds
2 teaspoons sesame seeds	1½ teaspoons sesame seeds
1 tablespoon dough enhancer (optional)	½ tablespoon dough enhancer (optional)
1 cup barley flour	⅔ cup barley flour
½ teaspoon garlic salt	¼ teaspoon garlic salt
1 teaspoon salt	½ teaspoon salt
1 tablespoon nonfat dry milk	½ tablespoon nonfat dry milk
1 cup + 1 tablespoon warm water	5½ ounces warm water
1½ tablespoons butter	1 tablespoon butter

Notes:
1. For machines with yeast dispensers, use 3 teaspoons of yeast for the 1½-pound loaf.
2. This bread is somewhat crumbly. The addition of the dough enhancer, if available, will help the bread stick together, and give it a smoother texture.

NUTRITIONAL ANALYSIS			
	1½-POUND	1-POUND	
TOTAL CALORIES	1790	1192	
TOTAL PROTEIN	53	35	GRAMS
TOTAL CARBOHYDRATES	312	208	GRAMS
TOTAL FAT	31	21	GRAMS
TOTAL SATURATED FAT	12	8	GRAMS
TOTAL CHOLESTEROL	48	32	MILLIGRAMS
TOTAL SODIUM	3240	1622	MILLIGRAMS
TOTAL FIBRE	20	13	GRAMS
% CALORIES FROM FAT	16	16	

Brown-Rice Bread

A soft, moist texture and light brown color characterize this bread. White rice can be substituted for brown rice.

1½-pound

1½ teaspoons active dry yeast

1 teaspoon sugar

3 cups bread flour

1½ teaspoons salt

¾ cup cooked brown rice

1½ tablespoons olive oil

3 tablespoons honey

4½ ounces warm buttermilk

3 ounces warm water

1-pound

1 teaspoon active dry yeast

½ teaspoon sugar

2 cups bread flour

1 teaspoon salt

½ cup cooked brown rice

1 tablespoon olive oil

2 tablespoons honey

3 ounces warm buttermilk

¼ cup warm water

Note:

For machines with yeast dispensers, use 3 teaspoons of yeast for the 1½-pound loaf.

NUTRITIONAL ANALYSIS			
	1½-POUND	1-POUND	
TOTAL CALORIES	2098	1396	
TOTAL PROTEIN	60	40	GRAMS
TOTAL CARBOHYDRATES	394	262	GRAMS
TOTAL FAT	29	20	GRAMS
TOTAL SATURATED FAT	4	3	GRAMS
TOTAL CHOLESTEROL	12	8	MILLIGRAMS
TOTAL SODIUM	3295	2197	MILLIGRAMS
TOTAL FIBRE	7	5	GRAMS
% CALORIES FROM FAT	13	13	

Millet Bread

Millet is a small, round, hard grain that requires soaking before use. It is also available in ground form as millet flour. The texture of this bread is crunchy, though also light due to the mixture of whole-wheat and bread flours.

1½-pound

1½ teaspoons active dry yeast

1 cup whole-wheat flour

2 cups bread flour

1 teaspoon salt

1 cup warm water

½ cup raw millet (or millet cereal)

2 tablespoons olive oil

3 tablespoons honey

1 egg

1-pound

1 teaspoon active dry yeast

⅔ cup whole-wheat flour

1½ cups bread flour

½ teaspoon salt

⅔ cup warm water

⅓ cup raw millet (or millet cereal)

1½ tablespoons olive oil

2 tablespoons honey

1 egg

Notes:

1. For machines with yeast dispensers, use 3 teaspoons of yeast for the 1½-pound loaf.
2. Soak the millet in the warm water for 45–60 minutes before adding the grain and the water to the recipe.

NUTRITIONAL ANALYSIS			
	1½-POUND	1-POUND	
TOTAL CALORIES	2279	1645	
TOTAL PROTEIN	68	50	GRAMS
TOTAL CARBOHYDRATES	409	289	GRAMS
TOTAL FAT	43	33	GRAMS
TOTAL SATURATED FAT	7	5	GRAMS
TOTAL CHOLESTEROL	213	213	MILLIGRAMS
TOTAL SODIUM	2207	1137	MILLIGRAMS
TOTAL FIBRE	21	14	GRAMS
% CALORIES FROM FAT	17	18	

Sesame Quinoa Bread

Quinoa, native to South America, is one of the grains highest in protein. Since it contains no gluten, it must be combined with wheat flour. Sesame Quinoa Bread has a nutty, earthy flavor, making it an excellent sandwich bread.

1½-pound	1-pound
1½ teaspoons active dry yeast	1 teaspoon active dry yeast
3 tablespoons sugar	2 tablespoons sugar
2 cups bread flour	1⅓ cups bread flour
½ cup quinoa flour	⅓ cup quinoa flour
3 tablespoons sesame seeds	2 tablespoons sesame seeds
½ teaspoon oregano	¼ teaspoon oregano
½ teaspoon ground caraway seeds	¼ teaspoon ground caraway seeds
½ cup whole-wheat flour	⅓ cup whole-wheat flour
1½ teaspoons salt	1 teaspoon salt
1½ tablespoons nonfat dry milk	1 tablespoon nonfat dry milk
9 ounces warm water	¾ cup warm water
2 tablespoons butter	1½ tablespoons butter

Note:
For machines with yeast dispensers, use 3 teaspoons of yeast for the 1½-pound loaf.

NUTRITIONAL ANALYSIS			
	1½-POUND	1-POUND	
TOTAL CALORIES	2053	1379	
TOTAL PROTEIN	62	41	GRAMS
TOTAL CARBOHYDRATES	350	232	GRAMS
TOTAL FAT	47	33	GRAMS
TOTAL SATURATED FAT	17	13	GRAMS
TOTAL CHOLESTEROL	64	48	MILLIGRAMS
TOTAL SODIUM	3256	2171	MILLIGRAMS
TOTAL FIBRE	14	9	GRAMS
% CALORIES FROM FAT	21	22	

Soy Bread

This white bread is enriched by the addition of high-protein soy flour.

1½-pound

1½ teaspoons active dry yeast

1½ tablespoons sugar

½ cup soy flour

2½ cups bread flour

1½ teaspoons salt

9 ounces warm milk

1½ tablespoons butter

1-pound

1 teaspoon active dry yeast

1 tablespoon sugar

⅓ cup soy flour

1⅔ cups bread flour

1 teaspoon salt

¾ cup warm milk

1 tablespoon butter

Note:

For machines with yeast dispensers, use 3 teaspoons of yeast for the 1½-pound loaf.

NUTRITIONAL ANALYSIS			
	1½-POUND	1-POUND	
TOTAL CALORIES	1746	1165	
TOTAL PROTEIN	75	50	GRAMS
TOTAL CARBOHYDRATES	300	200	GRAMS
TOTAL FAT	27	18	GRAMS
TOTAL SATURATED FAT	13	9	GRAMS
TOTAL CHOLESTEROL	58	39	MILLIGRAMS
TOTAL SODIUM	3355	2236	MILLIGRAMS
TOTAL FIBRE	8	5	GRAMS
% CALORIES FROM FAT	14	14	

MULTIPLE-GRAIN BREADS

This section features seven mixed-grain breads in which the taste of grain dominates. These unique combinations of grains are especially designed for whole-grain-bread lovers.

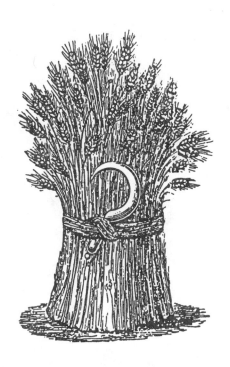

Bran & Rye Bread

This light wheat-rye bread has added oat bran for texture, flavor, and nutrients. It has a light wheat taste and texture.

1½-pound	1-pound
1½ teaspoons active dry yeast	1 teaspoon active dry yeast
2½ tablespoons brown sugar	1½ tablespoons brown sugar
1 cup + 1½ tablespoons bread flour	⅔ cup + 1 tablespoon bread flour
½ cup whole-wheat flour	⅓ cup whole-wheat flour
¾ cup rye flour	½ cup rye flour
¾ cup oat bran	½ cup oat bran
2 teaspoons salt	1½ teaspoons salt
2 tablespoons butter	1½ tablespoons butter
9 ounces warm buttermilk	¾ cup warm buttermilk

Notes:

1. For machines with yeast dispensers, use 3 teaspoons of yeast for the 1½-pound loaf.
2. If your machine is equipped with a whole-grain cycle, use it for this bread.

NUTRITIONAL ANALYSIS			
	1½-POUND	1-POUND	
TOTAL CALORIES	1691	1130	
TOTAL PROTEIN	60	40	GRAMS
TOTAL CARBOHYDRATES	300	197	GRAMS
TOTAL FAT	35	25	GRAMS
TOTAL SATURATED FAT	17	12	GRAMS
TOTAL CHOLESTEROL	85	62	MILLIGRAMS
TOTAL SODIUM	4460	3328	MILLIGRAMS
TOTAL FIBRE	31	21	GRAMS
% CALORIES FROM FAT	18	20	

Corn, Wheat, & Rye Bread

This is a very crunchy whole-grain bread with a good wheat flavor and a hint of rye.

1½-pound

2 teaspoons active dry yeast

3 tablespoons brown sugar

½ cup cornmeal

1¼ cups whole-wheat flour

1¼ cups rye flour

1½ teaspoons salt

3 tablespoons butter

9 ounces warm water

1-pound

1½ teaspoons active dry yeast

2 tablespoons brown sugar

¼ cup + 2 tablespoons cornmeal

1 cup whole-wheat flour

¾ cup rye flour

1 teaspoon salt

2 tablespoons butter

¾ cup warm water

Notes:

1. For machines with yeast dispensers, use 4 teaspoons of yeast for the 1½-pound loaf.
2. If your machine is equipped with a whole-grain cycle, use it for this bread.

NUTRITIONAL ANALYSIS			
	1½-POUND	1-POUND	
TOTAL CALORIES	1648	1158	
TOTAL PROTEIN	40	29	GRAMS
TOTAL CARBOHYDRATES	296	210	GRAMS
TOTAL FAT	42	28	GRAMS
TOTAL SATURATED FAT	22	15	GRAMS
TOTAL CHOLESTEROL	93	62	MILLIGRAMS
TOTAL SODIUM	3242	2164	MILLIGRAMS
TOTAL FIBRE	45	32	GRAMS
% CALORIES FROM FAT	230	22	

Mixed-Grain Bread

This bread combines many different grains for a full-grain taste. It doesn't rise much, due to the low-gluten content of the ingredients, but it is a wonderful, healthful bread with an earthy aroma.

1½-pound

2½ teaspoons active dry yeast

⅔ cup bread flour

½ teaspoon caraway seeds

2 teaspoons salt

½ cup rice flour

⅔ cup buckwheat flour

⅔ cup oat flour

⅔ cup rye flour

5 tablespoons molasses

1 egg

7 ounces warm water

3 tablespoons raisins

2 tablespoons gluten powder (optional)

1-pound

1½ teaspoons active dry yeast

½ cup bread flour

½ teaspoon caraway seeds

1½ teaspoons salt

⅓ cup rice flour

½ cup buckwheat flour

½ cup oat flour

½ cup rye flour

4 tablespoons molasses

1 egg

4½ ounces warm water

2 tablespoons raisins

1½ tablespoons gluten powder (optional)

Notes:

1. For machines with yeast dispensers, use 4½ teaspoons of yeast for the 1½-pound loaf.
2. If your machine is equipped with a whole-grain cycle, use it for this bread.
3. Raisins may be added at the mix-cycle beep, if your machine is so equipped.

NUTRITIONAL ANALYSIS			
	1½-POUND	1-POUND	
TOTAL CALORIES	1877	1403	
TOTAL PROTEIN	52	39	GRAMS
TOTAL CARBOHYDRATES	392	289	GRAMS
TOTAL FAT	13	11	GRAMS
TOTAL SATURATED FAT	3	2	GRAMS
TOTAL CHOLESTEROL	213	213	MILLIGRAMS
TOTAL SODIUM	4414	3329	MILLIGRAMS
TOTAL FIBRE	27	20	GRAMS
% CALORIES FROM FAT	6	7	

Oat, Rice & Rye Bread

This bread doesn't rise much, but with its tight texture and flat top, it tastes delicious.

1½-pound

2 teaspoons active dry yeast

1½ tablespoons gluten powder

¾ cup bread flour

1 teaspoon ground caraway seeds

¾ cup rice flour

¾ cup oat flour

¾ cup rye flour

1½ teaspoons salt

2 tablespoons brown sugar

2 tablespoons butter

9 ounces warm water

1-pound

1½ teaspoons active dry yeast

1 tablespoon gluten powder

½ cup bread flour

½ teaspoon ground caraway seeds

½ cup rice flour

½ cup oat flour

½ cup rye flour

1 teaspoon salt

1½ tablespoons brown sugar

1½ tablespoons butter

¾ ounces warm water

Notes:

1. For machines with yeast dispensers, use 4 teaspoons of yeast for the 1½-pound loaf.
2. If your machine is equipped with a whole-grain cycle, use it for this bread.
3. For a slightly higher rise, try adding an extra ½ teaspoon of yeast.

NUTRITIONAL ANALYSIS			
	1½-POUND	1-POUND	
TOTAL CALORIES	1774	1208	
TOTAL PROTEIN	51	34	GRAMS
TOTAL CARBOHYDRATES	330	222	GRAMS
TOTAL FAT	30	22	GRAMS
TOTAL SATURATED FAT	15	11	GRAMS
TOTAL CHOLESTEROL	62	47	MILLIGRAMS
TOTAL SODIUM	3217	2146	MILLIGRAMS
TOTAL FIBRE	30	20	GRAMS
% CALORIES FROM FAT	15	16	

Whole-Wheat & Rice Bread

This bread uses only wheat and rice flours, so the result is a bread similar to 100 percent–wheat bread, both in texture and flavor. The rice flour has a smoothing effect on the texture, but it contains no gluten, so the loaf will rise slightly less than a normal 100 percent–wheat loaf.

1½-pound	1-pound
2 teaspoons active dry yeast	1½ teaspoons active dry yeast
2¼ cups whole-wheat flour	1½ cups whole-wheat flour
½ teaspoon mace	¼ teaspoon mace
¾ cup rice flour	½ cup rice flour
2 teaspoons salt	1½ teaspoons salt
2 tablespoons butter	1½ tablespoons butter
3 tablespoons honey	2 tablespoons honey
1 cup warm water	5½ ounces warm water
¼ cup raisins	3 tablespoons raisins

Notes:
1. For machines with yeast dispensers, use 4 teaspoons of yeast for the 1½-pound loaf.
2. If your machine is equipped with a whole-grain cycle, use it for this bread.
3. Raisins may be added at the mix-cycle beep, if your machine is so equipped.
4. For machines with low-power motors, add 2 tablespoons of warm water for the 1½-pound loaf.

NUTRITIONAL ANALYSIS			
	1½-POUND	1-POUND	
TOTAL CALORIES	1852	1289	
TOTAL PROTEIN	47	32	GRAMS
TOTAL CARBOHYDRATES	369	256	GRAMS
TOTAL FAT	30	22	GRAMS
TOTAL SATURATED FAT	16	12	GRAMS
TOTAL CHOLESTEROL	62	47	MILLIGRAMS
TOTAL SODIUM	4276	3208	MILLIGRAMS
TOTAL FIBRE	40	27	GRAMS
% CALORIES FROM FAT	14	15	

Whole-Wheat, Bran & Oat Bread

This bread has a soft texture and a mild wheat-oat flavor. Because bread flour comprises half the flour, it rises well and yields a nice-looking, good-tasting loaf.

1½-pound

2 teaspoons active dry yeast

3 tablespoons brown sugar

1½ tablespoons gluten powder

1½ cups bread flour

⅓ cup oat bran

¾ cup oat flour

¾ cup whole-wheat flour

2 teaspoons salt

3½ tablespoons butter

1¼ cups warm water

1-pound

1½ teaspoons active dry yeast

2 tablespoons brown sugar

1 tablespoon gluten powder

1 cup bread flour

¼ cup oat bran

½ cup oat flour

½ cup whole-wheat flour

1½ teaspoons salt

2½ tablespoons butter

6½ ounces warm water

Note:

For machines with yeast dispensers, use 3½ teaspoons of yeast for the 1½-pound loaf.

NUTRITIONAL ANALYSIS			
	1½-POUND	1-POUND	
TOTAL CALORIES	2031	1406	
TOTAL PROTEIN	67	45	GRAMS
TOTAL CARBOHYDRATES	344	238	GRAMS
TOTAL FAT	50	35	GRAMS
TOTAL SATURATED FAT	26	18	GRAMS
TOTAL CHOLESTEROL	109	78	MILLIGRAMS
TOTAL SODIUM	4289	3217	MILLIGRAMS
TOTAL FIBRE	32	22	GRAMS
% CALORIES FROM FAT	22	22	

Whole-Wheat, Rye & Oat Bread

A good dense texture and hearty flavor characterize this bread. It's excellent eaten warm or toasted, and it's especially good with all kinds of cheese.

1½-pound	1-pound
2 teaspoons active dry yeast	1½ teaspoons active dry yeast
¾ cup oat flour	½ cup oat flour
¾ cup rye flour	½ cup rye flour
1½ cups whole-wheat flour	1 cup whole-wheat flour
1½ teaspoons salt	1 teaspoon salt
3 tablespoons butter	2 tablespoons butter
3 tablespoons honey	2 tablespoons honey
1 cup + 1 tablespoon warm water	5½ ounces warm water

Notes:
1. For machines with yeast dispensers, use 4 teaspoons of yeast for the 1½-pound loaf.
2. If your machine is equipped with a whole-grain cycle, use it for this bread.

NUTRITIONAL ANALYSIS			
	1½-POUND	1-POUND	
TOTAL CALORIES	1675	1118	
TOTAL PROTEIN	45	30	GRAMS
TOTAL CARBOHYDRATES	304	203	GRAMS
TOTAL FAT	41	27	GRAMS
TOTAL SATURATED FAT	22	15	GRAMS
TOTAL CHOLESTEROL	93	62	MILLIGRAMS
TOTAL SODIUM	3209	2139	MILLIGRAMS
TOTAL FIBRE	47	31	GRAMS
% CALORIES FROM FAT	22	22	

SPICE AND SWEET BREADS

If you like a lot of different flavors in your breads, these recipes will appeal to you. The spice breads use many different types of spices and seasonings to give them unique flavors. The sweet breads combine natural sweeteners with other bread ingredients to give you bread that will satisfy your sweet tooth in a low-calorie and natural way.

Cumin Spice Bread

Cumin, a relative of oregano, is a common spice in most Mexican foods. This bread has a distinct cumin flavor while still possessing the wonderful texture and taste of whole-grain flours.

1½-pound

3 teaspoons active dry yeast

2 teaspoons dried orange peel

1 teaspoon sugar

2 teaspoons cumin powder

½ cup rye flour

1 teaspoon salt

½ cup whole-wheat flour

2 cups bread flour

7 ounces warm milk

5 tablespoons honey

3 tablespoons olive oil

1-pound

2 teaspoons active dry yeast

1½ teaspoons dried orange peel

1 teaspoon sugar

1¼ teaspoons cumin powder

½ cup rye flour

½ teaspoon salt

½ cup whole-wheat flour

1¼ cups bread flour

6 ounces warm milk

3 tablespoons + 1 teaspoon honey

2 tablespoons olive oil

NUTRITIONAL ANALYSIS			
	1½-POUND	1-POUND	
TOTAL CALORIES	2200	1583	
TOTAL PROTEIN	61	46	GRAMS
TOTAL CARBOHYDRATES	385	281	GRAMS
TOTAL FAT	51	35	GRAMS
TOTAL SATURATED FAT	8	6	GRAMS
TOTAL CHOLESTEROL	9	8	MILLIGRAMS
TOTAL SODIUM	2257	1170	MILLIGRAMS
TOTAL FIBRE	14	12	GRAMS
% CALORIES FROM FAT	21	20	

Dilly Bread

This is an old family favorite. The cottage cheese (I use low-fat) gives it a great texture and flavor that is perfect with a salad. Note that all-purpose flour is used to maintain the original texture.

1½-pound

2½ teaspoons active dry yeast

3 cups all-purpose flour

½ teaspoon baking soda

1½ teaspoons salt

1½ tablespoons dill weed

2½ tablespoons sugar

2 tablespoons warm water

3 eggs

1 cup cottage cheese

1-pound

1½ teaspoon active dry yeast

2 cups all-purpose flour

¼ teaspoon baking soda

1 teaspoon salt

1 tablespoon dill weed

1½ tablespoons sugar

1 tablespoon warm water

2 eggs

¾ cup cottage cheese

Note:
For Panasonic/National machines, use 3½ teaspoons of yeast for the 1½-pound loaf.

NUTRITIONAL ANALYSIS			
	1½-POUND	1-POUND	
TOTAL CALORIES	2056	1379	
TOTAL PROTEIN	100	69	GRAMS
TOTAL CARBOHYDRATES	343	227	GRAMS
TOTAL FAT	26	18	GRAMS
TOTAL SATURATED FAT	8	5	GRAMS
TOTAL CHOLESTEROL	669	449	MILLIGRAMS
TOTAL SODIUM	4425	3035	MILLIGRAMS
TOTAL FIBRE	7	5	GRAMS
% CALORIES FROM FAT	11	12	

Peppy Cheese Bread

This bread has a snappy cheese flavor and is great for a ham or tuna sandwich. Cut it into small pieces for tasty and attractive appetizer sandwiches.

1½-pound

1½ teaspoons active dry yeast

3 cups bread flour

3 tablespoons Parmesan cheese

¼ cup grated Swiss cheese

1½ teaspoons oregano

¼ cup grated cheddar cheese

3 tablespoons wheat germ

4 teaspoons sugar

1½ teaspoons Louisiana-style hot sauce

2½ tablespoons butter

9 ounces warm water

1-pound

1 teaspoon active dry yeast

2 cups bread flour

2 tablespoons Parmesan cheese

2 tablespoons grated Swiss cheese

1 teaspoon oregano

2 tablespoons grated cheddar cheese

2 tablespoons wheat germ

1 tablespoon sugar

1 teaspoon Louisiana-style hot sauce

1½ tablespoons butter

¾ cup warm water

Notes:

1. For Panasonic/National machines, use 2½ teaspoons of yeast for the 1½-pound loaf.
2. Because of the fresh cheese content, use a lighter crust setting.
3. Because of the wetter dough caused by the melting cheese, the top of the loaf may fall during baking. This will not affect the taste of the bread.
4. The fresh cheeses may be added at the mix cycle, if desired.

NUTRITIONAL ANALYSIS			
	1½-POUND	1-POUND	
TOTAL CALORIES	2162	1395	
TOTAL PROTEIN	77	49	GRAMS
TOTAL CARBOHYDRATES	329	221	GRAMS
TOTAL FAT	60	35	GRAMS
TOTAL SATURATED FAT	33	19	GRAMS
TOTAL CHOLESTEROL	144	82	MILLIGRAMS
TOTAL SODIUM	747	444	MILLIGRAMS
TOTAL FIBRE	9	6	GRAMS
% CALORIES FROM FAT	25	23	

Taco Bread

The cornmeal and taco seasoning in this bread actually give it the flavor of a taco. It goes great with hot Southwestern chili.

1½-pound

1½ teaspoons active dry yeast

2 cups bread flour

3 tablespoons taco seasoning

¼ cup whole-wheat flour

¾ cup cornmeal

1 teaspoon garlic salt

2 tablespoons sugar

1½ tablespoons olive oil

9 ounces warm water

1-pound

1 teaspoon active dry yeast

1¼ cups bread flour

2 tablespoons taco seasoning

2 tablespoons whole-wheat flour

½ cup cornmeal

½ teaspoon garlic salt

4 teaspoons sugar

1 tablespoon olive oil

¾ cup warm water

Note:

For Panasonic/National machines, use 2½ teaspoons of yeast for the 1½-pound loaf.

NUTRITIONAL ANALYSIS			
	1½-POUND	1-POUND	
TOTAL CALORIES	1803	1254	
TOTAL PROTEIN	47	32	GRAMS
TOTAL CARBOHYDRATES	337	236	GRAMS
TOTAL FAT	30	21	GRAMS
TOTAL SATURATED FAT	4	3	GRAMS
TOTAL CHOLESTEROL	0	0	MILLIGRAMS
TOTAL SODIUM	5740	3482	MILLIGRAMS
TOTAL FIBRE	18	15	GRAMS
% CALORIES FROM FAT	15	15	

Cheddar-Parmesan Bread

Watch out here! This is a rich bread (due to the cheese content), and no butter is needed. Just pop this bread right in your mouth. It is an excellent bread for a ham sandwich (no cheese needed), and the flavor will remind you of Cheese-It crackers.

1½-pound

2 teaspoons active dry yeast

2½ cups bread flour

2½ tablespoons dried minced onion

1¼ cups grated cheddar cheese

1½ teaspoons paprika

2½ tablespoons Parmesan cheese

1 teaspoon dry mustard

½ teaspoon salt

3½ teaspoons sugar

2½ tablespoons butter

7 ounces warm milk

1-pound

1½ teaspoons active dry yeast

1¾ cups bread flour

5 teaspoons dried minced onion

¾ cup grated cheddar cheese

1 teaspoon paprika

5 teaspoons Parmesan cheese

½ teaspoon dry mustard

½ teaspoon salt

2½ teaspoons sugar

5 teaspoons butter

4½ ounces warm milk

Notes:

1. For Panasonic/National machines, use 3 teaspoons of yeast for the 1½-pound loaf.
2. Use a light-crust setting, because the cheese content of this bread gives it a tendency to bake to a dark-brown crust.

NUTRITIONAL ANALYSIS			
	1½-POUND	1-POUND	
TOTAL CALORIES	2329	1556	
TOTAL PROTEIN	93	61	GRAMS
TOTAL CARBOHYDRATES	289	202	GRAMS
TOTAL FAT	89	56	GRAMS
TOTAL SATURATED FAT	52	33	GRAMS
TOTAL CHOLESTEROL	245	153	MILLIGRAMS
TOTAL SODIUM	2296	1826	MILLIGRAMS
TOTAL FIBRE	7	5	GRAMS
% CALORIES FROM FAT	34	32	

Herb Bread

If you like herbs and spices, you will love this bread. It combines small amounts of herbs for just the right flavor. If you have any left over, dry it, and use it for turkey stuffing.

1½-pound	1-pound
1 teaspoon active dry yeast	½ teaspoon active dry yeast
2 tablespoons sugar	4 teaspoons sugar
3 cups bread flour	2 cups bread flour
2 teaspoons celery seed	1½ teaspoons celery seed
1 teaspoon ground sage	½ teaspoon ground sage
½ teaspoon nutmeg	¼ teaspoon nutmeg
1½ teaspoons salt	1 teaspoon salt
1 teaspoon parsley	½ teaspoon parsley
1 egg	1 egg
¾ cup warm milk	½ cup warm milk
2 tablespoons butte	1½ tablespoons butter
2 ounces warm water	3 tablespoons warm water

Notes:
1. For Panasonic/National machines, use 2 teaspoons of yeast for the 1½-pound loaf.
2. For DAK/Welbilt machines, use 3 ounces of warm water for the 1½-pound loaf.

NUTRITIONAL ANALYSIS			
	1½-POUND	1-POUND	
TOTAL CALORIES	1960	1347	
TOTAL PROTEIN	64	44	GRAMS
TOTAL CARBOHYDRATES	335	223	GRAMS
TOTAL FAT	38	29	GRAMS
TOTAL SATURATED FAT	19	14	GRAMS
TOTAL CHOLESTEROL	283	265	MILLIGRAMS
TOTAL SODIUM	3369	2267	MILLIGRAMS
TOTAL FIBRE	7	5	GRAMS
% CALORIES FROM FAT	18	19	

Pumpkin-Pie Bread

My kids eat this bread before it has a chance to cool off. It tastes like pumpkin pie and makes a great after-school treat.

1½-pound	1-pound
2 teaspoons active dry yeast	1½ teaspoons active dry yeast
9 tablespoons sugar	6 tablespoons sugar
½ teaspoon ginger	¼ teaspoon ginger
1 teaspoon cinnamon	½ teaspoon cinnamon
½ teaspoon dried lemon peel	¼ teaspoon dried lemon peel
¾ cup whole-wheat flour	½ cup whole-wheat flour
1 teaspoon salt	½ teaspoon salt
2½ cups bread flour	1½ cups bread flour
¼ cup + 2 tablespoons canned pumpkin	¼ cup canned pumpkin
3 ounces orange juice	¼ cup orange juice
3 ounces warm water	¼ cup warm water
2 eggs	1 egg
1½ tablespoons butter	1 tablespoon butter

Notes:

1. For Panasonic/National machines, use 3½ teaspoons of yeast for the 1½-pound loaf.
2. For DAK/Welbilt machines, use ½ cup warm water in the 1½-pound loaf.

NUTRITIONAL ANALYSIS			
	1½-POUND	1-POUND	
TOTAL CALORIES	2225	1458	
TOTAL PROTEIN	66	42	GRAMS
TOTAL CARBOHYDRATES	419	279	GRAMS
TOTAL FAT	35	21	GRAMS
TOTAL SATURATED FAT	15	9	GRAMS
TOTAL CHOLESTEROL	473	244	MILLIGRAMS
TOTAL SODIUM	2269	1136	MILLIGRAMS
TOTAL FIBRE	17	11	GRAMS
% CALORIES FROM FAT	14	13	

Hawaiian Bread

This bread works well when you want a sweet substitute for white bread. It's great with jelly or jam.

1½-pound

1½ teaspoons active dry yeast

5 tablespoons sugar

3 cups bread flour

½ teaspoon salt

2 tablespoons dry milk

2 tablespoons instant-mashed
    potato flakes

¼ teaspoon lemon extract

¼ teaspoon vanilla extract

2 eggs

4 tablespoons butter

1 cup warm water

1-pound

1 teaspoon active dry yeast

3 tablespoons sugar

2 cups bread flour

½ teaspoon salt

4 teaspoons dry milk

4 teaspoons instant-mashed
    potato flakes

¼ teaspoon lemon extract

¼ teaspoon vanilla extract

1 egg

2½ tablespoons butter

5 ounces warm water

Note:

For Panasonic/National machines, use 3 teaspoons of yeast for the 1½-pound loaf.

NUTRITIONAL ANALYSIS			
	1½-POUND	1-POUND	
TOTAL CALORIES	2351	1511	
TOTAL PROTEIN	68	44	GRAMS
TOTAL CARBOHYDRATES	371	243	GRAMS
TOTAL FAT	64	39	GRAMS
TOTAL SATURATED FAT	33	20	GRAMS
TOTAL CHOLESTEROL	552	292	MILLIGRAMS
TOTAL SODIUM	1356	1238	MILLIGRAMS
TOTAL FIBRE	7	4	GRAMS
% CALORIES FROM FAT	25	23	

Peanut-Butter-and-Jelly Bread

This is a fun bread. You can vary it by adding different types of jelly or jam each time you make it.

1½-pound

2 teaspoons active dry yeast

3½ tablespoons peanut butter

3 tablespoons jelly or jam

2½ cups bread flour

1½ teaspoons salt

2 tablespoons sugar

½ cup warm milk

½ cup warm water

1-pound

1½ teaspoons active dry yeast

2½ tablespoons peanut butter

2 tablespoons jelly or jam

1½ cups bread flour

1 teaspoons salt

3½ teaspoons sugar

¼ cup warm milk

2½ ounces warm water

Note:

For Panasonic/National machines, use 3½ teaspoons of yeast for the 1½-pound loaf.

NUTRITIONAL ANALYSIS			
	1½-POUND	1-POUND	
TOTAL CALORIES	1886	1175	
TOTAL PROTEIN	60	38	GRAMS
TOTAL CARBOHYDRATES	333	203	GRAMS
TOTAL FAT	35	24	GRAMS
TOTAL SATURATED FAT	7	5	GRAMS
TOTAL CHOLESTEROL	5	3	MILLIGRAMS
TOTAL SODIUM	3289	2183	MILLIGRAMS
TOTAL FIBRE	10	6	GRAMS
% CALORIES FROM FAT	17	19	

Apple-Pie Bread

This is so much like the real thing that it even contains apple-pie filling. It is moist, tangy, and a great breakfast bread.

1½-pound

1½ teaspoons active dry yeast

1½ teaspoons cinnamon

5 tablespoons sugar

3¼ cups + 2 tablespoons bread flour

1½ tablespoons salt

3 tablespoons buttermilk powder
    or dry milk

¾ cup apple-pie filling

1½ tablespoons butter

4½ ounces apple juice

1-pound

1 teaspoon active dry yeast

1 teaspoon cinnamon

3½ tablespoons sugar

2¼ cups bread flour

1 tablespoon salt

4 teaspoons buttermilk powder
    or dry milk

½ cup apple-pie filling

1 tablespoon butter

3 ounces apple juice

Note:
For Panasonic/National machines, use 3 teaspoons of yeast for the 1½-pound loaf.

NUTRITIONAL ANALYSIS			
	1½-POUND	1-POUND	
TOTAL CALORIES	2376	1591	
TOTAL PROTEIN	62	42	GRAMS
TOTAL CARBOHYDRATES	468	314	GRAMS
TOTAL FAT	26	17	GRAMS
TOTAL SATURATED FAT	12	8	GRAMS
TOTAL CHOLESTEROL	57	38	MILLIGRAMS
TOTAL SODIUM	3382	2255	MILLIGRAMS
TOTAL FIBRE	9	6	GRAMS
% CALORIES FROM FAT	10	10	

FRUIT AND VEGETABLE BREADS

These recipes focus on the variety of flavors available using fruits and vegetables in breads. They vary greatly in their content and texture, but you will find that they all contain natural, nutritious ingredients that are sure to please your palate.

Cinnamon-Raisin-Nut Bread

Although not an extremely sweet bread, it is very flavorful. The nuts give it a great crunch, especially if added during the mix cycle.

1½-pound

2 teaspoons active dry yeast

3½ tablespoons sugar

2 cups bread flour

2 teaspoons dry milk

1½ teaspoons cinnamon

1 teaspoon salt

2½ tablespoons honey

2 tablespoons butter

1 egg

3 tablespoons warm water

3 ounces warm milk

½ cup raisins

½ cup chopped nuts

1-pound

1½ teaspoons active dry yeast

2½ tablespoons sugar

1½ cups bread flour

1½ teaspoons dry milk

1 teaspoon cinnamon

½ teaspoon salt

1½ tablespoons honey

1½ tablespoons butter

1 egg

2 tablespoons warm water

2½ ounces warm milk

¼ cup raisins

¼ cup chopped nuts

Notes:

1. For Panasonic/National machines, use 3½ teaspoons of yeast for the 1½-pound loaf.
2. For DAK/Welbilt machines, use 5 tablespoons of warm water for the 1½-pound loaf.
3. For best results, add the raisins and chopped nuts after the first mixing. If your machine has a mix cycle, use it and add the raisins and nuts at the "mix" beep.

NUTRITIONAL ANALYSIS			
	1½-POUND	1-POUND	
TOTAL CALORIES	2253	1532	
TOTAL PROTEIN	57	42	GRAMS
TOTAL CARBOHYDRATES	360	246	GRAMS
TOTAL FAT	71	45	GRAMS
TOTAL SATURATED FAT	20	15	GRAMS
TOTAL CHOLESTEROL	279	263	MILLIGRAMS
TOTAL SODIUM	2287	1198	MILLIGRAMS
TOTAL FIBRE	12	8	GRAMS
% CALORIES FROM FAT	28	27	

Apple Bread

A very tangy, tart-tasting bread with low calories, it has a strong apple flavor. This bread goes great with pork chops or pork roast.

1½-pound

2½ teaspoons active dry yeast

4 tablespoons sugar

2½ cups bread flour

¼ teaspoon nutmeg

1 teaspoon cinnamon

½ teaspoon salt

½ cup whole-wheat flour

1 tablespoon butter

1 cup + 2 tablespoons apple sauce

1-pound

1½ teaspoons active dry yeast

2½ tablespoons sugar

1¾ cups bread flour

¼ teaspoon nutmeg

½ teaspoon cinnamon

¼ teaspoon salt

¼ cup whole-wheat flour

1 tablespoon butter

¾ cup apple sauce

Note:

For Panasonic/National machines, use 3½ teaspoons of yeast for the 1½-pound loaf.

NUTRITIONAL ANALYSIS			
	1½-POUND	1-POUND	
TOTAL CALORIES	1864	1275	
TOTAL PROTEIN	53	35	GRAMS
TOTAL CARBOHYDRATES	366	243	GRAMS
TOTAL FAT	20	17	GRAMS
TOTAL SATURATED FAT	8	8	GRAMS
TOTAL CHOLESTEROL	31	31	MILLIGRAMS
TOTAL SODIUM	1077	540	MILLIGRAMS
TOTAL FIBRE	14	8	GRAMS
% CALORIES FROM FAT	10	12	

Whole-Wheat Oat Cinnamon Raisin Bread

This bread bread combines the great taste and texture of whole wheat with the nutrition of oats and raisins for a naturally sweet loaf.

1½-pound

2 teaspoons active dry yeast

2 teaspoons gluten (optional)

2 teaspoons dough enhancer
    (optional)

2 cups whole-wheat flour

1 tablespoons cinnamon

½ cup rolled oats

1 teaspoon salt

2 tablespoons olive oil

2 tablespoons honey

1 cup warm water

¾ cup raisins

1-pound

1½ teaspoons active dry yeast

1½ teaspoons gluten (optional)

1½ teaspoons dough enhancer
    (optional)

1½ cups whole-wheat flour

2 teaspoons cinnamon

¼ cup rolled oats

1 teaspoon salt

4 teaspoons olive oil

4 teaspoons honey

5½ ounces warm water

½ cup raisins

Notes:
1. For Panasonic/National machines, use 3½ teaspoons of yeast for the 1½-pound loaf.
2. For best results, add the raisins at the end of the first mixing or use the mix cycle. If your machine has a mix cycle, add the raisins at the "mix" beep.

NUTRITIONAL ANALYSIS			
	1½-POUND	1-POUND	
TOTAL CALORIES	1685	1166	
TOTAL PROTEIN	45	32	GRAMS
TOTAL CARBOHYDRATES	327	228	GRAMS
TOTAL FAT	35	23	GRAMS
TOTAL SATURATED FAT	5	3	GRAMS
TOTAL CHOLESTEROL	0	0	MILLIGRAMS
TOTAL SODIUM	2155	2147	MILLIGRAMS
TOTAL FIBRE	43	30	GRAMS
% CALORIES FROM FAT	19	18	

Cranberry Bread

The tart, tangy flavor of cranberries is predominant in this light, pink bread. A slice is excellent with meat, especially poultry or pork.

1½-pound

1 teaspoon active dry yeast

¼ cup sugar

3 cups bread flour

2 teaspoons orange peel

½ teaspoon salt

½ cup canned cranberries

3 ounces warm water

1 tablespoon olive oil

3 ounces orange juice

1 egg

2 tablespoons chopped nuts

1-pound

½ teaspoon active dry yeast

2 tablespoons sugar

2 cups bread flour

1½ teaspoons orange peel

½ teaspoon salt

¼ cup canned cranberries

¼ cup warm water

2 teaspoons olive oil

¼ cup orange juice

1 egg

4 teaspoons chopped nuts

Notes:
1. For Panasonic/National machines, use 3 teaspoons of yeast for the 1½-pound loaf.
2. Nuts are best added during the mix cycle, if your machine has one. If your machine does not have a mix cycle, you can either add the nuts at the beginning (with the rest of the ingredients) or after the initial mixing has taken place.

NUTRITIONAL ANALYSIS			
	1½-POUND	1-POUND	
TOTAL CALORIES	2098	1377	
TOTAL PROTEIN	59	41	GRAMS
TOTAL CARBOHYDRATES	382	243	GRAMS
TOTAL FAT	35	25	GRAMS
TOTAL SATURATED FAT	5	4	GRAMS
TOTAL CHOLESTEROL	213	213	MILLIGRAMS
TOTAL SODIUM	1158	1145	MILLIGRAMS
TOTAL FIBRE	7	5	GRAMS
% CALORIES FROM FAT	15	16	

Banana Oat-Bran Bread

This bread is nutricious and delicious, with a light banana flavor and a great oat texture.

1½-pound

2 teaspoons active dry yeast

2 bananas

2 cups bread flour

½ teaspoon salt

5 tablespoons oat bran

½ cup + 2 tablespoons oat flour

½ teaspoon vanilla

2 tablespoons olive oil

2 eggs

½ cup warm water

2½ tablespoons honey

1-pound

1½ teaspoons active dry yeast

1½ bananas

1½ cups bread flour

¼ teaspoon salt

3 tablespoons oat bran

¼ cup + 2½ tablespoons oat flour

½ teaspoon vanilla

4 teaspoons olive oil

2 eggs

3 ounces warm water

2 tablespoons honey

Note:

For Panasonic/National machines, use 3 teaspoons of yeast for the 1½-pound loaf.

NUTRITIONAL ANALYSIS			
	1½-POUND	1-POUND	
TOTAL CALORIES	2103	1558	
TOTAL PROTEIN	64	49	GRAMS
TOTAL CARBOHYDRATES	367	268	GRAMS
TOTAL FAT	46	34	GRAMS
TOTAL SATURATED FAT	8	6	GRAMS
TOTAL CHOLESTEROL	426	426	MILLIGRAMS
TOTAL SODIUM	1203	667	MILLIGRAMS
TOTAL FIBRE	23	15	GRAMS
% CALORIES FROM FAT	20	20	

Apple-Butter Bread

This is a sweet bread with a distinct apple flavor, enhanced with nuts.

1½-pound

2 teaspoons active dry yeast

½ cup sugar

1 teaspoon cinnamon

3 cups bread flour

½ teaspoon salt

3 tablespoons warm water

¾ cup apple butter

1 egg

1 teaspoon vanilla

3 tablespoons butter

½ cup chopped nuts

1-pound

1½ teaspoons active dry yeast

½ cup sugar

½ teaspoon cinnamon

2 cups bread flour

¼ teaspoon salt

2 tablespoons warm water

½ cup apple butter

1 egg

½ teaspoon vanilla

2 tablespoons butter

¼ cup chopped nuts

Note:

For Panasonic/National machines, use 3½ teaspoons of yeast for the 1½-pound loaf.

NUTRITIONAL ANALYSIS			
	1½-POUND	1-POUND	
TOTAL CALORIES	2799	1767	
TOTAL PROTEIN	67	45	GRAMS
TOTAL CARBOHYDRATES	445	280	GRAMS
TOTAL FAT	84	51	GRAMS
TOTAL SATURATED FAT	27	18	GRAMS
TOTAL CHOLESTEROL	306	275	MILLIGRAMS
TOTAL SODIUM	1178	628	MILLIGRAMS
TOTAL FIBRE	10	7	GRAMS
% CALORIES FROM FAT	27	26	

Orange Bread

The light-orange color and aroma of this bread complement its distinctive orange flavor. It goes well with fruit salad, and it is great for breakfast toast.

1½-pound

1 teaspoon active dry yeast

3 cups bread flour

½ teaspoon salt

¼ cup + 1 tablespoon sugar

1 tablespoon orange peel

1 egg

2 tablespoons butter

3 ounces orange juice

¾ cup warm water

1-pound

½ teaspoon active dry yeast

2 cups bread flour

½ teaspoon salt

3 tablespoons sugar

2 teaspoons orange peel

1 egg

1½ tablespoons butter

¼ cup orange juice

½ cup warm water

Note:

For Panasonic/National machines, use 2½ teaspoons of yeast for the 1½-pound loaf.

NUTRITIONAL ANALYSIS			
	1½-POUND	1-POUND	
TOTAL CALORIES	2039	1385	
TOTAL PROTEIN	57	40	GRAMS
TOTAL CARBOHYDRATES	369	242	GRAMS
TOTAL FAT	35	27	GRAMS
TOTAL SATURATED FAT	17	13	GRAMS
TOTAL CHOLESTEROL	275	260	MILLIGRAMS
TOTAL SODIUM	1138	1135	MILLIGRAMS
TOTAL FIBRE	6	4	GRAMS
% CALORIES FROM FAT	15	18	

Carrot-Celery Bread

The light taste of celery and carrots combined with whole wheat makes this a great sandwich bread, especially for cold cuts. Try it with a bacon-lettuce-tomato sandwich for a unique treat.

1½-pound

1½ teaspoons active dry yeast

1½ cups whole-wheat flour

1½ cups bread flour

½ cup grated carrots

1 teaspoon salt

1 teaspoon celery seed

1 tablespoon olive oil

2 tablespoons honey

1 cup warm water

1-pound

1 teaspoon active dry yeast

1 cup whole-wheat flour

1 cup bread flour

¼ cup grated carrots

½ teaspoon salt

½ teaspoon celery seed

2 teaspoons olive oil

1½ tablespoons honey

5½ ounces warm water

Note:

For Panasonic/National machines, use 3 teaspoons of yeast for the 1½-pound loaf.

NUTRITIONAL ANALYSIS			
	1½-POUND	1-POUND	
TOTAL CALORIES	1635	1094	
TOTAL PROTEIN	52	34	GRAMS
TOTAL CARBOHYDRATES	320	215	GRAMS
TOTAL FAT	21	14	GRAMS
TOTAL SATURATED FAT	3	2	GRAMS
TOTAL CHOLESTEROL	0	0	MILLIGRAMS
TOTAL SODIUM	2160	1081	MILLIGRAMS
TOTAL FIBRE	28	19	GRAMS
% CALORIES FROM FAT	12	11	

Cheddar Olive Bread

Olives and cheese have always been a great combination, and they are both present in this tasty bread. This was one of the tasters' favorites.

1½-pound	1-pound
1½ teaspoons active dry yeast	1 teaspoon active dry yeast
3 cups bread flour	2 cups bread flour
4 teaspoons cornmeal	1 tablespoon cornmeal
1 teaspoon salt	½ teaspoon salt
1 teaspoon basil	½ teaspoon basil
1 tablespoon olive oil	2 teaspoons olive oil
2 eggs	1 egg
¾ cup warm water	½ cup warm water
½ cup sliced or grated black olives	¼ cup sliced or grated black olives
¾ cup grated cheddar cheese	½ cup grated cheddar cheese

Notes:

1. For Panasonic/National machines, use 3 teaspoons of yeast for the 1½-pound loaf.
2. For DAK/Welbilt machines, use one extra tablespoon of warm water if the machine seems to labor with the 1½-pound loaf.
3. The dough will seem very stiff at first; however, once the cheese melts, the consistency will be about right.
4. For best results, add the olives during the mix cycle. If your machine does not have a mix cycle, add the olives after the initial mixing has completed.

NUTRITIONAL ANALYSIS			
	1½-POUND	1-POUND	
TOTAL CALORIES	2213	1441	
TOTAL PROTEIN	86	55	GRAMS
TOTAL CARBOHYDRATES	314	209	GRAMS
TOTAL FAT	66	41	GRAMS
TOTAL SATURATED FAT	25	16	GRAMS
TOTAL CHOLESTEROL	515	273	MILLIGRAMS
TOTAL SODIUM	3393	1786	MILLIGRAMS
TOTAL FIBRE	10	6	GRAMS
% CALORIES FROM FAT	27	26	

V-8 Bread

If you like tomato and V-8 juice, you'll like this bread. It uses V-8 juice as the liquid and combines that flavor with some seasonings to produce a light-orange bread with a distinctively vegetable taste.

1½-pound	1-pound
2 teaspoons active dry yeast	1½ teaspoons active dry yeast
1½ tablespoons sugar	1 tablespoon sugar
3 cups bread flour	2 cups bread flour
1 teaspoon dried onion	½ teaspoon dried onion
1 teaspoon garlic powder	½ teaspoon garlic powder
3 tablespoons dry milk	2 tablespoons dry milk
2 teaspoons Italian spice	1½ teaspoons Italian spice
2 tablespoons Parmesan cheese	1½ tablespoons Parmesan cheese
1 teaspoon garlic salt	½ teaspoon garlic salt
3 tablespoons olive oil	2 tablespoons olive oil
¼ cup warm water	¼ cup warm water
7 ounces V-8 juice	5 ounces V-8 juice

Notes:

1. For Panasonic/National machines, use 3 teaspoons of yeast for the 1½-pound loaf.
2. If you like the taste but want to lower the salt content, buy salt-free V-8 juice and eliminate the garlic salt from the recipe.

NUTRITIONAL ANALYSIS			
	1½-POUND	1-POUND	
TOTAL CALORIES	2085	1396	
TOTAL PROTEIN	63	42	GRAMS
TOTAL CARBOHYDRATES	339	227	GRAMS
TOTAL FAT	51	34	GRAMS
TOTAL SATURATED FAT	8	6	GRAMS
TOTAL CHOLESTEROL	11	8	MILLIGRAMS
TOTAL SODIUM	3084	1748	MILLIGRAMS
TOTAL FIBRE	7	5	GRAMS
% CALORIES FROM FAT	22	22	

Carrot Bread

This bread is bright orange in color. It has all the nutrients and flavor of fresh carrots. Prepare the carrot puree by steaming or boiling them. Then liquefy them in your blender or food processor.

1½-pound

1 teaspoon active dry yeast

1 tablespoon sugar

3 cups bread flour

½ teaspoon nutmeg

½ teaspoon salt

¾ cup carrot puree

1 egg

2 tablespoons + 1 teaspoon butter

3 tablespoons warm milk

1½ tablespoons warm water

1-pound

½ teaspoon active dry yeast

2 teaspoons sugar

2 cups bread flour

¼ teaspoon nutmeg

½ teaspoon salt

½ cup carrot puree

1 egg

1½ tablespoons butter

2 tablespoons warm milk

1 tablespoon warm water

Notes:

1. For Panasonic/National machines, use 2 teaspoons of yeast for the 1½-pound loaf.
2. Be sure not to add the carrot puree while it is still hot from steaming. Let it cool so that you don't kill the yeast.

NUTRITIONAL ANALYSIS			
	1½-POUND	1-POUND	
TOTAL CALORIES	1907	1289	
TOTAL PROTEIN	59	41	GRAMS
TOTAL CARBOHYDRATES	323	215	GRAMS
TOTAL FAT	40	27	GRAMS
TOTAL SATURATED FAT	20	13	GRAMS
TOTAL CHOLESTEROL	287	261	MILLIGRAMS
TOTAL SODIUM	1190	1170	MILLIGRAMS
TOTAL FIBRE	9	6	GRAMS
% CALORIES FROM FAT	19	19	

Sweet-Potato Bread

If you like yams on the dinner table, try this bread instead. It's a great supplement to a turkey dinner.

1½-pound

1½ teaspoons active dry yeast

9 tablespoons brown sugar

½ teaspoon ginger

3 cups bread flour

1 teaspoon cinnamon

½ teaspoon dried orange peel

1 teaspoon salt

¼ cup + 2 tablespoons canned yams

3 ounces orange juice

3 ounces warm water

2 eggs

1½ tablespoons butter

1-pound

1 teaspoon active dry yeast

6 tablespoons brown sugar

¼ teaspoon ginger

2 cups bread flour

1 teaspoon cinnamon

½ teaspoon dried orange peel

½ teaspoon salt

¼ cup canned yams

¼ cup orange juice

¼ cup cwarm water

1 egg

1 tablespoon butter

Note:

For Panasonic/National machines, use 3 teaspoons of yeast for the 1½-pound loaf.

NUTRITIONAL ANALYSIS			
	1½-POUND	1-POUND	
TOTAL CALORIES	2359	1549	
TOTAL PROTEIN	65	41	GRAMS
TOTAL CARBOHYDRATES	445	297	GRAMS
TOTAL FAT	35	22	GRAMS
TOTAL SATURATED FAT	15	9	GRAMS
TOTAL CHOLESTEROL	473	244	MILLIGRAMS
TOTAL SODIUM	2320	1171	MILLIGRAMS
TOTAL FIBRE	7	5	GRAMS
% CALORIES FROM FAT	13	13	

Potato Bread

This is an old favorite, updated to use modern ingredients such as potato flakes. Still, the old-fashioned flavor persists, and this bread is great with soups.

1½-pound

1 teaspoon active dry yeast

2 tablespoons sugar

2¾ cups bread flour

1 teaspoon salt

4 tablespoons instant-mashed potato flakes

¼ cup dry milk

¼ cup buttermilk

2 eggs

2 tablespoons butter

5 ounces warm water

1-pound

½ teaspoon active dry yeast

4 teaspoons sugar

2 cups bread flour

½ teaspoon salt

2½ tablespoons instant-mashed potato flakes

2 tablespoons dry milk

2½ ounces buttermilk

1 egg

1 tablespoon butter

3½ ounces warm water

Notes:
1. For Panasonic/National machines, use 2 teaspoons of yeast for the 1½-pound loaf.
2. For DAK/Welbilt machines, use ¾ cup warm water for the 1½-pound loaf.

NUTRITIONAL ANALYSIS			
	1½-POUND	1-POUND	
TOTAL CALORIES	2073	1384	
TOTAL PROTEIN	79	51	GRAMS
TOTAL CARBOHYDRATES	334	236	GRAMS
TOTAL FAT	44	24	GRAMS
TOTAL SATURATED FAT	19	10	GRAMS
TOTAL CHOLESTEROL	513	259	MILLIGRAMS
TOTAL SODIUM	2727	1407	MILLIGRAMS
TOTAL FIBRE	6	4	GRAMS
% CALORIES FROM FAT	19	16	

Zucchini Bread

If one of your favorite summer vegetables is zucchini, here is a bread that will definitely have a place on your summer table.

1½-pound

1½ teaspoons active dry yeast

1½ tablespoons brown sugar

1¾ cups + 3 tablespoons bread flour

½ cup whole-wheat flour

1 cup shredded zucchini

1 teaspoon salt

1½ teaspoons ground coriander

2½ tablespoons dry milk

¼ cup wheat germ

1½ tablespoons butter

5½ ounces warm water

1-pound

1 teaspoon active dry yeast

1 tablespoon brown sugar

1¼ cups + 1 tablespoon bread flour

½ cup whole-wheat flour

¾ cup shredded zucchini

½ teaspoon salt

1 teaspoon ground coriander

1½ tablespoons dry milk

2 tablespoons wheat germ

1 tablespoon butter

3½ ounces warm water

Notes:
1. For Panasonic/National machines, use 3 teaspoons of yeast for the 1½-pound loaf.
2. For DAK/Welbilt machines, use 6½ ounces of warm water in the 1½-pound recipe.

NUTRITIONAL ANALYSIS			
	1½-POUND	1-POUND	
TOTAL CALORIES	1580	1112	
TOTAL PROTEIN	58	40	GRAMS
TOTAL CARBOHYDRATES	287	205	GRAMS
TOTAL FAT	27	18	GRAMS
TOTAL SATURATED FAT	12	8	GRAMS
TOTAL CHOLESTEROL	49	33	MILLIGRAMS
TOTAL SODIUM	2231	1127	MILLIGRAMS
TOTAL FIBRE	17	13	GRAMS
% CALORIES FROM FAT	15	15	

SOURDOUGH BREADS

Sourdough is a pioneer tradition in this country, made famous during the gold-rush days in California. Miners had to make bread, but they couldn't maintain leavening of any kind. So, they made sourdough, a live mixture of fermenting bacteria that acted much like yeast. They kept their starter alive year after year (it really does get better with age) and used it daily for baking breads, biscuits, and pancakes.

All the recipes in this section use sourdough starter (see recipe on following page). Even with a bread machine, sourdough-bread recipes require a little more patience than other bread recipes because the sourdough batter must be prepared. Here is the procedure for making sourdough batter for your recipes:

1. Remove your sourdough starter from the refrigerator and allow it to reach room temperature (allow for about 6 hours).
2. Place 1½ cups of starter in a 2-quart mixing bowl.
3. Return the remaining starter to the refrigerator.
4. Add 1½ cups of all-purpose flour and 1 cup of warm skim milk and mix well. The batter should have the consistency of a light pancake batter.
5. Cover the bowl lightly and let the batter proof for 8–12 hours in an 85–90 degree environment.
6. After proofing, use what batter you need for your bread (it can remain out for 1–3 days), but make sure you save at least 1½ cups of batter to replenish your starter.
7. Return the remaining batter to your starter pot. Stir and refrigerate.

Many people will place the starter directly into the ingredients. While this method will certainly work, it is not the best way to keep the starter active, because after you remove the starter, you have to add flour and milk and again proof the starter.

I have found it better to use the batter method described above. It tends to keep my starter more active and gives me plenty of batter to use in my recipes. If you use the batter method, place batter in the recipe any time sourdough starter is called for.

Sourdough Starter

This recipe will give you enough starter to begin with. Each time you remove starter to make batter, don't forget to replenish the starter with the leftover batter.

1. Warm a quart jar or similar container by filling it with hot tap water and letting it sit for a few minutes.

2. In a pan or microwave oven, heat 1 cup skim or low-fat milk to 100–110 degrees. Then, remove it from the heat and add 3 table-spoons of plain yogurt to the mix.

3. Drain the warm water from the jar and wipe it dry.

4. Pour the milk-yogurt mixture into the jar and cover. Note that it is preferable to use a plastic lid, but if your jar has a metal lid, place plastic wrap or waxed paper under the lid before screwing it tight.

5. Place the mixture in a warm place, and allow it to proof for 24 hours.

6. Stir 1 cup of all-purpose flour into the milk-yogurt mixture. Cover, and leave in a warm place to proof for 3 to 5 days.

7. At the end of 5 days, your starter should be bubbly and about the consistency of pancake batter. When it has reached this point, place the jar in the refrigerator for storage.

Sourdough French Bread

An old favorite, this bread has a long history. Its simple ingredients made it a favorite of the forty-niners and a San Francisco staple.

1½-pound

1½ teaspoons active dry yeast

1 teaspoon sugar

3 cups bread flour

1 teaspoon salt

½ cup sourdough starter

¾ cup warm water

1-pound

1 teaspoon active dry yeast

1 teaspoon sugar

2 cups bread flour

1 teaspoon salt

¼ cup sourdough starter

½ cup warm water

Notes:
1. For Panasonic/National machines, use 2½ teaspoons of yeast for the 1½-pound loaf.
2. If your machine has a "French bread" setting, use that setting for this recipe.

NUTRITIONAL ANALYSIS			
	1½-POUND	1-POUND	
TOTAL CALORIES	1758	1136	
TOTAL PROTEIN	59	38	GRAMS
TOTAL CARBOHYDRATES	353	228	GRAMS
TOTAL FAT	8	5	GRAMS
TOTAL SATURATED FAT	1	1	GRAMS
TOTAL CHOLESTEROL	0	0	MILLIGRAMS
TOTAL SODIUM	2141	2138	MILLIGRAMS
TOTAL FIBRE	8	5	GRAMS
% CALORIES FROM FAT	4	4	

Sourdough Rye Bread

This sourdough-and-rye combination is excellent for morning toast or for ham-and-cheese sandwiches. It has the flavor and texture of rye bread and a distinct sourdough aroma and taste.

1½-pound

2 teaspoons active dry yeast

2½ cups bread flour

1½ tablespoons unsweetened cocoa

1 teaspoon salt

2 teaspoons dill weed

1½ teaspoons caraway seed

¾ cup rye flour

1 tablespoon butter

1 egg

2 teaspoons molasses

1 tablespoon olive oil

3 ounces warm water

¾ cup sourdough starter

1-pound

1½ teaspoons active dry yeast

1½ cups bread flour

1 tablespoon unsweetened cocoa

½ teaspoon salt

1½ teaspoons dill weed

1 teaspoon caraway seed

½ cup rye flour

2 teaspoons butter

1 egg

½ tablespoon molasses

½ tablespoon olive oil

¼ cup warm water

½ cup sourdough starter

Note:

For Panasonic/National machines, use 3 teaspoons of yeast for the 1½-pound loaf.

NUTRITIONAL ANALYSIS			
	1½-POUND	1-POUND	
TOTAL CALORIES	2275	1473	
TOTAL PROTEIN	74	52	GRAMS
TOTAL CARBOHYDRATES	401	256	GRAMS
TOTAL FAT	41	27	GRAMS
TOTAL SATURATED FAT	12	8	GRAMS
TOTAL CHOLESTEROL	244	234	MILLIGRAMS
TOTAL SODIUM	2241	1148	MILLIGRAMS
TOTAL FIBRE	9	6	GRAMS
% CALORIES FROM FAT	16	16	

Sourdough Onion Rye Bread

If you are looking for a tangy bread, look no further. This bread combines the tart flavor of sourdough with the distinct taste of onion, rye and caraway seed. The result is a flavorful bread that is great for sandwiches. This was a favorite of the rye-bread tasters.

1½-pound

1½ teaspoons active dry yeast

1½ tablespoons gluten (optional)

1 teaspoon caraway seeds

1½ cups bread flour

3 tablespoons onion-soup mix

1 cup rye flour

½ cup whole-wheat flour

½ cup sourdough starter

2 tablespoons warm milk

1 tablespoon olive oil

1 tablespoon vinegar

2 teaspoons molasses

7 ounces warm water

1-pound

1 teaspoon active dry yeast

1 tablespoons gluten (optional)

½ teaspoon caraway seeds

¾ cup bread flour

2 tablespoons onion-soup mix

¾ cup rye flour

¼ cup whole-wheat flour

¼ cup sourdough starter

1½ tablespoons warm milk

2 teaspoons olive oil

2 teaspoons vinegar

1 teaspoon molasses

4½ ounces warm water

Note:

For Panasonic/National machines, use 3 teaspoons of yeast for the 1½-pound loaf.

NUTRITIONAL ANALYSIS			
	1½-POUND	1-POUND	
TOTAL CALORIES	1919	1137	
TOTAL PROTEIN	72	46	GRAMS
TOTAL CARBOHYDRATES	364	212	GRAMS
TOTAL FAT	24	16	GRAMS
TOTAL SATURATED FAT	3	2	GRAMS
TOTAL CHOLESTEROL	1	1	MILLIGRAMS
TOTAL SODIUM	2898	1918	MILLIGRAMS
TOTAL FIBRE	15	8	GRAMS
% CALORIES FROM FAT	11	13	

Sourdough Whole-Wheat Bread

Sourdough lovers will enjoy this variation of ordinary whole-wheat bread. This is a simple, low-calorie, low-fat bread that is nutritious as well as delicious.

1½-pound

1½ teaspoons active dry yeast

1 tablespoon gluten (optional)

1 tablespoon dough enhancer (optional)

½ cup bread flour

2½ cups whole-wheat flour

1 teaspoon salt

1½ teaspoons olive oil

1 cup warm water

½ cup sourdough starter

1-pound

1 teaspoon active dry yeast

2 teaspoons gluten (optional)

2 teaspoons dough enhancer (optional)

½ cup bread flour

1½ cups whole-wheat flour

1 teaspoon salt

1 teaspoon olive oil

5½ ounces warm water

¼ cup sourdough starter

Note:

For Panasonic/National machines, use 2½ teaspoons of yeast for the 1½-pound loaf.

NUTRITIONAL ANALYSIS			
	1½-POUND	1-POUND	
TOTAL CALORIES	1559	1152	
TOTAL PROTEIN	58	42	GRAMS
TOTAL CARBOHYDRATES	318	231	GRAMS
TOTAL FAT	12	10	GRAMS
TOTAL SATURATED FAT	2	2	GRAMS
TOTAL CHOLESTEROL	0	0	MILLIGRAMS
TOTAL SODIUM	2138	2137	MILLIGRAMS
TOTAL FIBRE	40	25	GRAMS
% CALOR ES FROM FAT	7	8	

Sourdough Sesame Bread

This is a combination of sourdough and whole wheat, enhanced with the nutty flavor of sesame seeds. Serve it warm with any soup or salad.

1½-pound	1-pound
1½ teaspoons active dry yeast	1 teaspoon active dry yeast
½ cup sesame seeds	5 tablespoons sesame seeds
1 cup whole-wheat flour	¾ cup whole-wheat flour
1½ cups rye flour	1 cup rye flour
1 teaspoon salt	½ teaspoon salt
1 egg	1 egg
2 tablespoons lemon juice	4 teaspoons lemon juice
2 tablespoons honey	4 teaspoons honey
5 ounces warm water	3½ ounces warm water
½ cup sourdough starter	¼ cup sourdough starter

Notes:

1. For Panasonic/National machines, use 3 teaspoons of yeast for the 1½-pound loaf.
2. For DAK/Welbilt machines, use ¾ cup of warm water for the 1½-pound loaf.

NUTRITIONAL ANALYSIS			
	1½-POUND	1-POUND	
TOTAL CALORIES	2019	1346	
TOTAL PROTEIN	70	48	GRAMS
TOTAL CARBOHYDRATES	337	223	GRAMS
TOTAL FAT	48	32	GRAMS
TOTAL SATURATED FAT	7	5	GRAMS
TOTAL CHOLESTEROL	213	213	MILLIGRAMS
TOTAL SODIUM	2210	1139	MILLIGRAMS
TOTAL FIBRE	23	16	GRAMS
% CALORIES FROM FAT	21	21	

Sourdough Dill Bread

Here, you'll find the classic taste of dill bread with a trace of sourdough aroma. This is a splendid variation of dill bread that is excellent for sandwiches, particularly tuna salad.

1½-pound

1½ teaspoons active dry yeast

2 tablespoons sugar

3 cups bread flour

1 teaspoon salt

2 tablespoons dill weed

1 egg

¾ cup cottage cheese

3 ounces warm water

½ cup sourdough starter

1-pound

1 teaspoon active dry yeast

1½ tablespoons sugar

2 cups bread flour

½ teaspoon salt

4 teaspoons dill weed

1 egg

½ cup cottage cheese

½ cup warm water

¼ cup sourdough starter

Note:

For Panasonic/National machines, use 2½ teaspoons of yeast for the 1½-pound loaf.

NUTRITIONAL ANALYSIS			
	1½-POUND	1-POUND	
TOTAL CALORIES	2078	1377	
TOTAL PROTEIN	87	59	GRAMS
TOTAL CARBOHYDRATES	383	249	GRAMS
TOTAL FAT	16	12	GRAMS
TOTAL SATURATED FAT	4	3	GRAMS
TOTAL CHOLESTEROL	236	228	MILLIGRAMS
TOTAL SODIUM	2981	1653	MILLIGRAMS
TOTAL FIBRE	8	5	GRAMS
% CALORIES FROM FAT	7	8	

BREAD DOUGHS
YOU FINISH YOURSELF

If you get tired of making the same-shaped breads and are willing to do a little bit of the work, you can use your machine to make the dough and then you can take it from there. Actually, any recipe in this book can be finished by hand, but this section primarily contains recipes that, because of their shape, can't be finished in the bread machine. Two of the recipes, French Bread and Bohemian Rye, could be finished in the machine, but are more authentic in their traditional shapes.

French Bread

A traditional French bread recipe, this is easy to make and yields a beautiful and tasty loaf.

1½-pound

2½ teaspoons active dry yeast

3 cups bread flour

1½ teaspoons salt

1 cup warm water

1-pound

1½ teaspoons active dry yeast

2 cups bread flour

1 teaspoon salt

5½ ounces warm water

Note:

For Panasonic/National machines, use 3 teaspoons of yeast for the 1½-pound loaf.

Instructions for baking: Remove from the machine after the first rise is complete (or use the dough cycle if your machine has one). After removal from the machine, knead the dough for 5—10 minutes. Shape the dough into a large loaf; then place the dough on a baking pan or sheet that has been liberally sprinkled with cornmeal. Cover with a cloth and let the dough rise for 30—40 minutes.

After the bread has risen, use a sharp knife or razor blade to make diagonal cuts on the top of the loaf. Bake the loaf at 410 degrees for 30—40 minutes.

If a hard crust is desired, place a pan of water in the oven with the bread while it is baking. For a soft crust, cover the outside of the loaf with a water-and-egg mixture before baking.

To enhance the flavor and appearance, apply a fine spray of water before baking and then sprinkle the bread with a coating of sesame seeds

NUTRITIONAL ANALYSIS			
	1½-POUND	1-POUND	
TOTAL CALORIES	1503	1001	
TOTAL PROTEIN	52	34	GRAMS
TOTAL CARBOHYDRATES	300	200	GRAMS
TOTAL FAT	7	5	GRAMS
TOTAL SATURATED FAT	1	1	GRAMS
TOTAL CHOLESTEROL	0	0	MILLIGRAMS
TOTAL SODIUM	3207	2138	MILLIGRAMS
TOTAL FIBRE	7	5	GRAMS
% CALORIES FROM FAT	4	4	

Pizza Dough

A high-rising pizza dough that makes one large pizza (using the 1½ pound recipe) or one medium pizza (using the 1-pound recipe). It is simple to make and lets you create your own pizzas, using the toppings you like.

1½-pound

3 teaspoons active dry yeast

2 tablespoons sugar

3 cups all-purpose flour

1 teaspoon salt

2 teaspoons olive oil

1 cup warm water

1-pound

2 teaspoons active dry yeast

1½ tablespoons sugar

2 cups all-purpose flour

1 teaspoon salt

1½ teaspoons olive oil

5½ ounces warm water

Note:

Use the dough cycle, if your machine has one, or remove the dough from the bread machine after the first rise has been completed.

Instructions for baking: After removing the pizza dough from the bread machine, punch the dough down. Then place it in a greased bowl, cover it with a cloth, and let it rise in a warm place for 30-40 minutes.

Remove the dough from the bowl and roll it out flat. Place the dough on a pizza pan that has been sprinkled with cornmeal, and finish stretching the dough until it is a uniform thickness throughout. Spread tomato sauce on the pizza and finish with toppings of your choice. Bake the pizza at 350 degrees for 10-15 minutes or until the crust turns light brown.

NUTRITIONAL ANALYSIS (Not including Pizza Toppings)			
	1½-POUND	1-POUND	
TOTAL CALORIES	1585	1064	
TOTAL PROTEIN	52	35	GRAMS
TOTAL CARBOHYDRATES	301	201	GRAMS
TOTAL FAT	16	12	GRAMS
TOTAL SATURATED FAT	2	2	GRAMS
TOTAL CHOLESTEROL	0	0	MILLIGRAMS
TOTAL SODIUM	2142	2139	MILLIGRAMS
TOTAL FIBRE	7	5	GRAMS
% CALORIES FROM FAT	9	10	

Breadsticks

Instead of sliced bread, try serving breadsticks with your spaghetti or lasagna dinner. These are easy and fun to make.

1½-pound	1-pound
1½ teaspoons active dry yeast	1 teaspoon active dry yeast
3 cups bread flour	2 cups bread flour
1½ teaspoons salt	1 teaspoon salt
1 cup warm water	5 ounces warm water
2 tablespoons olive oil	4 teaspoons olive oil

Notes:

1. For Panasonic/National machines, use 3 teaspoons of yeast for the 1½-pound loaf.
2. For DAK/Welbilt machines, use an extra 2 tablespoons of water with the 1½-pound recipe.
3. Use the dough cycle, if your machine has one, or remove the dough from the bread machine after the first rise is completed.
4. Try substituting garlic salt for regular salt for a garlic-bread taste.
5. Add 3 tablespoons of onion soup mix for onion-flavored breadsticks.

Instructions for baking: Remove the dough from the machine and knead it for approximately 5—6 minutes, punching the dough to remove all the air. Form the dough into sticks by pinching balls of dough and rolling them with your hands into cylinder-shaped pieces. Lay the sticks in a pan that has been dusted with cornmeal. Place the sticks about 1 inch from each other in the pan.

Let the breadsticks rise for approximately 45 minutes or until almost doubled in size. Bake them in a 375-degree oven for 15—20 minutes or until golden brown. For a crunchy crust, place a pan of water in the oven with the breadsticks while baking. If desired, brush a water-and-eggwhite mixture on the breadsticks before baking and coat with sesame seeds.

NUTRITIONAL ANALYSIS			
	1½-POUND	1-POUND	
TOTAL CALORIES	1734	1156	
TOTAL PROTEIN	51	34	GRAMS
TOTAL CARBOHYDRATES	300	200	GRAMS
TOTAL FAT	34	23	GRAMS
TOTAL SATURATED FAT	5	3	GRAMS
TOTAL CHOLESTEROL	0	0	MILLIGRAMS
TOTAL SODIUM	3206	2137	MILLIGRAMS
TOTAL FIBRE	7	4	GRAMS
% CALORIES FROM FAT	18	18	

Bagels

These are traditional water bagels with a dense texture and great flavor. They are great in the morning with cream cheese or butter.

1½-pound	1-pound
2½ teaspoons active dry yeast	1½ teaspoons active dry yeast
3 cups all-purpose flour	2 cups all-purpose flour
1½ teaspoons salt	1 teaspoons salt
1½ tablespoons sugar	1 tablespoon sugar
9 ounces warm water	¾ cup warm water

Notes:

1. For Panasonic/National machines, use 3 teaspoons of yeast for the 1½-pound loaf.
2. For DAK/Welbilt machines, use 10 ounces of warm water for the 1½-pound loaf.
3. If your machine has one, use the dough cycle. If it does not, remove the dough at the end of the first rise.
4. For onion bagels, add 3 tablespoons of onion-soup mix.
5. For garlic bagels, use garlic salt instead of regular salt.

Instructions for baking: Remove the bread from the dough machine. Punch it down and knead it for 5—6 minutes. Form the dough into small (2 inches in diameter) balls. Flatten the balls slightly and use your thumb or finger to punch a hole into the middle of each bagel. Place the bagels on a lightly floured baking sheet, cover them with a cloth, and let them rise for approximately 30 minutes.

In the meantime, prepare a water-and-sugar mixture consisting of 6 cups of water and ½ tablespoon of sugar. Bring this mixture to a boil in a pan and adjust the heat to maintain a steady boil. Boil each bagel for approximately 5 minutes in the solution, turning frequently. Then place the bagels on a baking sheet coated with cornmeal. Brush the bagels with egg (whole eggs whipped) and bake in a 400-degree oven for 20—25 minutes or until brown.

NUTRITIONAL ANALYSIS			
	1½-POUND	1-POUND	
TOTAL CALORIES	1572	1047	
TOTAL PROTEIN	52	34	GRAMS
TOTAL CARBOHYDRATES	318	212	GRAMS
TOTAL FAT	7	5	GRAMS
TOTAL SATURATED FAT	1	1	GRAMS
TOTAL CHOLESTEROL	0	0	MILLIGRAMS
TOTAL SODIUM	3207	2138	MILLIGRAMS
TOTAL FIBRE	7	5	GRAMS
% CALORIES FROM FAT	4	4	

Bohemian Rye Bread

This bread is made with 100-percent rye flour. Since rye flour doesn't rise much, it is best to bake this loaf in the traditional round shape. Rye lovers will enjoy the pure rye flavor and authentic Bohemian taste of this loaf.

1½-pound

2 teaspoons active dry yeast

3 tablespoons gluten

2 teaspoons sugar

2 teaspoons caraway seed

3 cups rye flour

2 teaspoons salt

5 ounces warm water

½ cup sour cream

1-pound

1½ teaspoons active dry yeast

2 tablespoons gluten

1½ teaspoons sugar

1½ teaspoons caraway seed

2 cups rye flour

1½ teaspoons salt

½ cup warm water

¼ cup sour cream

Notes:
1. For Panasonic/National machines, use 3 teaspoons of yeast for the 1½-pound loaf.
2. For DAK/Welbilt machines, use 6 ounces of warm water for the 1½-pound loaf.
3. Use the dough cycle, if your machine has one, or remove the dough after the first rise is complete.

Instructions for baking: Remove the dough from the bread machine. Punch it down and knead it for approximately 5—6 minutes. Place the kneaded dough in a greased bowl and cover it with a cloth. Let it rise in a warm location for approximately 60 minutes.

Remove the dough from the bowl and shape it into a round or oblong loaf. Place the loaf on a baking sheet that has been liberally sprinkled with cornmeal. Cut two or three slits in the top of the loaf with a sharp knife or razor blade. Bake in a 375-degree oven for 30—35 minutes.

NUTRITIONAL ANALYSIS			
	1½-POUND	1-POUND	
TOTAL CALORIES	1700	1097	
TOTAL PROTEIN	83	55	GRAMS
TOTAL CARBOHYDRATES	294	196	GRAMS
TOTAL FAT	37	20	GRAMS
TOTAL SATURATED FAT	16	8	GRAMS
TOTAL CHOLESTEROL	51	26	MILLIGRAMS
TOTAL SODIUM	4336	3236	MILLIGRAMS
TOTAL FIBRE	9	6	GRAMS
% CALORIES FROM FAT	19	17	

AMERICAN PIONEER BREADS

The recipes in this section are based on old American favorites from various parts of the United States. Because these recipes pre-date the commercial development of yeast for baking, most of these breads probably started out as baking-powder breads, baking-soda breads, or sourdough breads. In fact, the recipe for *Forty-Niner Sourdough Bread* has changed little since the days of the California gold rush.

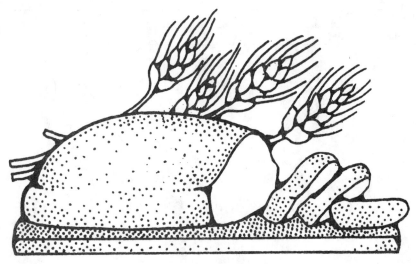

Adobe Bread

Originally designed for the adobe ovens of the American Southwest, this bread tastes just as good when baked in your machine.

1½-pound

1½ teaspoons active dry yeast

3 cups all-purpose flour

1 teaspoon salt

3 tablespoons olive oil

1 cup warm water

1-pound

1 teaspoon active dry yeast

2 cups all-purpose flour

½ teaspoon salt

2 tablespoons olive oil

5 ounces warm water

Notes:

1. For Panasonic/National machines, use 3 teaspoons of yeast for the 1½-pound loaf.
2. For DAK/Welbilt machines, add 2 extra tablespoons of warm water to the 1½-pound loaf.

NUTRITIONAL ANALYSIS			
	1½-POUND	1-POUND	
TOTAL CALORIES	1853	1235	
TOTAL PROTEIN	51	34	GRAMS
TOTAL CARBOHYDRATES	300	200	GRAMS
TOTAL FAT	48	32	GRAMS
TOTAL SATURATED FAT	6	4	GRAMS
TOTAL CHOLESTEROL	0	0	MILLIGRAMS
TOTAL SODIUM	2140	1071	MILLIGRAMS
TOTAL FIBRE	7	4	GRAMS
% CALORIES FROM FAT	23	23	

Adobe Bread II

This is a variation of the adobe-bread recipe. The main difference is the addition of sugar and the deletion of olive oil.

1½-pound

1½ teaspoons active dry yeast

3 cups all-purpose flour

2 teaspoons salt

2 teaspoons sugar

9 ounces warm water

1-pound

1 teaspoon active dry yeast

2 cups all-purpose flour

1 teaspoon salt

1½ teaspoons sugar

6 ounces warm water

Notes:
1. For Panasonic/National machines, use 3 teaspoons of yeast for the 1½-pound loaf.
2. For DAK/Welbilt machines, use 2 extra tablespoons of warm water for the 1½-pound loaf.

NUTRITIONAL ANALYSIS			
	1½-POUND	1-POUND	
TOTAL CALORIES	1526	1020	
TOTAL PROTEIN	51	34	GRAMS
TOTAL CARBOHYDRATES	307	206	GRAMS
TOTAL FAT	7	5	GRAMS
TOTAL SATURATED FAT	1	1	GRAMS
TOTAL CHOLESTEROL	0	0	MILLIGRAMS
TOTAL SODIUM	4272	2137	MILLIGRAMS
TOTAL FIBRE	7	4	GRAMS
% CALORIES FROM FAT	4	4	

Amish Bread

Here is a simple, tasty, white bread with a sweet taste and a wonderfully fluffy texture.

1½-pound

1½ teaspoons active dry yeast

3¼ cups bread flour

1 teaspoon salt

3 tablespoons sugar

4 tablespoons olive oil

9 ounces warm water

1-pound

1 teaspoon active dry yeast

2 cups + 2 tablespoons bread flour

½ teaspoon salt

2 tablespoons sugar

2½ tablespoons olive oil

6 ounces warm water

Note:

For Panasonic/National machines, use 3 teaspoons of yeast for the 1½-pound loaf.

NUTRITIONAL ANALYSIS			
	1½-POUND	1-POUND	
TOTAL CALORIES	2233	1471	
TOTAL PROTEIN	55	37	GRAMS
TOTAL CARBOHYDRATES	360	240	GRAMS
TOTAL FAT	62	39	GRAMS
TOTAL SATURATED FAT	8	5	GRAMS
TOTAL CHOLESTEROL	0	0	MILLIGRAMS
TOTAL SODIUM	2140	1072	MILLIGRAMS
TOTAL FIBRE	7	5	GRAMS
% CALORIES FROM FAT	25	24	

Anadama Bread

The addition of cornmeal gives this rich white bread a somewhat crunchy texture.

1½-pound

1½ teaspoons active dry yeast

½ cup cornmeal

1 teaspoon salt

2¾ cups bread flour

3 tablespoons molasses

1 cup warm water

2½ tablespoons butter

1-pound

1 teaspoon active dry yeast

⅓ cup cornmeal

½ teaspoon salt

1¾ cups + 2 tablespoons bread flour

2 tablespoons molasses

6 ounces warm water

2 tablespoons butter

Notes:

1. For Panasonic/National machines, use 3 teaspoons of yeast for the 1½-pound loaf.
2. For DAK/Welbilt machines, add 2 tablespoons of warm water for the 1½-pound loaf.

NUTRITIONAL ANALYSIS			
	1½-POUND	1-POUND	
TOTAL CALORIES	2023	1403	
TOTAL PROTEIN	52	35	GRAMS
TOTAL CARBOHYDRATES	364	247	GRAMS
TOTAL FAT	37	29	GRAMS
TOTAL SATURATED FAT	19	15	GRAMS
TOTAL CHOLESTEROL	78	62	MILLIGRAMS
TOTAL SODIUM	2208	1117	MILLIGRAMS
TOTAL FIBRE	13	9	GRAMS
% CALORIES FROM FAT	17	18	

Cottage-Cheese Bread

Pioneers used what they had on hand to make bread. This recipe uses ingredients found in the typical pioneer kitchen. Because the loaf will really rise, try the 1-pound recipe first to make sure your machine can handle the size.

1½-pound

1½ teaspoons active dry yeast

¼ cup whole-wheat flour

2¾ cups bread flour

1½ teaspoons salt

½ teaspoon sugar

1 tablespoon sour cream

½ cup cottage cheese

1 egg

2 tablespoons butter

2 tablespoons honey

2 ounces warm milk

1-pound

1 teaspoon active dry yeast

¼ cup whole-wheat flour

1¾ cups bread flour

1 teaspoon salt

½ teaspoon sugar

½ tablespoon sour cream

6 tablespoons cottage cheese

1 egg

1 tablespoon butter

1½ tablespoons honey

1½ ounces warm milk

Note:

For Panasonic/National machines, use 3 teaspoons of yeast for the 1½-pound loaf.

NUTRITIONAL ANALYSIS			
	1½-POUND	1-POUND	
TOTAL CALORIES	1996	1357	
TOTAL PROTEIN	73	52	GRAMS
TOTAL CARBOHYDRATES	330	229	GRAMS
TOTAL FAT	40	25	GRAMS
TOTAL SATURATED FAT	20	11	GRAMS
TOTAL CHOLESTEROL	298	260	MILLIGRAMS
TOTAL SODIUM	3811	2610	MILLIGRAMS
TOTAL FIBRE	10	8	GRAMS
% CALORIES FROM FAT	18	16	

Country Bread

The specifics of the Midwestern origins of this bread are unknown, but it is a wonderfully rich white loaf sweetened by dates and nuts.

1½-pound

1½ teaspoons active dry yeast

2 teaspoons dried lemon peel

3 tablespoons sugar

3 cups bread flour

1½ teaspoons salt

2 eggs

5 tablespoons butter

7 ounces warm milk

3 tablespoons chopped nuts

3 tablespoons chopped dates

1-pound

1 teaspoon active dry yeast

1½ teaspoons dried lemon peel

1½ tablespoons sugar

2 cups bread flour

1 teaspoon salt

1 egg

3 tablespoons butter

5 ounces warm milk

2 tablespoons chopped nuts

2 tablespoons chopped dates

Notes:
1. For Panasonic/National machines, use 3 teaspoons of yeast for the 1½-pound loaf.
2. Dates and nuts may be added during the mix cycle or add them at the beep (if your machine is equipped with one).

NUTRITIONAL ANALYSIS			
	1½-POUND	1-POUND	
TOTAL CALORIES	2609	1662	
TOTAL PROTEIN	75	48	GRAMS
TOTAL CARBOHYDRATES	375	245	GRAMS
TOTAL FAT	90	55	GRAMS
TOTAL SATURATED FAT	42	25	GRAMS
TOTAL CHOLESTEROL	590	312	MILLIGRAMS
TOTAL SODIUM	3448	2282	MILLIGRAMS
TOTAL FIBRE	9	6	GRAMS
% CALORIES FROM FAT	31	30	

Grumbera Bread

This bread was originally made with real mashed potatoes. For the sake of simplicity, I developed a recipe using mashed-potato flakes. It retains the excellent flavor and light-yellowish color of the original.

1½-pound

1½ teaspoons active dry yeast

½ cup mashed-potato flakes or buds

3 cups + 2 tablespoons bread flour

1½ teaspoons salt

2 tablespoons sugar

5 ounces warm water

2 eggs

4 ounces warm milk

1 tablespoon butter

1-pound

1 teaspoon active dry yeast

¼ cup mashed-potato flakes or buds

2 cups + 2 tablespoons bread flour

1 teaspoon salt

1½ tablespoons sugar

3 ounces warm water

1 egg

3 ounces warm milk

½ tablespoon butter

Note:

For Panasonic/National machines, use 3 teaspoons of yeast for the 1½-pound loaf.

NUTRITIONAL ANALYSIS			
	1½-POUND	1-POUND	
TOTAL CALORIES	2080	1356	
TOTAL PROTEIN	72	47	GRAMS
TOTAL CARBOHYDRATES	360	243	GRAMS
TOTAL FAT	36	20	GRAMS
TOTAL SATURATED FAT	12	6	GRAMS
TOTAL CHOLESTEROL	462	232	MILLIGRAMS
TOTAL SODIUM	3755	2427	MILLIGRAMS
TOTAL FIBRE	7	5	GRAMS
% CALORIES FROM FAT	16	13	

Indian Bread

Cornmeal and cream give this bread a distinctive flavor and texture.

1½-pound

1½ teaspoons active dry yeast

2¼ cups + 2 tablespoons all-purpose flour

¾ cup cornmeal

1½ teaspoons salt

2 eggs

3 tablespoons butter

4 ounces cream

3 ounces warm water

2½ tablespoons honey

1-pound

1 teaspoon active dry yeast

1½ cups + 2 tablespoons all-purpose flour

½ cup cornmeal

1 teaspoon salt

1 egg

2 tablespoons butter

2½ ounces cream

2 ounces warm water

2 tablespoons honey

Note:

For Panasonic/National machines, use 3 teaspoons of yeast for the 1½-pound loaf.

NUTRITIONAL ANALYSIS			
	1½-POUND	1-POUND	
TOTAL CALORIES	2316	1520	
TOTAL PROTEIN	64	39	GRAMS
TOTAL CARBOHYDRATES	343	233	GRAMS
TOTAL FAT	76	49	GRAMS
TOTAL SATURATED FAT	41	26	GRAMS
TOTAL CHOLESTEROL	570	307	MILLIGRAMS
TOTAL SODIUM	3417	2261	MILLIGRAMS
TOTAL FIBRE	12	10	GRAMS
% CALORIES FROM FAT	30	29	

Plymouth Bread

An old New England favorite, this bread combines basic ingredients to produce a firm, tasty loaf.

1½-pound

1½ teaspoons active dry yeast

2¾ cups bread flour

1½ teaspoons salt

4 tablespoons cornmeal

4 tablespoons molasses

1½ tablespoons butter

7 ounces warm water

1-pound

1 teaspoon active dry yeast

2 cups bread flour

1 teaspoon salt

2½ tablespoons cornmeal

2½ tablespoons molasses

1 tablespoon butter

5 ounces warm water

Note:

For Panasonic/National machines, use 3 teaspoons of yeast for the 1½-pound loaf.

NUTRITIONAL ANALYSIS			
	1½-POUND	1-POUND	
TOTAL CALORIES	1872	1316	
TOTAL PROTEIN	49	35	GRAMS
TOTAL CARBOHYDRATES	354	249	GRAMS
TOTAL FAT	25	17	GRAMS
TOTAL SATURATED FAT	12	8	GRAMS
TOTAL CHOLESTEROL	47	31	MILLIGRAMS
TOTAL SODIUM	3278	2183	MILLIGRAMS
TOTAL FIBRE	9	6	GRAMS
% CALORIES FROM FAT	12	11	

Southern Bread

This fluffy white-bread recipe has been a favorite in the southern United States. It's excellent sandwich bread.

1½-pound	1-pound
1½ teaspoons active dry yeast	1 teaspoon active dry yeast
2 tablespoons wheat germ	5 teaspoons wheat germ
1 tablespoon sugar	½ tablespoon sugar
3 tablespoons dry milk	2 tablespoons dry milk
3 cups bread flour	2 cups bread flour
1 teaspoon salt	½ teaspoon salt
1 tablespoon butter	½ tablespoon butter
9 ounces warm water	6 ounces warm water

Notes:
1. For Panasonic/National machines, use 3 teaspoons of yeast for the 1½-pound loaf.
2. For DAK/Welbilt machines, use 2 additional tablespoons of warm water for the 1½-pound loaf.

NUTRITIONAL ANALYSIS			
	1½-POUND	1-POUND	
TOTAL CALORIES	1755	1154	
TOTAL PROTEIN	61	42	GRAMS
TOTAL CARBOHYDRATES	329	218	GRAMS
TOTAL FAT	20	12	GRAMS
TOTAL SATURATED FAT	8	4	GRAMS
TOTAL CHOLESTEROL	34	18	MILLIGRAMS
TOTAL SODIUM	2236	1135	MILLIGRAMS
TOTAL FIBRE	8	6	GRAMS
% CALORIES FROM FAT	10	9	

War Bread

Legend has it that this bread was first baked during the American Revolution. Oats and cornmeal were added to make the flour go further, creating a great loaf of healthful bread.

1½-pound

1½ teaspoons active dry yeast

2½ cups all-purpose flour

1 teaspoon salt

¼ cup whole-wheat flour

¼ cup cornmeal

¼ cup rolled oats

10 ounces warm water

1½ tablespoons molasses

½ tablespoon butter

1-pound

1 teaspoon active dry yeast

1¾ cups all-purpose flour

1 teaspoon salt

2½ tablespoons whole-wheat flour

2½ tablespoons cornmeal

2½ tablespoons rolled oats

7 ounces warm water

1 tablespoon molasses

½ tablespoon butter

Notes:
1. For Panasonic/National machines, use 3 teaspoons of yeast for the 1½-pound loaf.
2. For DAK/Welbilt machines, use 2 additional tablespoons of warm water for the 1½-pound loaf.

NUTRITIONAL ANALYSIS			
	1½-POUND	1-POUND	
TOTAL CALORIES	1678	1165	
TOTAL PROTEIN	52	36	GRAMS
TOTAL CARBOHYDRATES	330	226	GRAMS
TOTAL FAT	15	12	GRAMS
TOTAL SATURATED FAT	5	4	GRAMS
TOTAL CHOLESTEROL	16	16	MILLIGRAMS
TOTAL SODIUM	2174	2160	MILLIGRAMS
TOTAL FIBRE	15	10	GRAMS
% CALORIES FROM FAT	8	9	

MEDITERRANEAN BREADS

The area that surrounds the Mediterranean encompasses a wide variety of cultures. Each country produces different types of bread. In this section, you'll find breads from Greece, Italy, and Portugal.

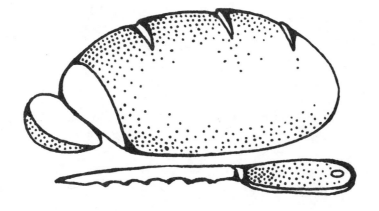

Christopsomo (Greek Christmas Bread)

The slight cherry aroma makes this sweet-tasting bread perfect for parties or special occasions.

1½-pound	1-pound
1½ teaspoons active dry yeast	1 teaspoon active dry yeast
3 chopped candied cherries	2 chopped candied cherries
1 tablespoon chopped walnuts	2 teaspoons chopped walnuts
3¼ cups all-purpose flour	2¼ cups all-purpose flour
1 teaspoon crushed anise seed	½ teaspoon crushed anise seed
½ teaspoon salt	½ teaspoon salt
½ cup sugar	5 tablespoons sugar
2 eggs	1 egg
3 ounces warm water	2 ounces warm water
5 tablespoons butter	3½ tablespoons butter
½ cup warm milk	3 ounces warm milk

Note:

For Panasonic/National machines, use 3 teaspoons of yeast for the 1½-pound loaf.

NUTRITIONAL ANALYSIS			
	1½-POUND	1-POUND	
TOTAL CALORIES	2736	1839	
TOTAL PROTEIN	73	47	GRAMS
TOTAL CARBOHYDRATES	428	289	GRAMS
TOTAL FAT	81	54	GRAMS
TOTAL SATURATED FAT	41	28	GRAMS
TOTAL CHOLESTEROL	586	325	MILLIGRAMS
TOTAL SODIUM	1268	1184	MILLIGRAMS
TOTAL FIBRE	7	5	GRAMS
% CALORIES FROM FAT	26	26	

Italian Whole-Wheat Bread

If you like whole-grain breads, this wheat bread will please your palate. It has a light, wheat flavor and somewhat crumbly texture. If you prefer a smoother texture, add the optional dough enhancer.

1½-pound

1½ teaspoons active dry yeast

1½ tablespoons dough enhancer (optional)

2 cups all-purpose flour

1 cup whole-wheat flour

2 tablespoons wheat germ

1½ teaspoons salt

1½ teaspoons brown sugar

1 tablespoon butter

9 ounces warm water

1-pound

1 teaspoon active dry yeast

1 tablespoon dough enhancer (optional)

1¼ cups all-purpose flour

¾ cup whole-wheat flour

1½ tablespoons wheat germ

1 teaspoon salt

1 teaspoon brown sugar

½ tablespoon butter

6 ounces warm water

Notes:
1. For Panasonic/National machines, use 3 teaspoons of yeast for the 1½-pound loaf.
2. For DAK/Welbilt machines, use 2 additional tablespoons of warm water for the 1½-pound loaf.

NUTRITIONAL ANALYSIS			
	1½-POUND	1-POUND	
TOTAL CALORIES	1585	1037	
TOTAL PROTEIN	55	37	GRAMS
TOTAL CARBOHYDRATES	302	201	GRAMS
TOTAL FAT	20	12	GRAMS
TOTAL SATURATED FAT	8	4	GRAMS
TOTAL CHOLESTEROL	31	16	MILLIGRAMS
TOTAL SODIUM	3209	2139	MILLIGRAMS
TOTAL FIBRE	21	15	GRAMS
% CALORIES FROM FAT	11	10	

Pane Italiano

This simple bread is a staple in Italy. It is easy to make and yields the kind of loaf you associate with traditional Italian bread. It is an excellent base for garlic bread.

1½-pound

1½ teaspoons active dry yeast

3 cups + 2 tablespoons bread flour

1½ teaspoons salt

9 ounces warm water

1-pound

1 teaspoon active dry yeast

2 cups + 2 tablespoons bread flour

1 teaspoon salt

6 ounces warm water

Notes:

1. For Panasonic/National machines, use 3 teaspoons of yeast for the 1½-pound loaf.
2. For DAK/Welbilt machines, use 1 additional tablespoon of warm water for the 1½-pound loaf.

NUTRITIONAL ANALYSIS			
	1½-POUND	1-POUND	
TOTAL CALORIES	1560	1061	
TOTAL PROTEIN	53	36	GRAMS
TOTAL CARBOHYDRATES	312	213	GRAMS
TOTAL FAT	7	5	GRAMS
TOTAL SATURATED FAT	1	1	GRAM
TOTAL CHOLESTEROL	0	0	MILLIGRAMS
TOTAL SODIUM	3206	2138	MILLIGRAMS
TOTAL FIBRE	7	5	GRAMS
% CALORIES FROM FAT	4	4	

Panettone

Because it has a sweet, nutty flavor, this Italian bread is particularly enjoyable as a breakfast toast served with butter and jam.

1½-pound	1-pound
1½ teaspoons active dry yeast	1 teaspoon active dry yeast
½ teaspoon dried orange peel	½ teaspoon dried orange peel
1½ teaspoons dried lemon peel	1 teaspoon dried lemon peal
½ teaspoon salt	½ teaspoon salt
3 cups + 3 tablespoons all-purpose flour	2 cups + 2 tablespoons all-purpose flour
6 tablespoons sugar	4 tablespoons sugar
2 eggs	1 egg
7½ tablespoons butter	5 tablespoons butter
6 ounces warm milk	½ cup warm milk
6 tablespoons raisins	4 tablespoons raisins
4 tablespoons shredded almonds	3 tablespoons shredded almonds

Notes:
1. For Panasonic/National machines, use 3 teaspoons of yeast for the 1½-pound loaf.
2. If your machine has a mix cycle, you may add the almonds and raisins at the beep.

NUTRITIONAL ANALYSIS			
	1½-POUND	1-POUND	
TOTAL CALORIES	3196	2060	
TOTAL PROTEIN	79	49	GRAMS
TOTAL CARBOHYDRATES	448	287	GRAMS
TOTAL FAT	124	82	GRAMS
TOTAL SATURATED FAT	60	40	GRAMS
TOTAL CHOLESTEROL	666	373	MILLIGRAMS
TOTAL SODIUM	1310	1208	MILLIGRAMS
TOTAL FIBRE	11	7	GRAMS
% CALORIES FROM FAT	35	36	

Portuguese Corn Bread

Here is a good, dense, corn bread with a crunchy texture and rich flavor. It is very good with soup or with butter and jelly or jam.

1½-pound

1½ teaspoons active dry yeast

2 cups bread flour

1½ teaspoons salt

1½ cups cornmeal

1 tablespoon sugar

1 tablespoon olive oil

9 ounces warm water

1-pound

1 teaspoon active dry yeast

1¼ cups bread flour

1 teaspoon salt

1 cup cornmeal

2 teaspoons sugar

2 teaspoons olive oil

6 ounces warm water

Notes:

1. For Panasonic/National machines, use 3 teaspoons of yeast for the 1½-pound loaf.
2. For DAK/Welbilt machines, use 2 additional tablespoons of warm water for the 1½-pound loaf.

NUTRITIONAL ANALYSIS			
	1½-POUND	1-POUND	
TOTAL CALORIES	1829	1178	
TOTAL PROTEIN	49	31	GRAMS
TOTAL CARBOHYDRATES	353	227	GRAMS
TOTAL FAT	25	16	GRAMS
TOTAL SATURATED FAT	3	2	GRAMS
TOTAL CHOLESTEROL	0	0	MILLIGRAMS
TOTAL SODIUM	3268	2179	MILLIGRAMS
TOTAL FIBRE	25	16	GRAMS
% CALORIES FROM FAT	12	13	

Portuguese Sweet Bread

Light and sweet, this rich white bread is great at breakfast, spread with jam or jelly.

1½-pound

1½ teaspoons active dry yeast

3¼ cups bread flour

1 teaspoon salt

½ cup sugar

4 tablespoons butter

2 eggs

5 ounces warm milk

3 ounces warm water

3 tablespoons currants

1-pound

1 teaspoon active dry yeast

2 cups + 3 tablespoons bread flour

½ teaspoon salt

5½ tablespoons sugar

3 tablespoons butter

1 egg

3 ounces warm milk

2 ounces warm water

2 tablespoons currants

Note:

For Panasonic/National machines, use 3 teaspoons of yeast for the 1½-pound loaf.

NUTRITIONAL ANALYSIS			
	1½-POUND	1-POUND	
TOTAL CALORIES	2682	1810	
TOTAL PROTEIN	74	47	GRAMS
TOTAL CARBOHYDRATES	450	303	GRAMS
TOTAL FAT	65	45	GRAMS
TOTAL SATURATED FAT	34	24	GRAMS
TOTAL CHOLESTEROL	556	310	MILLIGRAMS
TOTAL SODIUM	2351	1186	MILLIGRAMS
TOTAL FIBRE	9	6	GRAMS
% CALORIES FROM FAT	22	23	

AFRICAN AND CAUCASIAN BREADS

These few recipes offer a glimpse into the cuisines of these exotic regions. You've probably never tried these recipes before, so here's your chance to please and surprise friends and family with new and exciting tastes.

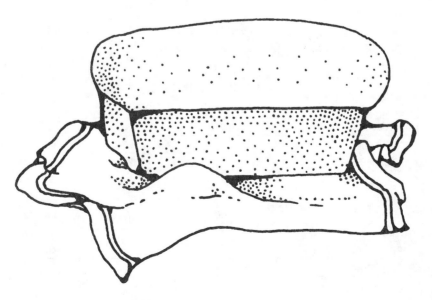

Armenian Pita

Pita cannot be baked in the bread machine, but you can use the dough cycle to mix it and to let it rise. After the first rise, remove the dough and follow the instructions below to bake the small pita loaves. I like to stuff this pocket bread with chicken, tomato, and lettuce.

1½-pound	1-pound
1½ teaspoons active dry yeast	1 teaspoon active dry yeast
1 tablespoon sugar	2½ teaspoons sugar
3 cups all-purpose flour	2 cups all-purpose flour
1 teaspoon salt	½ teaspoon salt
1 tablespoon olive oil	½ tablespoon olive oil
1 cup warm water	5½ ounces warm water

Notes:
1. For Panasonic/National machines, use 3 teaspoons of yeast for the 1½-pound loaf.
2. For DAK/Welbilt machines, use 2 additional tablespoons of warm water for the 1½-pound loaf.

Instructions for baking:

Remove the dough from the machine at the end of the dough cycle (after the first rise). Form the dough into individual balls approximately 2–3 inches in diameter. Place the balls on a greased cookie sheet. Flatten the balls with the palm of your hand until each is about ¾ inch thick. Cut the top of each with a razor blade. Cover them lightly and let the pitas rise for about 20–30 minutes or until about double in volume.

Bake in a preheated, 425 °F oven until brown and crusty (about 20 minutes). Cut the pita loaves in half and split the insides.

NUTRITIONAL ANALYSIS			
	1½-POUND	1-POUND	
TOTAL CALORIES	1661	1095	
TOTAL PROTEIN	51	34	GRAMS
TOTAL CARBOHYDRATES	311	210	GRAMS
TOTAL FAT	21	11	GRAMS
TOTAL SATURATED FAT	3	2	GRAMS
TOTAL CHOLESTEROL	0	0	MILLIGRAMS
TOTAL SODIUM	2140	1071	MILLIGRAMS
TOTAL FIBRE	7	4	GRAMS
% CALORIES FROM FAT	11	9	

Churek Bread

The sesame seeds in this Armenian recipe produce a basic white bread with a distinctive flavor. Traditionally, Churek is baked as a flat, crisp bread. This recipe gives you the flavor of Churek and allows you to bake it in your bread machine. As a variation, you can bake it by hand in a large, flat loaf.

1½-pound

1½ teaspoons active dry yeast

4 tablespoons sesame seeds

1 tablespoon sugar

3 cups all-purpose flour

2 teaspoons salt

1 cup warm water

4 tablespoons butter

1-pound

1 teaspoon active dry yeast

2½ tablespoons sesame seeds

½ tablespoon sugar

2 cups all-purpose flour

1½ teaspoons salt

5 ounces warm water

2½ tablespoons butter

Notes:

1. For Panasonic/National machines, use 3 teaspoons of yeast for the 1½-pound loaf.
2. For DAK/Welbilt machines, use 2 additional tablespoons of warm water for the 1½-pound loaf.

NUTRITIONAL ANALYSIS			
	1½-POUND	1-POUND	
TOTAL CALORIES	2150	1400	
TOTAL PROTEIN	58	38	GRAMS
TOTAL CARBOHYDRATES	320	211	GRAMS
TOTAL FAT	71	44	GRAMS
TOTAL SATURATED FAT	32	20	GRAMS
TOTAL CHOLESTEROL	124	78	MILLIGRAMS
TOTAL SODIUM	4280	3208	MILLIGRAMS
TOTAL FIBRE	8	5	GRAMS
% CALORIES FROM FAT	30	29	

Ethiopian Honey Bread

This African bread is complex to make by hand, but it works quite well in this version, adapted for the bread machine. It has a spicy, somewhat sweet taste.

1½-pound

1½ teaspoons active dry yeast

3¼ cups all-purpose flour

1 teaspoon salt

½ teaspoon ground cloves

½ teaspoon ground cinnamon

2 teaspoons ground coriander

3½ tablespoons butter

4½ ounces warm milk

6 tablespoons honey

1 egg

2 tablespoons warm water

1-pound

1 teaspoon active dry yeast

2¼ cups all-purpose flour

½ teaspoon salt

½ teaspoon ground cloves

½ teaspoon ground cinnamon

1½ teaspoons ground coriander

2½ tablespoons butter

3 ounces warm milk

4 tablespoons honey

1 egg

1½ tablespoons warm water

Note:

For Panasonic/National machines, use 3 teaspoons of yeast for the 1½-pound loaf.

NUTRITIONAL ANALYSIS			
	1½-POUND	1-POUND	
TOTAL CALORIES	2478	1738	
TOTAL PROTEIN	66	48	GRAMS
TOTAL CARBOHYDRATES	431	297	GRAMS
TOTAL FAT	55	40	GRAMS
TOTAL SATURATED FAT	28	21	GRAMS
TOTAL CHOLESTEROL	327	294	MILLIGRAMS
TOTAL SODIUM	2279	1186	MILLIGRAMS
TOTAL FIBRE	9	6	GRAMS
% CALORIES FROM FAT	20	21	

Ethiopian Spice Bread

The distinct and unusual blend of spices in this bread make it a great choice with soups or salads.

1½-pound

1½ teaspoons active dry yeast

3 cups all-purpose flour

½ teaspoon paprika

½ teaspoon salt

½ teaspoon ground cardamom

1 tablespoon ground coriander

½ teaspoon garlic salt

1½ teaspoons dried onion

1 teaspoon hot sauce (red pepper)

5½ tablespoons butter

7 ounces warm water

1-pound

1 teaspoon active dry yeast

2 cups all-purpose flour

½ teaspoon paprika

½ teaspoon salt

½ teaspoon ground cardamom

2 teaspoons ground coriander

½ teaspoon garlic salt

1 teaspoon dried onion

½ teaspoon hot sauce (red pepper)

3½ tablespoons butter

4½ ounces warm water

Notes:
1. For Panasonic/National machines, use 3 teaspoons of yeast for the 1½-pound loaf.
2. For DAK/Welbilt machines, use 2 additional tablespoons of warm water for the 1½-pound loaf.

NUTRITIONAL ANALYSIS			
	1½-POUND	1-POUND	
TOTAL CALORIES	2072	1365	
TOTAL PROTEIN	52	35	GRAMS
TOTAL CARBOHYDRATES	305	204	GRAMS
TOTAL FAT	71	45	GRAMS
TOTAL SATURATED FAT	40	26	GRAMS
TOTAL CHOLESTEROL	171	109	MILLIGRAMS
TOTAL SODIUM	2239	2189	MILLIGRAMS
TOTAL FIBRE	8	6	GRAMS
% CALORIES FROM FAT	31	30	

Georgian Cheese Bread

This favorite from the Caucasus is a very rich, flaky textured bread. The dough is made in the bread machine and then removed to be flattened, filled, and baked in the oven.

1½-pound

1½ teaspoons active dry yeast

1 tablespoon sugar

3 cups all-purpose flour

2 teaspoons salt

8 tablespoons butter

¾ cup warm milk

Filling(do not place in bread machine):

1¼ cup mozzarella or cheddar cheese (shredded)

1 egg

2½ tablespoons butter

1-pound

1 teaspoon active dry yeast

2 teaspoons sugar

2 cups all-purpose flour

1½ teaspoons salt

5½ tablespoons butter

½ cup warm milk

¾ cup mozzarella or cheddar cheese (shredded)

1 egg

1½ tablespoons butter

Notes:
1. For Panasonic/National machines, use 3 teaspoons of yeast for the 1½-pound loaf.
2. Use the dough cycle and remove the dough when complete. Finish the bread according to the baking instructions below.

Instructions for baking:

Remove the dough from the bread machine. Flatten the dough into a round shape, about ¼ inch thick. Place the dough on a greased pie plate in much the same manner as you would a piecrust. Gently press the dough down into the bottom of the pie plate, shaping it to conform to the contour of the plate. Prepare the filling, mix it well, and spoon it into the crust in the pie plate. Fold the remaining crust over the top of the filling until the filling is completely covered. Let rise 15–20 minutes in a warm location (cover with a towel or cloth). Bake in a preheated 375 °F oven for 60 minutes or until brown on top.

NUTRITIONAL ANALYSIS			
	1½-POUND	1-POUND	
TOTAL CALORIES	3312	2195	
TOTAL PROTEIN	99	66	GRAMS
TOTAL CARBOHYDRATES	323	215	GRAMS
TOTAL FAT	181	119	GRAMS
TOTAL SATURATED FAT	108	71	GRAMS
TOTAL CHOLESTEROL	695	524	MILLIGRAMS
TOTAL SODIUM	5314	3861	MILLIGRAMS
TOTAL FIBRE	7	4	GRAMS
% CALORIES FROM FAT	49	49	

WESTERN EUROPEAN BREADS

Germany, Austria, and France are represented by breads in this section. You will find a great variety of recipes, including everything from soft, sweet, white breads to dense, sour ryes.

Feather Bread

This French recipe gets its name from the airy loaf it produces. Experiment with the amount of yeast to get just the lightness you desire. Try the 1-pound loaf first to make sure the volume of the larger loaf won't overflow your machine.

1½-pound

2 teaspoons active dry yeast

1½ teaspoons sugar

3 cups bread flour

1½ teaspoons salt

3 tablespoons butter

1 cup warm water

1-pound

1½ teaspoons active dry yeast

1 teaspoon sugar

2 cups bread flour

1 teaspoon salt

2 tablespoons butter

5 ounces warm water

Notes:
1. For Panasonic/National machines, use 4 teaspoons of yeast for the 1½-pound loaf.
2. For DAK/Welbilt machines, use 2 additional tablespoons of warm water for the 1½-pound loaf.

NUTRITIONAL ANALYSIS			
	1½-POUND	1-POUND	
TOTAL CALORIES	1822	1216	
TOTAL PROTEIN	52	35	GRAMS
TOTAL CARBOHYDRATES	306	204	GRAMS
TOTAL FAT	41	28	GRAMS
TOTAL SATURATED FAT	22	15	GRAMS
TOTAL CHOLESTEROL	93	62	MILLIGRAMS
TOTAL SODIUM	3210	2140	MILLIGRAMS
TOTAL FIBRE	7	5	GRAMS
% CALORIES FROM FAT	20	20	

Hausbrot

Hausbrot could be any homemade bread. This loaf combines a light wheat and rye flavor and texture with a touch of potato for a basic, traditional German bread.

1½-pound

2 teaspoons active dry yeast

1½ tablespoons gluten powder

1 teaspoon caraway seed

1½ cups bread flour

1½ tablespoons sugar

¾ cup whole-wheat flour

½ teaspoon salt

¾ cup rye flour

¾ cup potato flakes or buds

10 ounces warm water

1-pound

1½ teaspoons active dry yeast

1 tablespoon gluten powder

½ teaspoon caraway seed

1 cup bread flour

1 tablespoon sugar

½ cup whole-wheat flour

½ teaspoon salt

½ cup rye flour

½ cup potato flakes or buds

7 ounces warm water

Note:

For Panasonic/National machines, use 3 teaspoons of yeast for the 1½-pound loaf.

NUTRITIONAL ANALYSIS			
	1½-POUND	1-POUND	
TOTAL CALORIES	1688	1126	
TOTAL PROTEIN	62	41	GRAMS
TOTAL CARBOHYDRATES	329	219	GRAMS
TOTAL FAT	16	11	GRAMS
TOTAL SATURATED FAT	1	1	GRAMS
TOTAL CHOLESTEROL	0	0	MILLIGRAMS
TOTAL SODIUM	1615	1432	MILLIGRAMS
TOTAL FIBRE	27	18	GRAMS
% CALORIES FROM FAT	9	9	

Heidelberg Rye Bread

Although similar to German country-rye bread, this bread has a slightly different combination of ingredients.

1½-pound

3 teaspoons active dry yeast

½ tablespoon caraway seeds

1½ cups bread flour

½ tablespoon salt

½ tablespoon sugar

2 tablespoons unsweetened cocoa

1½ cups rye flour

1 tablespoon butter

2½ tablespoons molasses

1 cup warm water

3 tablespoons gluten (optional)

1-pound

2 teaspoons active dry yeast

1 teaspoon caraway seeds

1 cup bread flour

1 teaspoon salt

1 teaspoon sugar

4 teaspoons unsweetened cocoa

1 cup rye flour

1 tablespoon butter

1½ tablespoons molasses

5½ ounces warm water

2 tablespoons gluten (optional)

Notes:
1. For Panasonic/National machines, use 4 teaspoons of yeast for the 1½-pound loaf.
2. For DAK/Welbilt machines, use 2 additional tablespoons of warm water for the 1½-pound loaf.

NUTRITIONAL ANALYSIS			
	1½-POUND	1-POUND	
TOTAL CALORIES	1715	1166	
TOTAL PROTEIN	58	39	GRAMS
TOTAL CARBOHYDRATES	332	219	GRAMS
TOTAL FAT	22	19	GRAMS
TOTAL SATURATED FAT	8	8	GRAMS
TOTAL CHOLESTEROL	31	31	MILLIGRAMS
TOTAL SODIUM	3248	2163	MILLIGRAMS
TOTAL FIBRE	8	5	GRAMS
% CALORIES FROM FAT	12	14	

Kugelhopf Bread

A slightly sweet white bread, *Kugelhopf* is an excellent breakfast bread. It is particularly good spread with jam or jelly.

1½-pound	1-pound
1½ teaspoons active dry yeast	1 teaspoon active dry yeast
½ teaspoon dried lemon peel	½ teaspoon dried lemon peel
3 cups + 2 tablespoons bread flour	2 cups + 2 tablespoons bread flour
½ teaspoon salt	½ teaspoon salt
3 tablespoons sugar	2 tablespoons sugar
2 eggs	1 egg
4 tablespoons butter	2½ tablespoons butter
2 ounces warm water	2 ounces warm water
½ cup warm milk	2 ounces warm milk
¼ cup slivered almonds	2 tablespoons slivered almonds
½ cup currants	¼ cup currants

Notes:
1. For Panasonic/National machines, use 3 teaspoons of yeast for the 1½-pound loaf.
2. Almonds and currants may be added at the mix beep (if your machine is equipped with one). They may also be added at the beginning with the other ingredients.

NUTRITIONAL ANALYSIS			
	1½-POUND	1-POUND	
TOTAL CALORIES	2706	1706	
TOTAL PROTEIN	76	48	GRAMS
TOTAL CARBOHYDRATES	418	271	GRAMS
TOTAL FAT	83	49	GRAMS
TOTAL SATURATED FAT	35	21	GRAMS
TOTAL CHOLESTEROL	555	293	MILLIGRAMS
TOTAL SODIUM	1278	1174	MILLIGRAMS
TOTAL FIBRE	12	7	GRAMS
% CALORIES FROM FAT	28	26	

La Fouace

This French hearth bread is a hearty white bread with a slight wheat flavor. Toasting it brings out the walnut and wheat flavors.

1½-pound

1½ teaspoons active dry yeast

¼ cup whole-wheat flour

6 tablespoons chopped walnuts

2 teaspoons salt

2¾ cups bread flour

4 tablespoons butter

6 ounces warm milk

3 ounces warm water

1-pound

1 teaspoon active dry yeast

3 tablespoons whole-wheat flour

4 tablespoons chopped walnuts

1½ teaspoons salt

1¾ cups + 2 tablespoons bread flour

2½ tablespoons butter

4 ounces warm milk

2 ounces warm water

Note:

For Panasonic/National machines, use 3 teaspoons of yeast for the 1½-pound loaf.

NUTRITIONAL ANALYSIS			
	1½-POUND	1-POUND	
TOTAL CALORIES	2239	1483	
TOTAL PROTEIN	64	43	GRAMS
TOTAL CARBOHYDRATES	314	210	GRAMS
TOTAL FAT	82	53	GRAMS
TOTAL SATURATED FAT	33	21	GRAMS
TOTAL CHOLESTEROL	132	83	MILLIGRAMS
TOTAL SODIUM	4372	3270	MILLIGRAMS
TOTAL FIBRE	12	8	GRAMS
% CALORIES FROM FAT	33	32	

Milk Bread

This traditional Austrian bread is most often baked in a braided loaf, but the flavor, aroma, and texture come through in the bread machine, too.

1½-pound	1-pound
1½ teaspoons active dry yeast	1 teaspoon active dry yeast
1 teaspoon ground caraway	½ teaspoon ground caraway
1 teaspoon anise seed	½ teaspoon anise seed
3 cups bread flour	2 cups bread flour
½ teaspoon salt	½ teaspoon salt
2 tablespoons sugar	4 teaspoons sugar
6 tablespoons butter	4 tablespoons butter
8 ounces warm milk	5 ounces warm milk

Note:

For Panasonic/National machines, use 3 teaspoons of yeast for the 1½-pound loaf.

NUTRITIONAL ANALYSIS			
	1½-POUND	1-POUND	
TOTAL CALORIES	2297	1526	
TOTAL PROTEIN	60	39	GRAMS
TOTAL CARBOHYDRATES	336	223	GRAMS
TOTAL FAT	78	52	GRAMS
TOTAL SATURATED FAT	45	30	GRAMS
TOTAL CHOLESTEROL	196	130	MILLIGRAMS
TOTAL SODIUM	1203	1152	MILLIGRAMS
TOTAL FIBRE	7	5	GRAMS
% CALORIES FROM FAT	31	31	

Muenster-Cheese Loaf

Fresh Muenster cheese characterizes this rich white bread. It makes an outstanding sandwich.

1½-pound

1½ teaspoons active dry yeast

1 teaspoon sugar

3 cups + 3 tablespoons bread flour

2 teaspoons salt

½ cup shredded Muenster cheese

2 eggs

1½ tablespoons butter

½ cup plain yogurt

1-pound

1 teaspoon active dry yeast

½ teaspoon sugar

2 cups + 2 tablespoons bread flour

1½ teaspoons salt

¼ cup shredded Muenster cheese

2 eggs

1 tablespoon butter

¼ cup plain yogurt

Note:

For Panasonic/National machines, use 3 teaspoons of yeast for the 1½-pound loaf.

NUTRITIONAL ANALYSIS			
	1½-POUND	1-POUND	
TOTAL CALORIES	2203	1466	
TOTAL PROTEIN	87	59	GRAMS
TOTAL CARBOHYDRATES	332	220	GRAMS
TOTAL FAT	55	37	GRAMS
TOTAL SATURATED FAT	28	17	GRAMS
TOTAL CHOLESTEROL	539	490	MILLIGRAMS
TOTAL SODIUM	4830	3546	MILLIGRAMS
TOTAL FIBRE	7	5	GRAMS
% CALORIES FROM FAT	23	22	

Soft Pumpernickel Bread

The addition of wheat flour softens this traditional rye bread, giving it a higher rise and a softer texture than pure rye bread.

1½-pound

2 teaspoons active dry yeast

¾ cup whole-wheat flour

1½ cups bread flour

¾ cup rye flour

2 teaspoons salt

1 tablespoon butter

1½ tablespoons molasses

3 tablespoons honey

1 cup warm water

1-pound

1½ teaspoons active dry yeast

½ cup whole-wheat flour

1 cup bread flour

½ cup rye flour

1½ teaspoons salt

½ tablespoon butter

1 tablespoon molasses

1½ tablespoons honey

6 ounces warm water

Note:

For Panasonic/National machines, use 3 teaspoons of yeast for the 1½-pound loaf.

NUTRITIONAL ANALYSIS			
	1½-POUND	1-POUND	
TOTAL CALORIES	1712	1096	
TOTAL PROTEIN	45	30	GRAMS
TOTAL CARBOHYDRATES	347	223	GRAMS
TOTAL FAT	18	10	GRAMS
TOTAL SATURATED FAT	8	4	GRAMS
TOTAL CHOLESTEROL	31	16	MILLIGRAMS
TOTAL SODIUM	4295	3219	MILLIGRAMS
TOTAL FIBRE	26	18	GRAMS
% CALORIES FROM FAT	9	8	

Sour Rye Bread

Although you can use various types of starter for this recipe, sourdough starter works well and is used here. See page 44 for the sourdough starter recipe. This is a very densely textured excellent-tasting, rye bread.

1½-pound

1½ teaspoons active dry yeast

¾ cup sourdough starter batter

1½ cups bread flour

1½ cups rye flour

1½ teaspoons salt

7½ ounces warm water

2 tablespoons molasses

1-pound

1 teaspoon active dry yeast

½ cup sourdough starter batter

1 cup bread flour

1 cup rye flour

1 teaspoon salt

4½ ounces warm water

4 teaspoons molasses

Notes:

1. For Panasonic/National machines, use 3 teaspoons of yeast for the 1½-pound loaf.
2. For DAK/Welbilt machines, use 2 additional tablespoons of warm water for the 1½-pound loaf.

Instructions for baking:

Mix ingredients through the end of the mix cycle. Turn off the bread machine and reset it to start a complete cycle in 4–5 hours (completion in 8–9 hours). The long first rise gives the sourdough and the yeast time to interact and to proof.

NUTRITIONAL ANALYSIS			
	1½-POUND	1-POUND	
TOTAL CALORIES	1867	1245	
TOTAL PROTEIN	65	44	GRAMS
TOTAL CARBOHYDRATES	385	257	GRAMS
TOTAL FAT	10	7	GRAMS
TOTAL SATURATED FAT	1	1	GRAMS
TOTAL CHOLESTEROL	0	0	MILLIGRAMS
TOTAL SODIUM	3237	2158	MILLIGRAMS
TOTAL FIBRE	8	5	GRAMS
% CALORIES FROM FAT	5	5	

Viennese Hausbrot

This bread is half rye and doesn't rise much (hence the need for extra gluten). The taste and texture are wonderful, particularly if you like rye breads. Add caraway seed, if you like.

1½-pound

2 teaspoons active dry yeast

1 teaspoon anise seed

1½ tablespoons gluten powder

1 tablespoon sugar

1½ cups bread flour

1½ cups rye flour

½ teaspoon salt

¾ cup potato flakes or buds

11 ounces warm water

1-pound

1½ teaspoons active dry yeast

½ teaspoon anise seed

1 tablespoon gluten powder

½ tablespoon sugar

1 cup bread flour

1 cup rye flour

½ teaspoon salt

½ cup potato flakes or buds

1 cup warm water

Note:

For Panasonic/National machines, use 3½ teaspoons of yeast for the 1½-pound loaf.

NUTRITIONAL ANALYSIS			
	1½-POUND	1-POUND	
TOTAL CALORIES	1634	1083	
TOTAL PROTEIN	55	37	GRAMS
TOTAL CARBOHYDRATES	318	210	GRAMS
TOTAL FAT	16	10	GRAMS
TOTAL SATURATED FAT	1	0	GRAMS
TOTAL CHOLESTEROL	0	0	MILLIGRAMS
TOTAL SODIUM	1615	1432	MILLIGRAMS
TOTAL FIBRE	27	18	GRAMS
% CALORIES FROM FAT	9	9	

Viennese Potato Bread (Erdapfelbrot)

This simple white bread is rich with cream and butter, with a somewhat sweet taste provided by the raisins.

1½-pound

1½ teaspoons active dry yeast

3 cups bread flour

2 tablespoons raisins

¾ cup potato flakes or buds

½ cup whipping cream

2 tablespoons butter

7 ounces warm water

1-pound

1 teaspoon active dry yeast

2 cups bread flour

4 teaspoons raisins

½ cup potato flakes or buds

2½ ounces whipping cream

1½ tablespoons butter

4½ ounces warm water

Note:

For Panasonic/National machines, use 3 teaspoons of yeast for the 1½-pound loaf.

NUTRITIONAL ANALYSIS			
	1½-POUND	1-POUND	
TOTAL CALORIES	2191	1467	
TOTAL PROTEIN	60	40	GRAMS
TOTAL CARBOHYDRATES	344	229	GRAMS
TOTAL FAT	63	43	GRAMS
TOTAL SATURATED FAT	30	21	GRAMS
TOTAL CHOLESTEROL	113	78	MILLIGRAMS
TOTAL SODIUM	614	407	MILLIGRAMS
TOTAL FIBRE	8	5	GRAMS
% CALORIES FROM FAT	26	26	

Viennese Striezel Bread

Striezel bread is braided, but the texture and flavor develop well in the bread machine. This recipe is a plain *striezel*, using only basic ingredients.

1½-pound

1½ teaspoons active dry yeast

4 tablespoons sugar

2½ cups bread flour

½ teaspoon salt

¾ cup barley flour

3 tablespoons butter

1 egg

1 cup warm milk

1-pound

1 teaspoon active dry yeast

2½ tablespoons sugar

1¾ cups bread flour

½ teaspoon salt

½ cup barley flour

2 tablespoons butter

1 egg

5 ounces warm milk.

Note:
For Panasonic/National machines, use 3 teaspoons of yeast for the 1½-pound loaf.

NUTRITIONAL ANALYSIS			
	1½-POUND	1-POUND	
TOTAL CALORIES	2209	1527	
TOTAL PROTEIN	68	48	GRAMS
TOTAL CARBOHYDRATES	362	248	GRAMS
TOTAL FAT	49	35	GRAMS
TOTAL SATURATED FAT	25	17	GRAMS
TOTAL CHOLESTEROL	316	281	MILLIGRAMS
TOTAL SODIUM	1263	1214	MILLIGRAMS
TOTAL FIBRE	16	11	GRAMS
% CALORIES FROM FAT	20	20	

Weissbrot mit Kümmel

White bread with caraway is a favorite in Austria and Germany. It is excellent as a sandwich bread.

1½-pound

1½ teaspoons active dry yeast

2 teaspoons caraway seeds

1½ tablespoons sugar

3 cups bread flour

2 teaspoons salt

5 tablespoons butter

1 egg

5 ounces warm milk

2 ounces warm water

1-pound

1 teaspoon active dry yeast

1½ teaspoons caraway seeds

1 tablespoon sugar

2 cups bread flour

1½ teaspoons salt

3 tablespoons butter

1 egg

3 ounces warm milk

1½ ounces warm water

Notes:

1. For Panasonic/National machines, use 3 teaspoons of yeast for the 1½-pound loaf.
2. For DAK/Welbilt machines, use 2 additional tablespoons of warm water for the 1½-pound loaf.

NUTRITIONAL ANALYSIS			
	1½-POUND	1-POUND	
TOTAL CALORIES	2217	1467	
TOTAL PROTEIN	63	44	GRAMS
TOTAL CARBOHYDRATES	328	218	GRAMS
TOTAL FAT	71	45	GRAMS
TOTAL SATURATED FAT	39	24	GRAMS
TOTAL CHOLESTEROL	374	310	MILLIGRAMS
TOTAL SODIUM	4417	3315	MILLIGRAMS
TOTAL FIBRE	7	5	GRAMS
% CALORIES FROM FAT	29	28	

Zeppelin Bread

Similar to French bread, this recipe is typically baked in long loaves that resemble German zeppelin airships. In the bread machine, of course, the shape is different, but the wonderful taste remains the same.

1½-pound

1½ teaspoons active dry yeast

3 cups + 2 tablespoons bread flour

1½ teaspoons salt

½ tablespoon dry milk

¼ teaspoon sugar

1 tablespoon olive oil

9 ounces warm water

1-pound

1 teaspoon active dry yeast

2 cups bread flour

1 teaspoon salt

1 teaspoon dry milk

¼ teaspoon sugar

2 teaspoons olive oil

6 ounces warm water

Notes:
1. For Panasonic/National machines, use 3 teaspoons of yeast for the 1½-pound loaf.
2. For DAK/Welbilt machines, use 2 additional tablespoons of warm water for the 1½-pound loaf.
3. Use the French-bread setting (if your machine is equipped with one).

NUTRITIONAL ANALYSIS			
	1½-POUND	1-POUND	
TOTAL CALORIES	1693	1087	
TOTAL PROTEIN	54	34	GRAMS
TOTAL CARBOHYDRATES	315	202	GRAMS
TOTAL FAT	21	14	GRAMS
TOTAL SATURATED FAT	3	2	GRAMS
TOTAL CHOLESTEROL	1	0	MILLIGRAMS
TOTAL SODIUM	3222	2148	MILLIGRAMS
TOTAL FIBRE	7	4	GRAMS
% CALORIES FROM FAT	11	11	

SCANDINAVIAN AND FINNISH BREADS

The breads in this section are from Denmark, Finland, and Sweden. These countries have a rich tradition of bread baking. You will find these recipes delightfully different from any other breads.

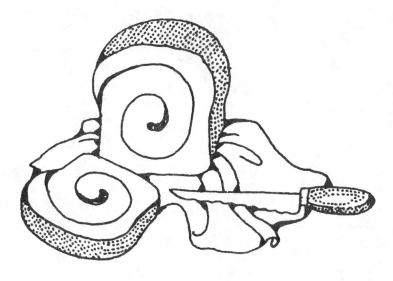

Danish Sour Bread

This dense, whole-grain bread doesn't rise much. It has a hearty, tart flavor. The rice flour called for is generally available in health-food stores.

1½-pound

1½ teaspoons active dry yeast

3 tablespoons gluten (optional)

¾ cup sourdough starter batter

1 teaspoon ground caraway seed

1 teaspoon salt

½ cup rice flour

½ cup rye flour

2 cups whole-wheat flour

9 ounces warm water

3 tablespoons butter

1-pound

1 teaspoon active dry yeast

2 tablespoons gluten (optional)

½ cup sourdough starter batter

½ teaspoon ground caraway seed

½ teaspoon salt

¼ cup rice flour

¼ cup rye flour

1½ cups whole-wheat flour

6 ounces warm water

2 tablespoons butter

Notes:
1. For Panasonic/National machines, use 3 teaspoons of yeast for the 1½-pound loaf.
2. For DAK/Welbilt machines, use 2 additional tablespoons of warm water for the 1½-pound loaf.

NUTRITIONAL ANALYSIS			
	1½-POUND	1-POUND	
TOTAL CALORIES	1918	1276	
TOTAL PROTEIN	65	43	GRAMS
TOTAL CARBOHYDRATES	339	226	GRAMS
TOTAL FAT	44	29	GRAMS
TOTAL SATURATED FAT	23	15	GRAMS
TOTAL CHOLESTEROL	93	62	MILLIGRAMS
TOTAL SODIUM	2142	1073	MILLIGRAMS
TOTAL FIBRE	35	25	GRAMS
% CALORIES FROM FAT	21	21	

Finnish Cardamom Loaf

Cardamom, the seed of an East Indian herb, lightly flavors this loaf of white bread, which is particularly good for breakfast, especially if eaten warm.

1½-pound	1-pound
1½ teaspoons active dry yeast	1 teaspoon active dry yeast
2½ tablespoons sugar	1½ tablespoons sugar
1 teaspoon cardamom	½ teaspoon cardamom
3 cups + 3 tablespoons bread flour	2 cups + 2 tablespoons bread flour
1 teaspoon salt	½ teaspoon salt
1 egg	1 egg
2 tablespoons butter	1½ tablespoons butter
1 cup warm water	5 ounces warm water

Note:

For Panasonic/National machines, use 3 teaspoons of yeast for the 1½-pound loaf.

NUTRITIONAL ANALYSIS			
	1½-POUND	1-POUND	
TOTAL CALORIES	1978	1353	
TOTAL PROTEIN	60	42	GRAMS
TOTAL CARBOHYDRATES	349	231	GRAMS
TOTAL FAT	35	27	GRAMS
TOTAL SATURATED FAT	17	13	GRAMS
TOTAL CHOLESTEROL	275	260	MILLIGRAMS
TOTAL SODIUM	2205	1136	MILLIGRAMS
TOTAL FIBRE	7	5	GRAMS
% CALORIES FROM FAT	16	18	

Finnish Easter-Crown Bread

Traditionally, Finns bake this bread in the spring to celebrate the arrival of the new calves and the abundance of dairy products. It is delicious with cream cheese or other soft, spreadable cheeses.

1½-pound

1½ teaspoons active dry yeast

¾ cup rye flour

¼ teaspoon dried orange peel

¼ teaspoon dried lemon peel

½ teaspoon cardamom

½ teaspoon salt

6 tablespoons sugar

2 cups all-purpose flour

1 egg yolk

4½ tablespoons butter

1 ounce warm water

6 ounces whipping cream

4 tablespoons chopped almonds

¼ cup raisins

1-pound

1 teaspoon active dry yeast

½ cup rye flour

¼ teaspoon dried orange peel

¼ teaspoon dried lemon peel

½ teaspoon cardamom

½ teaspoon salt

4 tablespoons sugar

1½ cups all-purpose flour

1 egg yolk

3 tablespoons butter

1 ounce warm water

4 ounces whipping cream

2½ tablespoons chopped almonds

2 tablespoons raisins

Notes:

1. For Panasonic/National machines, use 3 teaspoons of yeast for the 1½-pound loaf.
2. For DAK/Welbilt machines, use 2 additional tablespoons of warm water for the 1½-pound loaf.
3. Add the raisins and almonds at the mix-cycle beep or at the end of the initial mix cycle, if your machine is not equipped with an automatic mix cycle.

NUTRITIONAL ANALYSIS			
	1½-POUND	1-POUND	
TOTAL CALORIES	2784	1937	
TOTAL PROTEIN	65	48	GRAMS
TOTAL CARBOHYDRATES	380	265	GRAMS
TOTAL FAT	118	80	GRAMS
TOTAL SATURATED FAT	59	40	GRAMS
TOTAL CHOLESTEROL	429	357	MILLIGRAMS

TOTAL SODIUM	1241	1203	MILLIGRAMS
TOTAL FIBRE	9	6	GRAMS
% CALORIES FROM FAT	38	37	

Finnish Rye Bread

A traditional rye, this bread is simple and tasty. The combination of bread flour and rye flour helps to give it a wonderful texture.

1½-pound	1-pound
1½ teaspoons active dry yeast	1 teaspoon active dry yeast
1½ cups bread flour	1 cup bread flour
1½ cups rye flour	1 cup rye flour
1½ teaspoons salt	1 teaspoon salt
2 tablespoons sugar	4 teaspoons sugar
2 tablespoons butter	1½ tablespoons butter
1 cup warm water	5½ ounces warm water

Notes:
1. For Panasonic/National machines, use 3 teaspoons of yeast for the 1½-pound loaf.
2. For DAK/Welbilt machines, use 2 additional tablespoons of warm water for the 1½-pound loaf.

NUTRITIONAL ANALYSIS			
	1½-POUND	1-POUND	
TOTAL CALORIES	1606	1087	
TOTAL PROTEIN	39	26	GRAMS
TOTAL CARBOHYDRATES	297	198	GRAMS
TOTAL FAT	29	21	GRAMS
TOTAL SATURATED FAT	15	11	GRAMS
TOTAL CHOLESTEROL	62	47	MILLIGRAMS
TOTAL SODIUM	3208	2139	MILLIGRAMS
TOTAL FIBRE	26	17	GRAMS
% CALORIES FROM FAT	16	17	

Rieska Bread

Rieska bread is normally baked in flat cakes using pure barley flour. This recipe produces some of the same flavor in a yeast-based, fully baked loaf.

1½-pound

1½ teaspoons active dry yeast

1 tablespoon sugar

1½ cups barley flour

1½ cups bread flour

1 teaspoon salt

3 tablespoons butter

9 ounces half-and-half

1-pound

1 teaspoon active dry yeast

2 teaspoons sugar

1 cup barley flour

1 cup bread flour

¾ teaspoon salt

2 tablespoons butter

6 ounces half-and-half

Notes:

1. For Panasonic/National machines, use 3 teaspoons of yeast for the 1½-pound loaf.
2. For DAK/Welbilt machines, use 2 additional tablespoons of warm water for the 1½-pound loaf.

NUTRITIONAL ANALYSIS			
	1½-POUND	1-POUND	
TOTAL CALORIES	2254	1502	
TOTAL PROTEIN	56	37	GRAMS
TOTAL CARBOHYDRATES	278	186	GRAMS
TOTAL FAT	95	63	GRAMS
TOTAL SATURATED FAT	56	37	GRAMS
TOTAL CHOLESTEROL	208	139	MILLIGRAMS
TOTAL SODIUM	2281	1699	MILLIGRAMS
TOTAL FIBRE	25	17	GRAMS
% CALORIES FROM FAT	38	38	

Rieska Bread II

This recipe lets you mix the dough in your bread machine and then bake the bread in your oven. The result is an authentically shaped and flavored loaf.

1½-pound	1-pound
3 teaspoons baking powder	2 teaspoons baking powder
1½ teaspoons salt	1 teaspoon salt
2 tablespoons sugar	4 teaspoons sugar
3 cups barley flour	2 cups barley flour
9 ounces cream	6 ounces cream
3 tablespoons butter	2 tablespoons butter

Baking instructions:

Remove the dough from the bread machine after the mixing is completed. Flour your hands and form the dough into a ball. Place the dough ball on a greased cookie sheet and flatten it until it is about ½ inch thick. Use a fork to poke holes in the surface of the dough.

Bake in a preheated, 450 °F oven until it is crisp and golden brown. To serve, cut the loaf into wedges while it is still hot. Butter it liberally.

NUTRITIONAL ANALYSIS			
	1½-POUND	1-POUND	
TOTAL CALORIES	2147	1431	
TOTAL PROTEIN	51	34	GRAMS
TOTAL CARBOHYDRATES	245	163	GRAMS
TOTAL FAT	94	63	GRAMS
TOTAL SATURATED FAT	55	37	GRAMS
TOTAL CHOLESTEROL	208	139	MILLIGRAMS
TOTAL SODIUM	3345	2230	MILLIGRAMS
TOTAL FIBRE	43	29	GRAMS
% CALORIES FROM FAT	40	40	

Suomalaisleipaa Bread

Rye grain grows well in Finland's cold climate. This bread combines rye flour and brown sugar to create a loaf that's deep brown in color. It's great served warm with fresh butter.

1½-pound

1½ teaspoons active dry yeast

1¾ cups bread flour

1½ teaspoons salt

1½ tablespoons brown sugar

1½ cups rye flour

1 tablespoon butter

9 ounces warm water

1-pound

1 teaspoon active dry yeast

1 cup + 2 tablespoons bread flour

1 teaspoon salt

1 tablespoon brown sugar

1 cup rye flour

½ tablespoon butter

6 ounces warm water

Notes:

1. For Panasonic/National machines, use 3 teaspoons of yeast for the 1½-pound loaf.
2. For DAK/Welbilt machines, use 2 additional tablespoons of warm water for the 1½-pound loaf.

NUTRITIONAL ANALYSIS			
	1½-POUND	1-POUND	
TOTAL CALORIES	1676	1082	
TOTAL PROTEIN	57	38	GRAMS
TOTAL CARBOHYDRATES	327	215	GRAMS
TOTAL FAT	21	12	GRAMS
TOTAL SATURATED FAT	8	4	GRAMS
TOTAL CHOLESTEROL	31	16	MILLIGRAMS
TOTAL SODIUM	3213	2142	MILLIGRAMS
TOTAL FIBRE	7	5	GRAMS
% CALORIES FROM FAT	11	10	

EASTERN EUROPEAN BREADS

Eastern Europe is famous for its wide variety of breads. This section includes breads from Bohemia, Hungary, and Russia. Rye, which grows well in cold climates, is a staple grain in this area and is included in many different recipes.

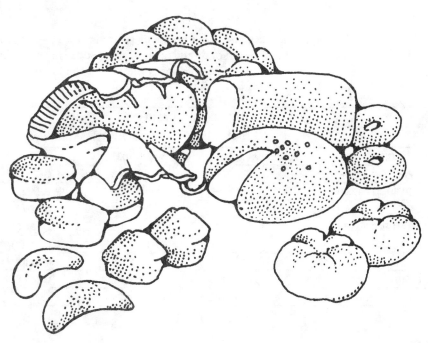

Bohemian Christmas Bread

This delightful bread is great for parties and celebrations. The raisins and nuts give it a festive flavor and texture that's hard to beat. Because this bread is an extremely high riser, a 1-pound loaf will easily fill a large bread-machine bucket. Test the small recipe first to see how the loaf rises in your machine.

1½-pound	1-pound
1½ teaspoons active dry yeast	1 teaspoon active dry yeast
3 cups bread flour	2 cups bread flour
1 teaspoon dried lemon peel	½ teaspoon dried lemon peel
1½ teaspoons salt	1 teaspoon salt
3½ tablespoons sugar	2½ tablespoons sugar
1 egg	1 egg
2 tablespoons butter	1½ tablespoons butter
6 ounces warm milk	½ cup warm milk
2 ounces warm water	1½ ounces warm water
4½ tablespoons chopped almonds	3 tablespoons chopped almonds
3½ tablespoons raisins	2½ tablespoons raisins

Notes:
1. For Panasonic/National machines, use 3 teaspoons of yeast for the 1½-pound loaf.
2. If your machine has a mix cycle, the almonds and raisins can be added at the beginning or at the mix beep. They can also be added towards the end of the mixing process.

NUTRITIONAL ANALYSIS			
	1½-POUND	1-POUND	
TOTAL CALORIES	2320	1600	
TOTAL PROTEIN	69	48	GRAMS
TOTAL CARBOHYDRATES	382	258	GRAMS
TOTAL FAT	58	42	GRAMS
TOTAL SATURATED FAT	20	15	GRAMS
TOTAL CHOLESTEROL	283	265	MILLIGRAMS
TOTAL SODIUM	3371	2268	MILLIGRAMS
TOTAL FIBRE	10	7	GRAMS
% CALORIES FROM FAT	22	24	

Bohemian Houska Bread

A high-rising, airy loaf, this bread is best when cut into thick slices and eaten with cream cheese or butter. Try the small recipe first to make sure you don't overflow your bread bucket.

1½-pound

1 teaspoon active dry yeast

3 cups + 2 tablespoons bread flour

½ teaspoon salt

2 teaspoons sugar

2 ounces warm water

1 egg

3 tablespoons olive oil

6 ounces warm milk

3 tablespoons chopped almonds

4 tablespoons raisins

1-pound

½ teaspoon active dry yeast

2 cups + 1 tablespoon bread flour

½ teaspoon salt

1½ teaspoons sugar

1 ounce warm water

1 egg

2 tablespoons olive oil

½ cup warm milk

2 tablespoons chopped almonds

2½ tablespoons raisins

Notes:

1. For Panasonic/National machines, use 2 teaspoons of yeast for the 1½-pound loaf.
2. You can use the mix cycle (if your machine has one) and add the raisins and almonds at the beep. You can also add them towards the end of the initial mix cycle.

NUTRITIONAL ANALYSIS			
	1½-POUND	1-POUND	
TOTAL CALORIES	2346	1576	
TOTAL PROTEIN	69	47	GRAMS
TOTAL CARBOHYDRATES	362	239	GRAMS
TOTAL FAT	69	47	GRAMS
TOTAL SATURATED FAT	10	7	GRAMS
TOTAL CHOLESTEROL	221	218	MILLIGRAMS
TOTAL SODIUM	1236	1200	MILLIGRAMS
TOTAL FIBRE	10	6	GRAMS
% CALORIES FROM FAT	26	27	

Kulich Bread

Also called *Russian Easter Bread*, this bread is very similar to Bohemian Christmas Bread. It is an extremely high riser, so try the small loaf first. A 1-pound loaf can fill a large bread-machine bucket.

1½-pound

1½ teaspoons active dry yeast

1 teaspoon grated lemon peel

¼ cup sugar

3 cups all-purpose flour

1 teaspoon salt

1 egg

2 tablespoons butter

½ cup warm water

5 ounces warm milk

4 tablespoons raisins

4 tablespoons chopped almonds

1-pound

1 teaspoon active dry yeast

½ teaspoon grated lemon peel

3 tablespoons sugar

2 cups all-purpose flour

½ teaspoon salt

1 egg

1½ tablespoons butter

2 ounces warm water

½ cup warm milk

2½ tablespoons raisins

2½ tablespoons chopped almonds

Notes:
1. For Panasonic/National machines, use 3 teaspoons of yeast for the 1½-pound loaf.
2. The raisins and almonds may be added with the other ingredients or you can add them at the beep (if your machine as a mix cycle).

NUTRITIONAL ANALYSIS			
	1½-POUND	1-POUND	
TOTAL CALORIES	2319	1599	
TOTAL PROTEIN	68	48	GRAMS
TOTAL CARBOHYDRATES	389	263	GRAMS
TOTAL FAT	55	40	GRAMS
TOTAL SATURATED FAT	19	15	GRAMS
TOTAL CHOLESTEROL	281	265	MILLIGRAMS
TOTAL SODIUM	2289	1202	MILLIGRAMS
TOTAL FIBRE	10	6	GRAMS
% CALORIES FROM FAT	21	22	

Pusstabrot

Hungarian white bread is light and airy. The fennel and garlic give it a great flavor. It is an excellent sandwich bread.

1½-pound

1½ teaspoons active dry yeast

3 cups bread flour

½ teaspoon garlic salt

1 teaspoon salt

¼ teaspoon fennel seed

5½ teaspoons sugar

1½ tablespoons olive oil

9 ounces warm water

1-pound

1 teaspoon active dry yeast

2 cups bread flour

½ teaspoon garlic salt

½ teaspoon salt

⅛ teaspoon fennel seed

4 teaspoons sugar

1 tablespoon olive oil

6 ounces warm water

Note:

For Panasonic/National machines, use 3 teaspoons of yeast for the 1½-pound loaf.

NUTRITIONAL ANALYSIS			
	1½-POUND	1-POUND	
TOTAL CALORIES	1758	1177	
TOTAL PROTEIN	51	34	GRAMS
TOTAL CARBOHYDRATES	321	216	GRAMS
TOTAL FAT	27	18	GRAMS
TOTAL SATURATED FAT	4	2	GRAMS
TOTAL CHOLESTEROL	0	0	MILLIGRAMS
TOTAL SODIUM	3206	2137	MILLIGRAMS
TOTAL FIBRE	7	4	GRAMS
% CALORIES FROM FAT	14	14	

Babovka

This sweet, lightly textured Czech bread is best served hot, sprinkled with a mixture of powdered sugar and cinnamon.

1½-pound

1 teaspoon active dry yeast

3 cups bread flour

½ teaspoon salt

5 tablespoons brown sugar

7 ounces warm milk

2 egg yolks

5 tablespoons butter

½ cup raisins

1-pound

½ teaspoon active dry yeast

2 cups bread flour

¼ teaspoon salt

3 tablespoons brown sugar

5 ounces warm milk

1 egg yolk

3 tablespoons butter

⅓ cup raisins

Notes:

1. For machines with yeast dispensers, use 2 teaspoons of yeast for the 1½-pound loaf.
2. Raisins can be added at the mix-cycle beep, if your machine is so equipped.

NUTRITIONAL ANALYSIS			
	1½-POUND	1-POUND	
TOTAL CALORIES	2203	1428	
TOTAL PROTEIN	72	46	GRAMS
TOTAL CARBOHYDRATES	434	285	GRAMS
TOTAL FAT	20	11	GRAMS
TOTAL SATURATED FAT	6	3	GRAMS
TOTAL CHOLESTEROL	435	219	MILLIGRAMS
TOTAL SODIUM	1336	695	MILLIGRAMS
TOTAL FIBRE	10	7	GRAMS
% CALORIES FROM FAT	8	7	

LATIN AMERICAN BREAD

Although most Latin American breads are not easily converted for baking in a bread machine, here's one recipe that demonstrates the distinctive nature of Latin American food.

Cuban Bread

Corn, the staple grain of Latin America, is the featured ingredient in this light and tasty bread. It is excellent with any Latin American dish and with foods from the American Southwest. The bread has a somewhat salty taste, so if you'd like less salt, feel free to cut down on the amount of it.

1½-pound

1½ teaspoons active dry yeast

1 tablespoon cornmeal

3 cups all-purpose flour

2 teaspoons salt

½ tablespoon sugar

9 ounces warm water

1-pound

1 teaspoon active dry yeast

½ tablespoon cornmeal

2 cups all-purpose flour

1½ teaspoons salt

1 teaspoon sugar

6 ounces warm water

Note:

For Panasonic/National machines, use 3 teaspoons of yeast for the 1½-pound loaf.

NUTRITIONAL ANALYSIS			
	1½-POUND	1-POUND	
TOTAL CALORIES	1546	1026	
TOTAL PROTEIN	51	34	GRAMS
TOTAL CARBOHYDRATES	311	207	GRAMS
TOTAL FAT	7	5	GRAMS
TOTAL SATURATED FAT	1	1	GRAMS
TOTAL CHOLESTEROL	0	0	MILLIGRAMS
TOTAL SODIUM	4275	3205	MILLIGRAMS
TOTAL FIBRE	7	5	GRAMS
% CALORIES FROM FAT	4	4	

Argentine Easter Bread

This festive bread makes a great breakfast toast and is particularly good with jam or jelly.

1½-pound

1 teaspoon active dry yeast

2¾ cups bread flour

1 teaspoon salt

½ teaspoon dried lemon peel

½ teaspoon dried orange peel

3½ tablespoons sugar

3 eggs

2½ tablespoons butter

4 ounces warm milk

¾ cup raisins

1-pound

½ teaspoon active dry yeast

1¾ cups bread flour

½ teaspoon salt

¼ teaspoon dried lemon peel

¼ teaspoon dried orange peel

2½ tablespoons sugar

2 eggs

1½ tablespoons butter

3 ounces warm milk

½ cup raisins

Notes:

1. For machines with yeast dispensers, use 2 teaspoons of yeast for the 1½-pound loaf.
2. Raisins can be added at the mix-cycle beep, if your machine is so equipped.

NUTRITIONAL ANALYSIS			
	1½-POUND	1-POUND	
TOTAL CALORIES	2330	1502	
TOTAL PROTEIN	69	44	GRAMS
TOTAL CARBOHYDRATES	404	263	GRAMS
TOTAL FAT	50	31	GRAMS
TOTAL SATURATED FAT	24	14	GRAMS
TOTAL CHOLESTEROL	717	473	MILLIGRAMS
TOTAL SODIUM	2344	1207	MILLIGRAMS
TOTAL FIBRE	12	8	GRAMS
% CALORIES FROM FAT	19	19	

BREADS OF THE BRITISH ISLES

The British Isles offer a wonderful variety of breads.

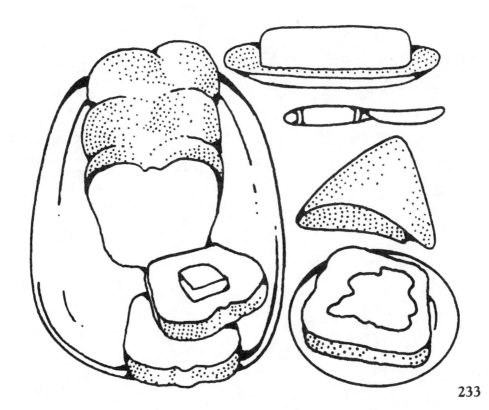

English Cobblestone Bread

This simple, fine-textured white bread makes excellent sandwiches and toast.

1½-pound

1½ teaspoons active dry yeast

3 cups bread flour

4 tablespoons sugar

1 teaspoon salt

5 tablespoons butter

½ cup warm milk

½ cup warm water

1-pound

1 teaspoon active dry yeast

2 cups bread flour

2½ tablespoons sugar

½ teaspoon salt

3½ tablespoons butter

3 ounces warm milk

2 ounces warm water

Notes:
1. For Panasonic/National machines, use 3 teaspoons of yeast for the 1½-pound loaf.
2. For DAK/Welbilt machines, use 2 additional tablespoons of warm water for the 1½-pound loaf.

NUTRITIONAL ANALYSIS			
	1½-POUND	1-POUND	
TOTAL CALORIES	2231	1500	
TOTAL PROTEIN	55	37	GRAMS
TOTAL CARBOHYDRATES	353	234	GRAMS
TOTAL FAT	65	46	GRAMS
TOTAL SATURATED FAT	37	26	GRAMS
TOTAL CHOLESTEROL	160	112	MILLIGRAMS
TOTAL SODIUM	2206	1121	MILLIGRAMS
TOTAL FIBRE	7	4	GRAMS
% CALORIES FROM FAT	26	27	

English Oatmeal Bread

Oatmeal and whole-wheat flour make this a tasty loaf. It's a great variation on white bread, yet the whole-grain flavors aren't overpowering.

1½-pound

2 teaspoons active dry yeast

1½ cups bread flour

½ cup whole-wheat flour

1½ teaspoons salt

1 cup rolled oats

3 tablespoons butter

3 ounces warm water

7 ounces warm milk

1-pound

1½ teaspoons active dry yeast

1 cup bread flour

¼ cup whole-wheat flour

1 teaspoon salt

¾ cup rolled oats

2 tablespoons butter

2 ounces warm water

5 ounces warm milk

Notes:
1. For Panasonic/National machines, use 3½ teaspoons of yeast for the 1½-pound loaf.
2. For DAK/Welbilt machines, use 2 additional tablespoons of warm water for the 1½-pound loaf.

NUTRITIONAL ANALYSIS			
	1½-POUND	1-POUND	
TOTAL CALORIES	1660	1104	
TOTAL PROTEIN	55	37	GRAMS
TOTAL CARBOHYDRATES	259	170	GRAMS
TOTAL FAT	46	31	GRAMS
TOTAL SATURATED FAT	24	16	GRAMS
TOTAL CHOLESTEROL	102	68	MILLIGRAMS
TOTAL SODIUM	3318	2217	MILLIGRAMS
TOTAL FIBRE	20	13	GRAMS
% CALORIES FROM FAT	25	25	

Irish Barmbrack

Although it doesn't rise much, this dense loaf is very sweet and quite tasty. Barmbrack ("yeast bread") is one of the rare examples of yeast being used in traditional Irish baking.

1½-pound

1½ teaspoons active dry yeast

¾ teaspoon dried lemon peel

¾ teaspoon allspice

1½ teaspoons salt

¾ cup sugar

3 cups bread flour

3½ tablespoons butter

2 ounces warm water

6 ounces warm milk

6 tablespoons seedless raisins

6 tablespoons currants

1-pound

1 teaspoon active dry yeast

½ teaspoon dried lemon peel

½ teaspoon allspice

1 teaspoon salt

½ cup sugar

2 cups bread flour

2½ tablespoons butter

1 ounce warm water

½ cup warm milk

¼ cup seedless raisins

¼ cup currants

Notes:
1. For Panasonic/National machines, use 3 teaspoons of yeast for the 1½-pound loaf.
2. Raisins and currants may be added in the beginning or at the mix beep (if your machine is equipped with one).

NUTRITIONAL ANALYSIS			
	1½-POUND	1-POUND	
TOTAL CALORIES	2765	1883	
TOTAL PROTEIN	60	40	GRAMS
TOTAL CARBOHYDRATES	528	358	GRAMS
TOTAL FAT	49	35	GRAMS
TOTAL SATURATED FAT	27	19	GRAMS
TOTAL CHOLESTEROL	116	83	MILLIGRAMS
TOTAL SODIUM	3314	2210	MILLIGRAMS
TOTAL FIBRE	12	8	GRAMS
% CALORIES FROM FAT	16	17	

Irish Barmbrack II

This variation of Irish Barmbrack features the wonderful flavor of dried fruit.

1½-pound

1½ teaspoons active dry yeast

1 teaspoon dried lemon peel

¼ cup sugar

3½ cups all-purpose flour

½ teaspoon salt

1 egg

½ cup warm milk

3 ounces warm water

3 tablespoons butter

3 tablespoons dried mixed fruit

½ cup currants

1-pound

1 teaspoon active dry yeast

½ teaspoon dried lemon peel

3 tablespoons sugar

2¼ cups + 2 tablespoons all-purpose flour

½ teaspoon salt

1 egg

3 ounces warm milk

2 ounces warm water

2 tablespoons butter

2 tablespoons dried mixed fruit

5 tablespoons currants

Notes:

1. For Panasonic/National machines, use 3 teaspoons of yeast for the 1½-pound loaf.
2. Chop the dried mixed fruit into small pieces before you add them.
3. You may add the dried fruit and currants at the beginning or at the mix beep (if your machine is equipped with one).

NUTRITIONAL ANALYSIS			
	1½-POUND	1-POUND	
TOTAL CALORIES	2651	1824	
TOTAL PROTEIN	73	51	GRAMS
TOTAL CARBOHYDRATES	482	328	GRAMS
TOTAL FAT	49	35	GRAMS
TOTAL SATURATED FAT	25	17	GRAMS
TOTAL CHOLESTEROL	311	279	MILLIGRAMS
TOTAL SODIUM	1215	1191	MILLIGRAMS
TOTAL FIBRE	13	8	GRAMS
% CALORIES FROM FAT	17	17	

Poor Irish Bread

This fairly standard white bread has a texture that's good for sandwiches or morning toast.

1½-pound	1-pound
1½ teaspoons active dry yeast	1 teaspoon active dry yeast
2½ tablespoons sugar	1½ tablespoons sugar
3 cups bread flour	2 cups bread flour
1 teaspoon salt	½ teaspoon salt
1 tablespoon butter	½ tablespoon butter
3 ounces warm milk	2 ounces warm milk
6 ounces warm water	½ cup warm water

Note:

For Panasonic/National machines, use 3 teaspoons of yeast for the 1½-pound loaf.

NUTRITIONAL ANALYSIS			
	1½-POUND	1-POUND	
TOTAL CALORIES	1749	1142	
TOTAL PROTEIN	54	36	GRAMS
TOTAL CARBOHYDRATES	334	220	GRAMS
TOTAL FAT	19	11	GRAMS
TOTAL SATURATED FAT	9	5	GRAMS
TOTAL CHOLESTEROL	35	18	MILLIGRAMS
TOTAL SODIUM	2187	1103	MILLIGRAMS
TOTAL FIBRE	7	4	GRAMS
% CALORIES FROM FAT	10	9	

Sugar Loaf

This interesting sweet bread, a variation on plain white bread, makes a good dessert bread. It is also excellent with jams or jellies. The chunks of sugar melt during the bake cycle, creating pockets of sweetness.

238

1½-pound

1½ teaspoons active dry yeast

3 cups bread flour

1 teaspoon salt

1 tablespoon sugar

2½ tablespoons dry milk

1½ tablespoons butter

9 ounces warm water

1-pound

1 teaspoon active dry yeast

2 cups bread flour

½ teaspoon salt

2 teaspoons sugar

1½ tablespoons dry milk

1 tablespoon butter

6 ounces warm water

Note:

For Panasonic/National machines, use 3 teaspoons of yeast for the 1½-pound loaf.

Instructions for baking:

Place ½ cup of sugar cubes and ½ tablespoon of cinnamon in a plastic bag. Crush the sugar cubes into coarse powder and shake the bag to mix the sugar with the cinnamon. Add the crushed mixture at the mix beep or towards the end of the mixing cycle.

Watch closely until the mixture is well blended into the dough. Larger pieces may jam the beater and must be released immediately to prevent motor damage. Large chunks may also scratch the surface of your pan. Make sure that none of the chunks is larger than 1/16 inch in diameter.

Alternately, you may use larger chunks of sugar and mix them into the dough by hand, replacing the dough when you are finished. It is not recommended that you use large chunks in the bread-machine mix cycle because of the danger of jamming the machine or scratching the bread bucket.

NUTRITIONAL ANALYSIS			
	1½-POUND	1-POUND	
TOTAL CALORIES	2110	1342	
TOTAL PROTEIN	56	37	GRAMS
TOTAL CARBOHYDRATES	414	260	GRAMS
TOTAL FAT	24	16	GRAMS
TOTAL SATURATED FAT	12	8	GRAMS
TOTAL CHOLESTEROL	49	33	MILLIGRAMS
TOTAL SODIUM	2219	1119	MILLIGRAMS
TOTAL FIBRE	7	4	GRAMS
% CALORIES FROM FAT	10	11	

Yorkshire Spice Bread

A raisin-bread lover's favorite, this makes an excellent breakfast bread.

1½-pound

1½ teaspoons active dry yeast

½ teaspoon cinnamon

2½ cups + 2 tablespoons bread flour

½ teaspoon nutmeg

1 tablespoon dried orange peel

½ cup powdered sugar

1 egg

2 tablespoons olive oil

3 tablespoons butter

½ tablespoon maple syrup

¾ cup warm milk

½ cup raisins

1-pound

1 teaspoon active dry yeast

½ teaspoon cinnamon

1¾ cups bread flour

½ teaspoon nutmeg

2 teaspoons dried orange peel

5 tablespoons powdered sugar

1 egg

4 teaspoons olive oil

2 tablespoons butter

1 teaspoon maple syrup

½ cup warm milk

¼ cup raisins

Notes:

1. For Panasonic/National machines, use 3 teaspoons of yeast for the 1½-pound loaf.
2. You may add the raisins at the beginning or at the mix beep (if your machine has one).

NUTRITIONAL ANALYSIS			
	1½-POUND	1-POUND	
TOTAL CALORIES	2485	1637	
TOTAL PROTEIN	60	41	GRAMS
TOTAL CARBOHYDRATES	397	253	GRAMS
TOTAL FAT	75	52	GRAMS
TOTAL SATURATED FAT	29	20	GRAMS
TOTAL CHOLESTEROL	314	280	MILLIGRAMS
TOTAL SODIUM	180	140	MILLIGRAMS
TOTAL FIBRE	10	6	GRAMS
% CALORIES FROM FAT	27	28	

Specialty Breads
for
2-lb Machines

BASIC BREADS

The breads in this section are old favorites and basic breads that are fitting for any occasion. If you are new to bread machines, try the breads in this section first.

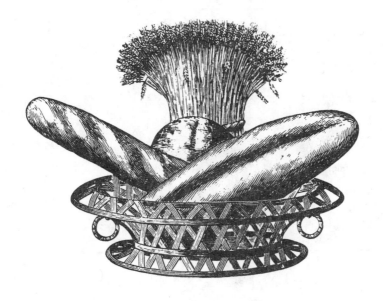

Air Bread

Based on a James Beard muffin recipe, modifications to the thick muffin batter yield this slightly sweet-tasting white bread, which is great toasted.

1 lb	1½ lb	2 lb
5 oz warm water	7½ oz warm water	10 oz warm water
2½ T butter	3½ T butter	⅓ C butter
1 egg	1 egg	2 eggs
2 C bread flour	3 C bread flour	4 C bread flour
¼ C nonfat dry milk	⅜ C nonfat dry milk	½ C nonfat dry milk
1½ T sugar	2½ T sugar	3 T sugar
1 t active dry yeast	1½ t active dry yeast	2 t active dry yeast

Nutritional Analysis (per loaf, approximate)

Item	1 lb	1½ lb	2 lb
total calories (kcal)	1496	2200	3026
total protein (g)	51	74	102
total carbohydrates (g)	235	356	470
total fat (g)	38	52	79
total saturated fat (g)	20	27	42
total cholesterol (mg)	263	297	536
total sodium (mg)	515	717	1069
total fiber (g)	8	12	15
% calories from fat	23	21	24

Basic White Bread

This basic white bread recipe should work in most bread machines and should give you good results. Use it as a gauge to tell how well your machine operates.

1 lb	1½ lb	2 lb
3 oz warm water	4½ oz warm water	6 oz warm water
3 oz milk	4½ oz milk	6 oz milk
1 T butter	1½ T butter	2 T butter
1 t salt	1½ t salt	2 t salt
2 C bread flour	3 C bread flour	4 C bread flour
2 T sugar	3 T sugar	¼ C sugar
½ t active dry yeast	1 t active dry yeast	1 t active dry yeast

Nutritional Analysis (per loaf, approximate)

Item	1 lb	1½ lb	2 lb
total calories (kcal)	1244	1870	2489
total protein (g)	37	55	73
total carbohydrates (g)	228	343	457
total fat (g)	19	28	38
total saturated fat (g)	10	14	19
total cholesterol (mg)	42	63	84
total sodium (mg)	2298	3448	4597
total fiber (g)	7	11	14
% calories from fat	14	14	14

Cornmeal Bread

This is a southwestern type bread that is excellent with a bowl of chili or a taco salad.

1 lb	1½ lb	2 lb
⅔ C milk	1 C milk	1⅓ C milk
½ C cottage cheese	¾ C cottage cheese	1 C cottage cheese
2 t dried onions	1 T dried onions	1⅓ T dried onions
1½ T green chili, diced	2 T green chili, diced	3 T green chili, diced
½ C cornmeal	⅔ C cornmeal	⅞ C cornmeal
2 t olive oil	1 T olive oil	1⅓ T olive oil
2 t sugar	1 T sugar	1⅓ T sugar
1¾ C bread flour	2⅔ C bread flour	3½ C bread flour
1 t active dry yeast	1½ t active dry yeast	2 t active dry yeast

Nutritional Analysis (per loaf, approximate)

Item	1 lb	1½ lb	2 lb
total calories (kcal)	1443	2164	2858
total protein (g)	57	86	114
total carbohydrates (g)	249	374	493
total fat (g)	22	33	44
total saturated fat (g)	7	10	14
total cholesterol (mg)	32	47	63
total sodium (mg)	549	823	1097
total fiber (g)	7	10	14
% calories from fat	14	14	14

Egg Bread

A staple white bread, simple to make and smooth in texture.

1 lb	1½ lb	2 lb
½ C milk	¾ C milk	1 C milk
2½ T butter	4 T butter	⅓ C butter
1 egg	1 egg	2 egg
½ t salt	¾ t salt	1 t salt
2 C bread flour	3 C bread flour	4 C bread flour
1 t active dry yeast	1½ active dry yeast	2 t active dry yeast

Nutritional Analysis (per loaf, approximate)			
Item	1 lb	1½ lb	2 lb
total calories (kcal)	1390	2079	2814
total protein (g)	44	63	88
total carbohydrates (g)	207	310	413
total fat (g)	42	63	87
total saturated fat (g)	22	34	47
total cholesterol (mg)	274	328	558
total sodium (mg)	1476	2216	2990
total fiber (g)	8	12	15
% calories from fat	27	28	28

Egg Bread II

A slightly sweeter version of the previous Egg Bread recipe.

1 lb	1½ lb	2 lb
1 oz warm water	1½ oz warm water	2 oz warm water
3 T butter	¼ C butter	⅜ C butter
⅓ C milk	½ C milk	⅔ C milk
1 egg	1 egg	2 eggs
1 T sugar	1½ T sugar	2 T sugar
½ t salt	¾ t salt	1 t salt
2 C bread flour	3 C bread flour	4 C bread flour
1 t active dry yeast	1½ t active dry yeast	3 t active dry yeast

Nutritional Analysis (per loaf, approximate)

Item	1 lb	1½ lb	2 lb
total calories (kcal)	1464	2114	2927
total protein (g)	43	61	85
total carbohydrates (g)	217	325	434
total fat (g)	46	61	92
total saturated fat (g)	25	33	50
total cholesterol (mg)	284	320	567
total sodium (mg)	1515	2188	3030
total fiber (g)	8	12	15
% calories from fat	28	26	28

English Loaf

Breads don't come much simpler than this. The story is that an English food editor, Elizabeth David, developed this recipe when she became frustrated with the quality of the bread she was finding accompanying her gourmet meals. She developed this recipe to be simple, almost foolproof, and to have a wonderful aroma while baking and a slightly salty taste.

1 lb	1½ lb	2 lb
6 oz warm water	9 oz warm water	12 oz warm water
2 C bread flour	3 C bread flour	4 C bread flour
1 t salt	1½ t salt	2 t salt
1½ t active dry yeast	2¼ t active dry yeast	1 T active dry yeast

Nutritional Analysis (per loaf, approximate)

Item	1 lb	1½ lb	2 lb
total calories (kcal)	1007	1510	2014
total protein (g)	35	53	70
total carbohydrates (g)	201	302	402
total fat (g)	5	7	10
total saturated fat (g)	1	1	1
total cholesterol (mg)	0	0	0
total sodium (mg)	2145	3218	4291
total fiber (g)	8	12	17
% calories from fat	4	4	4

Herb Bread

This bread makes excellent toast and has the hint of flavor from several different herbs, mixed together here in a wonderful combination.

1 lb	1½ lb	2 lb
3 oz milk	4½ oz milk	6 oz milk
1 T butter	1½ T butter	2 T butter
3 oz warm water	4½ oz warm water	6 oz warm water
1½ T sugar	2 T sugar	3 T sugar
1 t salt	1½ t salt	2 t salt
2 C whole wheat flour	3 C whole wheat flour	4 C whole wheat flour
½ each med. onions, chopped	¾ each med. onions, chopped	1 each med. onions, chopped
½ t dried dill weed	¾ t dried dill weed	1 t dried dill weed
½ t rosemary, crushed	¾ t rosemary, crushed	1 t rosemary, crushed
½ t basil	¾ t basil	1 t basil
1½ t active dry yeast	2¼ t active dry yeast	1 T active dry yeast

Nutritional Analysis (per loaf, approximate)

Item	1 lb	1½ lb	2 lb
total calories (kcal)	1072	1595	2143
total protein (g)	39	58	78
total carbohydrates (g)	202	300	405
total fat (g)	19	29	38
total saturated fat (g)	10	15	19
total cholesterol (mg)	42	63	84
total sodium (mg)	2504	3756	5009
total fiber (g)	32	48	64
% calories from fat	15	15	15

Honey Bread

A simple, somewhat sweet bread that is great eaten fresh and warm.

1 lb	1½ lb	2 lb
½ C milk	¾ C milk	1 C milk
3 T honey	¼ C honey	⅜ C honey
1½ T butter	2¼ T butter	3 T butter
½ t salt	¾ t salt	1 t salt
2 C bread flour	3 C bread flour	4 C bread flour
1½ t active dry yeast	2¼ t active dry yeast	1 T active dry yeast

Nutritional Analysis (per loaf, approximate)

Item	1 lb	1½ lb	2 lb
total calories (kcal)	1426	2106	2851
total protein (g)	40	59	79
total carbohydrates (g)	259	380	518
total fat (g)	26	39	52
total saturated fat (g)	14	21	28
total cholesterol (mg)	63	94	125
total sodium (mg)	1310	1965	2620
total fiber (g)	8	13	17
% calories from fat	16	16	16

Oatmeal Bran Bread

There are four favorite grains in this smoothly textured bread, a flavorful treat that makes excellent sandwich bread.

1 lb	1½ lb	2 lb
⅔ C warm water	1C warm water	1⅓ C warm water
1½ T butter	2½ T butter	3 T butter
1 T molasses	1½ T molasses	2 T molasses
1½ T brown sugar	2½ T brown sugar	3 T brown sugar
½ t salt	½ t salt	1 t salt
2 T dry milk	3 T dry milk	¼ C dry milk
3 T rolled oats	¼ C rolled oats	⅜ C rolled oats
1 T bran	1½ T bran	2 T bran
½ C whole wheat flour	¾ C whole wheat flour	1 C whole wheat flour
1½ C bread flour	2¼ C bread flour	3 C bread flour
1½ t active dry yeast	2¼ t active dry yeast	1 T active dry yeast

Nutritional Analysis (per loaf, approximate)

Item	1 lb	1½ lb	2 lb
total calories (kcal)	1316	1998	2362
total protein (g)	41	62	83
total carbohydrates (g)	239	359	479
total fat (g)	23	37	46
total saturated fat (g)	12	19	23
total cholesterol (mg)	48	79	95
total sodium (mg)	1314	1468	2629
total fiber (g)	17	25	34
% calories from fat	16	16	16

Old-Fashioned Buttermilk Bread

This basic buttermilk bread is a basic white bread with a thicker texture resulting from the use of buttermilk as the liquid instead of water.

1 lb	1½ lb	2 lb
7 oz buttermilk	10 oz buttermilk	14 oz buttermilk
2 T honey	3 T honey	¼ C honey
1 T butter	1½ T butter	2 T butter
2 t wheat gluten	1½ T wheat gluten	1½ T wheat gluten
2 C bread flour	3 C bread flour	4 C bread flour
1 t salt	1½ t salt	2 t salt
1½ t active dry yeast	2¼ t active dry yeast	1 T active dry yeast

Nutritional Analysis (per loaf, approximate)

Item	1 lb	1½ lb	2 lb
total calories (kcal)	1356	2028	2722
total protein (g)	50	74	102
total carbohydrates (g)	246	368	492
total fat (g)	19	28	37
total saturated fat (g)	9	13	18
total cholesterol (mg)	38	56	75
total sodium (mg)	2480	3705	4963
total fiber (g)	3	4	6
% calories from fat	12	12	12

Onion–Caraway Bread

The fresh onion in this bread gives it a great aroma while baking.

1 lb	1½ lb	2 lb
⅔ C cottage cheese	1 C cottage cheese	1⅓ C cottage cheese
½ T butter	2 t butter	1 T butter
5 T warm water	½ C warm water	⅝ C warm water
2 t sugar	1 T sugar	1⅓ T sugar
¾ t salt	1½ t salt	1½ t salt
2 C bread flour	3 C bread flour	4 C bread flour
½ t baking soda	¾ t baking soda	1 t baking soda
2 T chopped onion	3 T chopped onion	¼ C chopped onion
2 t caraway seed	1 T caraway seed	1⅓ T caraway seed
1 t active dry yeast	1½ t active dry yeast	2 t active dry yeast

Nutritional Analysis (per loaf, approximate)

Item	1 lb	1½ lb	2 lb
total calories (kcal)	1241	1853	2482
total protein (g)	56	84	112
total carbohydrates (g)	218	327	436
total fat (g)	14	20	28
total saturated fat (g)	6	9	12
total cholesterol (mg)	28	39	56
total sodium (mg)	2909	5153	5818
total fiber (g)	10	15	20
% calories from fat	10	10	10

Onion & Cheese Bread

This zesty bread has a moist consistency with the tangy flavor of cheddar and onion. Excellent bread for toasting.

1 lb	1½ lb	2 lb
7 oz water	1¼ C water	14 oz water
1⅓ T powdered milk	2 T powdered milk	2⅔ T powdered milk
2 t sugar	1 T sugar	1⅓ T sugar
½ t salt	1 t salt	1 t salt
2⅛ C bread flour	3¼ C bread flour	4½ C bread flour
2 t dried onions	1 T dried onions	1⅓ T dried onions
3 T shredded sharp cheddar cheese	¼ C shredded sharp cheddar cheese	⅜ C shredded sharp cheddar cheese
½ t active dry yeast	1 t active dry yeast	1½ t active dry yeast

Nutritional Analysis (per loaf, approximate)

Item	1 lb	1½ lb	2 lb
total calories (kcal)	1257	1888	2596
total protein (g)	48	67	92
total carbohydrates (g)	231	347	478
total fat (g)	15	22	30
total saturated fat (g)	8	11	14
total cholesterol (mg)	33	49	65
total sodium (mg)	1251	1345	2502
total fiber (g)	2	3	4
% calories from fat	11	11	11

Onion–Mustard Bread

This is a tangy bread that is particularly good for sandwiches.

1 lb	1½ lb	2 lb
⅔ C milk	1 C milk	1⅓ C milk
2 t prepared mustard	1 T prepared mustard	1½ T prepared mustard
½ T olive oil	2½ t olive oil	1 T olive oil
1 egg	1 egg	2 eggs
½ T sugar	2¼ t sugar	1 T sugar
½ t salt	¾ t salt	1 t salt
2 C bread flour	3 C bread flour	4 C bread flour
¼ t black pepper	½ t black pepper	½ t black pepper
1 T minced onion	1½ T minced onion	2 T minced onion
1 t active dry yeast	1½ t active dry yeast	2 t active dry yeast

Nutritional Analysis (per loaf, approximate)

Item	1 lb	1½ lb	2 lb
total calories (kcal)	1259	1871	2518
total protein (g)	46	66	91
total carbohydrates (g)	216	325	432
total fat (g)	22	32	43
total saturated fat (g)	6	9	13
total cholesterol (mg)	203	214	406
total sodium (mg)	1369	2027	2738
total fiber (g)	8	12	17
% calories from fat	16	15	16

Poppy Seed Dilly Bread

"Dilly bread" is bread made with dill weed. This variation features plenty of interesting flavors with the addition of poppy seeds and onions.

1 lb	1½ lb	2 lb
⅔ C warm water	1 C warm water	1⅓ C warm water
1½ T butter	2 T butter	3 T butter
2 C bread flour	3 C bread flour	4 C bread flour
1½ T instant dry milk	2 T instant dry milk	3 T instant dry milk
1 T sugar	2 T sugar	2 T sugar
1½ T dried onions	2 T dried onions	3 T dried onions
1 t dill weed	1½ t dill weed	2 t dill weed
1 t poppy seeds	1½ t poppy seeds	2 t poppy seeds
½ t salt	1 t salt	1 t salt
1 t active dry yeast	1½ t active dry yeast	2 t active dry yeast

Nutritional Analysis (per loaf, approximate)

Item	1 lb	1½ lb	2 lb
total calories (kcal)	1261	1883	2521
total protein (g)	38	57	76
total carbohydrates (g)	222	338	444
total fat (g)	23	32	46
total saturated fat (g)	12	15	23
total cholesterol (mg)	47	63	94
total sodium (mg)	1290	2433	2579
total fiber (g)	3	5	7
% calories from fat	17	15	17

Prune Bread

This is white bread with a zip to it. The addition of orange peel and chopped prunes gives it a mild fruit flavor that tastes great toasted and buttered.

1 lb	1½ lb	2 lb
5 oz warm water	7½ oz warm water	10 oz warm water
1 T honey	1½ T honey	2 T honey
½ t salt	¾ t salt	1 t salt
1¾ C bread flour	2⅝ C bread flour	3½ C bread flour
½ t orange peel	¾ t orange peel	1 t orange peel
½ C prunes, chopped	¾ C prunes, chopped	1 C prunes, chopped
1½ t active dry yeast	2¼ t active dry yeast	1 T active dry yeast

Nutritional Analysis (per loaf, approximate)

Item	1 lb	1½ lb	2 lb
total calories (kcal)	1122	1684	2245
total protein (g)	33	50	66
total carbohydrates (g)	240	360	479
total fat (g)	5	7	9
total saturated fat (g)	1	1	1
total cholesterol (mg)	0	0	0
total sodium (mg)	1082	1623	2163
total fiber (g)	13	19	25
% calories from fat	4	4	4

Quick Onion Bread

This easy bread has a great texture and wonderful onion flavor enhanced by the applesauce and honey.

1 lb	1½ lb	2 lb
½ C water	¾ C water	1 C water
1 T applesauce	1½ T applesauce	2 T applesauce
1 T honey	1½ T honey	2 T honey
1 egg	1 egg	2 eggs
3 T dried onions	¼ C dried onions	⅜ C dried onions
2 C bread flour	3 C bread flour	4 C bread flour
¼ T powdered milk	¾ t powdered milk	1¼ t powdered milk
1 t salt	1½ t salt	2 t salt
1½ t active dry yeast	2 t active dry yeast	1 T active dry yeast

Nutritional Analysis (per loaf, approximate)

Item	1 lb	1½ lb	2 lb
total calories (kcal)	1205	1765	2410
total protein (g)	43	61	86
total carbohydrates (g)	232	347	463
total fat (g)	10	13	21
total saturated fat (g)	3 g	3	5
total cholesterol (mg)	214	214	428
total sodium (mg)	2216	3291	4432
total fiber (g)	4	6	8
% calories from fat	8	7	8

Wheat–Corn Bread

The combination of wheat flour, white flour, and cornmeal make this bread a tasty variation of ordinary white bread, with a bit of crunchy texture.

1 lb	1½ lb	2 lb
3 T warm water	¼ C warm water	⅜ warm water
½ T honey	2½ t honey	1 T honey
1 egg	1 egg	2 egg
½ C milk	¾ C milk	1 C milk
1 T butter	2 T butter	2 T butter
½ t salt	¾ t salt	1 t salt
⅓ C white corn meal	½ C white corn meal	⅔ C white corn meal
3 T wheat germ	¼ C wheat germ	⅜ C wheat germ
½ C whole wheat flour	¾ C whole wheat flour	1 C whole wheat flour
1¼ C bread flour	1¾ C bread flour	2½ C bread flour
1 t active dry yeast	1½ t active dry yeast	2 t active dry yeast

Nutritional Analysis (per loaf, approximate)			
Item	1 lb	1½ lb	2 lb
total calories (kcal)	1340	1961	2680
total protein (g)	48	67	96
total carbohydrates (g)	230	332	459
total fat (g)	26	43	53
total saturated fat (g)	12	21	24
total cholesterol (mg)	228	267	456
total sodium (mg)	1309	1993	2617
total fiber (g)	18	27	37
% calories from fat	18	19	18

FESTIVE BREADS

These breads are traditional on special occasions or holidays.

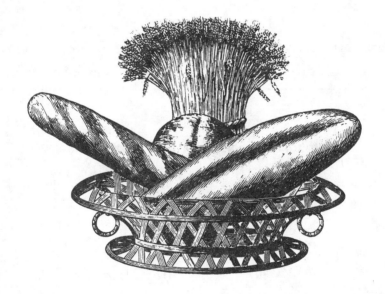

Alpine Easter Bread

A tangy white bread with the nutty flavor of almonds and the zest of lemon.

1 lb	1½ lb	2 lb
¼ C milk	⅜ C milk	½ C milk
4 T butter	½ C butter	½ C butter
1 oz warm water	1 oz warm water	2 oz warm water
1 egg	1 egg	2 eggs
½ t vanilla extract	¾ t vanilla extract	1 t vanilla extract
¼ t lemon extract	¼ t lemon extract	½ t lemon extract
¼ t sugar	½ t sugar	½ t sugar
2 C bread flour	3 C bread flour	4 C bread flour
½ t salt	½ t salt	1 t salt
1 t dried lemon peel	1½ t dried lemon peel	2 t dried lemon peel
1 T chopped almonds	1½ T chopped almonds	2 T chopped almonds
1 t active dry yeast	1½ t active dry yeast	2 t active dry yeast

Nutritional Analysis (per loaf, approximate)

Item	1 lb	1½ lb	2 lb
total calories (kcal)	1564	2516	3128
total protein (g)	44	64	88
total carbohydrates (g)	207	310	413
total fat (g)	61	112	122
total saturated fat (g)	32	62	64
total cholesterol (mg)	312	438	623
total sodium (mg)	1621	2103	3243
total fiber (g)	8	12	17
% calories from fat	36	40	36

Cinnamon Cranberry Bread

If you like the tart, distinctive taste of cranberries, you'll love this bread. It is only lightly sweetened, so the original flavor of the cranberries is highlighted.

1 lb	1½ lb	2 lb
1 C water	1½ C water	2 C water
1 T vegetable oil	1½ T vegetable oil	2 T vegetable oil
1 t cinnamon	1½ t cinnamon	2 t cinnamon
1½ t salt	2 t salt	1 T salt
1 T dry milk	1½ T dry milk	2 T dry milk
1 T orange peel	1½ T orange peel	2 T orange peel
1 T sugar	1½ T sugar	2 T sugar
2¼ C bread flour	3¼ C bread flour	4½ C bread flour
1 t active dry yeast	1½ t active dry yeast	2 t active dry yeast

Add at mix cycle:

2½T fresh cranberries	¼ C fresh cranberries	½ C fresh cranberries

Nutritional Analysis (per loaf, approximate)

Item	1 lb	1½ lb	2 lb
total calories (kcal)	1345	1955	2690
total protein (g)	41	59	81
total carbohydrates (g)	244	354	488
total fat (g)	21	32	42
total saturated fat (g)	4	5	7
total cholesterol (mg)	8	12	15
total sodium (mg)	3243	4332	6487
total fiber (g)	4	5	7
% calories from fat	14	15	14

Cinnamon Swirl Orange Bread

This glazed bread is excellent for an after-dinner treat.

1 lb	1½ lb	2 lb
1½ T warm water	2½ T warm water	3 T warm water
¼ C milk	⅜ C milk	½ C milk
1 T margarine	1½ T margarine	2 T margarine
¼ C orange juice	⅜ C orange juice	½ C orange juice
1 egg	1 egg	2 eggs
2 T sugar	3 T sugar	¼ C sugar
½ t salt	¾ t salt	1 t salt
2 C bread flour	3 C bread flour	4 C bread flour
½ T cinnamon	2¼ t cinnamon	1 T cinnamon
1½ t active dry yeast	2¼ t active dry yeast	1 T active dry yeast
½ T grated orange peel	2¼ t grated orange peel	1 T grated orange peel

Nutritional Analysis (per loaf, approximate)

Item	1 lb	1½ lb	2 lb
total calories (kcal)	1343	1982	2685
total protein (g)	43	62	86
total carbohydrates (g)	239	359	479
total fat (g)	23	32	45
total saturated fat (g)	5	7	11
total cholesterol (mg)	189	193	378
total sodium (mg)	1293	1913	2587
total fiber (g)	10	16	21
% calories from fat	15	15	15

Honey–Mustard Bread

This is a great sandwich bread with a light wheat consistency and the distinctive flavor of honey and mustard.

1 lb	1½ lb	2 lb
½ C water	¾ C water	1 C water
2½ T honey	3½ T honey	⅓ C honey
¼ C chicken broth	⅜ C chicken broth	½ C chicken broth
5 t honey mustard	2½ T honey mustard	3⅓ T honey mustard
1½ C bread flour	2¼ C bread flour	3 C bread flour
½ C whole wheat flour	¾ C whole wheat flour	1 C whole wheat flour
2 t dry milk	1 T dry milk	1⅓ T dry milk
1 t chives, dried	1½ t chives, dried	2 t chives, dried
½ t salt	¾ t salt	1 t salt
½ t active dry yeast	1 t active dry yeast	4 t active dry yeast

Nutritional Analysis (per loaf, approximate)

Item	1 lb	1½ lb	2 lb
total calories (kcal)	1183	1758	2367
total protein (g)	42	63	84
total carbohydrates (g)	243	360	486
total fat (g)	8	11	15
total saturated fat (g)	1	1	2
total cholesterol (mg)	1	2	2
total sodium (mg)	1830	2745	3660
total fiber (g)	10	16	21
% calories from fat	6	6	6

Multigrain Garlic–Dill Bread

This is a flavorful variation on a basic bread. The garlic, dill weed, and yogurt add a particular zest to the loaf.

1 lb	1½ lb	2 lb
½ C warm water	¾ C warm water	1 C warn water
⅓ C plain yogurt	½ C plain yogurt	⅔ C plain yogurt
1 T olive oil	1½ T olive oil	2 T olive oil
¼ C rolled oats	⅜ C rolled oats	½ C rolled oats
¼ C cracked wheat	⅜ C cracked wheat	½ C cracked wheat
1½ t brown sugar	2¼ t brown sugar	1 T brown sugar
¾ t salt	1¼ t salt	1½ t salt
1¾ C bread flour	2¾ C bread flour	3½ C bread flour
1½ t minced garlic	2¼ t minced garlic	1 T minced garlic
1 t dill weed	1½ t dill weed	2 t dill weed
1 t active dry yeast	1 t active dry yeast	2 t active dry yeast

Nutritional Analysis (per loaf, approximate)

Item	1 lb	1½ lb	2 lb
total calories (kcal)	1146	1781	2293
total protein (g)	37	57	73
total carbohydrates (g)	199	311	398
total fat (g)	22	33	43
total saturated fat (g)	4	6	9
total cholesterol (mg)	10	14	19
total sodium (mg)	1650	2741	3299
total fiber (g)	9	14	18
% calories from fat	17	17	17

Peanut Butter Bread

The peanut butter in this bread gives it a smooth texture. It is excellent for toasting.

1 lb	1½ lb	2 lb
1 egg	1 egg	2 eggs
6 oz milk	9 oz milk	12 oz milk
2 C bread flour	3 C bread flour	4 C bread flour
½ t salt	¾ t salt	1 t salt
½ C sugar	¾ C sugar	1 C sugar
¾ C peanut butter	1⅛ C peanut butter	1½ C peanut butter
1 t active dry yeast	1½ t active dry yeast	2 t active dry yeast

Nutritional Analysis (per loaf, approximate)

Item	1 lb	1½ lb	2 lb
total calories (kcal)	2694	4009	5387
total protein (g)	93	137	186
total carbohydrates (g)	349	523	697
total fat (g)	111	165	223
total saturated fat (g)	24	36	48
total cholesterol (mg)	204	215	408
total sodium (mg)	2136	3177	4272
total fiber (g)	19	29	38
% calories from fat	36	36	36

Poppy Seed Loaf

A great party bread that is especially good on the table with other finger foods.

Make poppy seed dip for the bread by combining 4 tablespoons of melted butter and ¼ cup poppy seeds. Get the bread from the bread machine while warm, tear or cut pieces from the loaf, and dip.

1 lb	1½ lb	2 lb
½ C warm water	¾ C warm water	1 C warm water
¼ C milk	⅜ C milk	½ C milk
½ T shortening	2 t shortening	1 T shortening
½ t salt	¾ t salt	1 t salt
1 T sugar	1½ T sugar	2 T sugar
2 C bread flour	3 C bread flour	4 C bread flour
½ T poppy seeds	2¼ t poppy seeds	1 T poppy seeds
1 t active dry yeast	1½ t active dry yeast	2 t active dry yeast

Nutritional Analysis (per loaf, approximate)

Item	1 lb	1½ lb	2 lb
total calories (kcal)	1167	1741	2334
total protein (g)	37	56	74
total carbohydrates (g)	217	325	433
total fat (g)	15	22	30
total saturated fat (g)	4	5	8
total cholesterol (mg)	8	12	17
total sodium (mg)	1108	1662	2216
total fiber (g)	9	14	18
% calories from fat	12	11	12

Soft Cheese Bread

This bread has the soft, spongy texture of oatmeal bread with the pizzazz of tangy cheese.

1 lb	1½ lb	2 lb
½ C water	¾ C water	1 C water
⅔ C shredded sharp cheddar cheese	1 C shredded sharp cheddar cheese	1⅓ C shredded sharp cheddar cheese
1 egg	1 egg	2 eggs
2 t olive oil	1 T olive oil	1⅓ T olive oil
1⅔ C bread flour	2½ C bread flour	3½ C bread flour
⅔ C rolled oats	1 C rolled oats	1⅓ C rolled oats
2⅔ T powdered milk	¼ C powdered milk	⅓ C powdered milk
1 t salt	1½ t salt	2 t salt
2 t sugar	1 T sugar	1⅓ T sugar
1 t active dry yeast	1½ t active dry yeast	2 t active dry yeast

Nutritional Analysis (per loaf, approximate)

Item	1 lb	1½ lb	2 lb
total calories (kcal)	1640	2422	3362
total protein (g)	68	99	139
total carbohydrates (g)	221	332	459
total fat (g)	52	76	105
total saturated fat (g)	24	34	47
total cholesterol (mg)	313	363	625
total sodium (mg)	2755	4103	5511
total fiber (g)	7	12	15
% calories from fat	29	28	28

Sweet Potato Wheat Twist

A soft-textured bread with a distinctive sweet potato flavor. Excellent with soup.

1 lb	1½ lb	2 lb
2½ T warm water	3¾ T warm water	⅓ C warm water
⅓ C yams	½ C yams	⅔ C yams
¼ C buttermilk	⅜ C buttermilk	½ C buttermilk
½ T butter	1 T butter	1 T butter
½ T honey	2½ t honey	1 T honey
1 egg	1 egg	2 eggs
½ t salt	¾ t salt	1 t salt
1¾ C bread flour	2⅝ C bread flour	3½ C bread flour
½ C whole wheat flour	¾ C whole wheat flour	1 C whole wheat flour
1½ t active dry yeast	2¼ t active dry yeast	1 T active dry yeast

Nutritional Analysis (per loaf, approximate)

Item	1 lb	1½ lb	2 lb
total calories (kcal)	1308	1961	2616
total protein (g)	47	68	95
total carbohydrates (g)	244	367	488
total fat (g)	16	25	32
total saturated fat (g)	6	10	12
total cholesterol (mg)	198	215	396
total sodium (mg)	1258	1889	2516
total fiber (g)	17	25	33
% calories from fat	11	11	11

Three Kings Bread

Called *Rosca de los Reyes* in Latin America, this bread is customarily baked to celebrate Twelfth Night (January 6th). In its normal form, the bread is baked in a ring shape and garnished with nuts and candied fruits. Often, a tiny doll or an uncooked lima bean is hidden in the bread. The person receiving the bean or doll hosts a party on February 2nd, *El dia de la candelaria.*

1 lb	1½ lb	2 lb
⅓ C warm water	½ C warm water	⅔ C warm water
4 T butter	½ C butter	½ C butter
1 egg	1 egg	2 eggs
1¾ C bread flour	2⅝ C bread flour	3½ C bread flour
1½ T dry milk	2½ T dry milk	3 T dry milk
2 T sugar	3 T sugar	¼ C sugar
½ t salt	¾ t salt	1 t salt
2½ T raisins	3½ T raisins	⅓ C raisins
2½ T walnuts, chopped	4 T walnuts, chopped	⅓ C walnuts, chopped
1 T candied cherries, chopped	1½ T candied cherries, chopped	2 T candied cherries, chopped
1 t grated orange peel	1½ t grated orange peel	2 t grated orange peel
1 t grated lemon rind	1½ t grated lemon rind	2 t grated lemon rind
1½ t active dry yeast	2¼ t active dry yeast	1 T active dry yeast

(Nutritional analysis is on next page).

Three Kings Bread Nutritional Analysis (per loaf, approximate)

Item	1 lb	1½ lb	2 lb
total calories (kcal)	1582	2542	3177
total protein (g)	41	60	82
total carbohydrates (g)	229	342	461
total fat (g)	57	106	114
total saturated fat (g)	31	59	61
total cholesterol (mg)	304	428	609
total sodium (mg)	1638	2667	3277
total fiber (g)	9	13	18
% calories from fat	32	37	32

Wild Rice Bread

Wild rice is difficult to find growing wild, and hence fairly expensive. This recipe is made even better if you can use wild rice flour instead of the regular white rice flour called for. If you have a grinder or food processor that can process grains into flour, you can simply make your own wild rice flour. Otherwise, use the commercially available rice flour and use the cooked wild rice to give the bread the wild rice flavor. Be sure to drain the cooked rice well and let it dry or a while before using it in the recipe. The cooked wild rice is included as a dry ingredient in the ratio, so you don't want wet rice or your bread will not rise properly.

1 lb	1½ lb	2 lb
¾ C warm water	9 oz warm water	1½ C warm water
1½ T vegetable oil	2½ T vegetable oil	3 T vegetable oil
¼ C rice flour	⅜ C rice flour	½ C rice flour
½ t salt	¾ t salt	1 t salt
1½ C bread flour	2½ C bread flour	3 C bread flour
⅓ C cooked wild rice	½ C cooked wild rice	⅔ C cooked wild rice
1 t active dry yeast	1½ t active dry yeast	2 t active dry yeast

Nutritional Analysis (per loaf, approximate)

Item	1 lb	1½ lb	2 lb
total calories (kcal)	1134	1855	2268
total protein (g)	31	50	61
total carbohydrates (g)	194	316	388
total fat (g)	25	41	50
total saturated fat (g)	3	5	6
total cholesterol (mg)	0	0	0
total sodium (mg)	1079	1619	2158
total fiber (g)	8	13	16
% calories from fat	20	20	20

Wild Rice Bread

Wild rice is difficult to find growing wild, and hence fairly expensive. This recipe is made even better if you can use wild rice flour instead of the regular white rice flour called for. If you have a grinder or food processor that can process grains into flour, you can simply make your own wild rice flour. Otherwise, use the commercially available rice flour and use the cooked wild rice to give the bread the wild rice flavor. Be sure to drain the cooked rice well and let it dry or a while before using it in the recipe. The cooked wild rice is included as a dry ingredient in the ratio, so you don't want wet rice or your bread will not rise properly.

1 lb	1½ lb	2 lb
¾ C warm water	9 oz warm water	1½ C warm water
1½ T vegetable oil	2½ T vegetable oil	3 T vegetable oil
¼ C rice flour	⅜ C rice flour	½ C rice flour
½ t salt	¾ t salt	1 t salt
1½ C bread flour	2½ C bread flour	3 C bread flour
⅓ C cooked wild rice	½ C cooked wild rice	⅔ C cooked wild rice
1 t active dry yeast	1½ t active dry yeast	2 t active dry yeast

Nutritional Analysis (per loaf, approximate)

Item	1 lb	1½ lb	2 lb
total calories (kcal)	1134	1855	2268
total protein (g)	31	50	61
total carbohydrates (g)	194	316	388
total fat (g)	25	41	50
total saturated fat (g)	3	5	6
total cholesterol (mg)	0	0	0
total sodium (mg)	1079	1619	2158
total fiber (g)	8	13	16
% calories from fat	20	20	20

INTERNATIONAL BREADS

These breads have their origins all around the world. Many are traditional loaves of their respective countries, modified for baking in the bread machine.

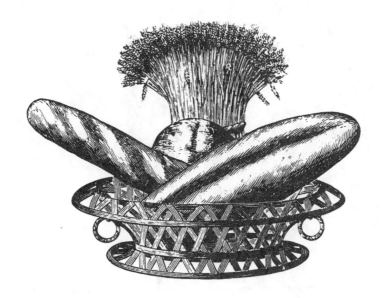

Armenian Sesame Bread

A hearty and rich white bread, perfect for sandwiches.

1 lb	1½ lb	2 lb
2 T warm water	3 T warm water	¼ C warm water
½ C milk	¾ C milk	1 C milk
1 T olive oil	1½ T olive oil	2 T olive oil
½ T butter	2½ t butter	1 T butter
2½ t sugar	1½ T sugar	1⅔ T sugar
¾ t salt	1 t salt	1½ t salt
2 C bread flour	3 C bread flour	4 C bread flour
1½ T sesame seeds	2⅓ T sesame seeds	3 T sesame seeds
1 t active dry yeast	1½ t active dry yeast	2 t active dry yeast

Nutritional Analysis (per loaf, approximate)

Item	1 lb	1½ lb	2 lb
total calories (kcal)	1368	2078	2737
total protein (g)	42	63	84
total carbohydrates (g)	218	330	435
total fat (g)	36	55	71
total saturated fat (g)	10	15	19
total cholesterol (mg)	32	50	64
total sodium (mg)	1731	2339	3461
total fiber (g)	8	12	15
% calories from fat	24	24	24

Broa: Portuguese Corn Bread

In Portugal, this bread frequently is served with caldo verde, a type of bean soup. It was brought to the United States by the descendants of Portuguese fishermen from the Azores. The bread goes well with almost any soup or salad, and is delicious by itself with butter and jam or jelly.

1 lb	1½ lb	2 lb
1 C boiling water	1½ C boiling water	2 C boiling water
1 T olive oil	1½ T olive oil	2 T olive oil
½ t sugar	¾ t sugar	1 t sugar
½ C yellow corn flour, whole grain	¾ C yellow corn flour, whole grain	1 C yellow corn flour, whole grain
½ t salt	¾ t salt	1 t salt
1½ C bread flour	2¼ C bread flour	3 C bread flour
1½ t active dry yeast	2¼ t active dry yeast	1 T active dry yeast

Nutritional Analysis (per loaf, approximate)

Item	1 lb	1½ lb	2 lb
total calories (kcal)	1098	1647	2196
total protein (g)	31	47	62
total carbohydrates (g)	198	298	397
total fat (g)	19	29	39
total saturated fat (g)	3	4	5
total cholesterol (mg)	0	0	0
total sodium (mg)	1083	1625	2166
total fiber (g)	14	22	29
% calories from fat	16	16	16

Chive and Garlic Bread

This is a zippy variation of white bread that is fantastic with pasta or soups. Saute the garlic in butter for 1–2 minutes; then let cool before adding to the mixture.

1 lb	1½ lb	2 lb
2 t butter	1 T butter	1½ T butter
7 oz milk	1¼ C milk	14 oz milk
3 cloves garlic	5 cloves garlic	6 cloves garlic
2 C bread flour	3 C bread flour	4 C bread flour
3½ T grated parmesan cheese	⅓ C grated parmesan cheese	½ C grated parmesan cheese
1½ T chopped fresh chives	2 T chopped fresh chives	3 T chopped fresh chives
2 t sugar	1 T sugar	1½ T sugar
½ t salt	¾ t salt	1 t salt
½ t active dry yeast	1 t active dry yeast	2 t active dry yeast

Nutritional Analysis (per loaf, approximate)

Item	1 lb	1½ lb	2 lb
total calories (kcal)	1332	2007	2700
total protein (g)	50	76	102
total carbohydrates (g)	221	333	446
total fat (g)	26	39	53
total saturated fat (g)	14	21	29
total cholesterol (mg)	65	98	135
total sodium (mg)	1661	2496	3344
total fiber (g)	2	3	5
% calories from fat	18	18	18

Crescia al Formaggio

Crescia is a conjugated form of the Italian verb *crescere*, which means "to grow." This bread, rich in cheese flavor, rises steadily. The cheese in the bread is best melted in the microwave ahead of time so that it adds to the liquidity of the bread during mixing. When the bread is not baked in the bread machine, the cheese is typically folded into the dough before the final rise and bake. Using the bread machine can work too, but as the cheese melts, it adds to the liquidity of the bread, which can cause the loaf to fall from a high rise. That's why it is better to melt the cheese before adding it to the machine.

1 lb	1½ lb	2 lb
7 oz warm water	1¼ C warm water	14 oz warm water
4 T butter	⅜ C butter	½ C butter
⅓ C Swiss cheese, shredded & melted	½ C Swiss cheese, shredded & melted	⅔ C Swiss cheese, shredded & melted
¼ t sugar	½ t sugar	½ t sugar
¼ t salt	½ t salt	½ t salt
⅓ C grated parmesan cheese	½ C grated parmesan cheese	⅔ C grated parmesan cheese
1¾ C bread flour	2¾ C bread flour	3½ C bread flour
1½ t active dry yeast	2¼ t active dry yeast	1 T active dry yeast

Nutritional Analysis (per loaf, approximate)

Item	1 lb	1½ lb	2 lb
total calories (kcal)	1552	2392	3104
total protein (g)	53	82	107
total carbohydrates (g)	180	282	359
total fat (g)	68	102	136
total saturated fat (g)	41	61	81
total cholesterol (mg)	178	267	357
total sodium (mg)	1604	2673	3208
total fiber (g)	7	12	15
% calories from fat	40	39	40

Feta–Garlic Bread

A traditional Greek bread that goes well with salad.

1 lb	1½ lb	2 lb
¾ C warm water	9 oz warm water	1½ C warm water
1½ t sugar	2¼ t sugar	1 T sugar
1½ t salt	2¼ t salt	1 T salt
2⅛ C bread flour	3¼ C bread flour	4½ C bread flour
1 T garlic, chopped	1½ T garlic, chopped	2 T garlic, chopped
¼ t ground pepper	¼ t ground pepper	½ t ground pepper
¼ C feta cheese	⅜ C feta cheese	½ C feta cheese
1 t active dry yeast	1½ t active dry yeast	2 t active dry yeast

Nutritional Analysis (per loaf, approximate)

Item	1 lb	1½ lb	2 lb
total calories (kcal)	1175	1792	2473
total protein (g)	41	63	86
total carbohydrates (g)	223	341	471
total fat (g)	11	17	23
total saturated fat (g)	5	8	10
total cholesterol (mg)	25	38	50
total sodium (mg)	3529	5293	7058
total fiber (g)	8	13	18
% calories from fat	9	9	8

Haidd: Welsh Barley Bread

Barley is a staple grain in many parts of the world. Making a loaf out of pure barley flour is difficult in the bread machine, since barley doesn't have the same rising characteristics as wheat flour. Although the authetic bread would be 100% barley flour, we have inserted some bread flour in the recipe to make it work better in the bread machine. The extra yeast (more than normal for the bread machine) is necessary because of the reduced rising capacity of the barley flour.

This bread is a favorite in Wales. Similar breads are found in Ireland, Scotland, Egypt, and many other parts of the world. If you want the authentic bread, substitute barley flour for the bread flour called for here, and use the dough setting on your machine. Remove the dough from the machine at the end of the cycle and bake the bread in a 400°F (204.4°C) oven for 25 minutes. It is best eaten hot with butter and honey.

1 lb	1½ lb	2 lb
7 oz warm water	11 oz warm water	14 oz warm water
2 t butter	1 T butter	1⅓ T butter
½ t sugar	¾ t sugar	1 t sugar
1⅔ C barley flour	2½ C barley flour	3⅓ C barley flour
½ t salt	¾ t salt	1 t salt
½ C bread flour	¾ C bread flour	1 C bread flour
2 t active dry yeast	1 T active dry yeast	1⅓ T active dry yeast
4 t gluten	2 T gluten	2⅔ T gluten

(Nutritional analysis is on next page).

Haidd Nutritional Analysis (per loaf, approximate)

Item	1 lb	1½ lb	2 lb
total calories (kcal)	1432	2147	2863
total protein (g)	50	75	99
total carbohydrates (g)	280	420	560
total fat (g)	16	24	32
total saturated fat (g)	6	10	13
total cholesterol (mg)	20	31	41
total sodium (mg)	1191	1787	2382
total fiber (g)	57	85	114
% calories from fat	10	10	10

Italian Herb Bread

This bread is great with any Italian dish or any salad. It's also good for making salad croutons.

1 lb	1½ lb	2 lbs
¾ C water	9 oz water	1½ C water
2 T applesauce	3 T applesauce	¼ C applesauce
1 T honey	1½ T honey	2 T honey
2 C whole wheat flour	3 C whole wheat flour	4 C whole wheat flour
1½ T wheat gluten	2¼ T wheat gluten	3 T wheat gluten
2 T dried onions	3 T dried onions	¼ C dried onions
2 t chives, freeze dried	1 T chives, freeze dried	1⅓ T chives, freeze dried
1 t salt	1½ t salt	2 t salt
¾ t garlic powder	1 t garlic powder	1½ t garlic powder
¾ t oregano	1¼ t oregano	1½ t oregano
¼ t basil	¼ t basil	½ t basil
1½ t active dry yeast	2¼ t active dry yeast	1 T active dry yeast

Nutritional Analysis (per loaf, approximate)

Item	1 lb	1½ lb	2 lb
total calories (kcal)	1048	1571	2095
total protein (g)	54	81	109
total carbohydrates (g)	210	314	420
total fat (g)	7	10	13
total saturated fat (g)	1	2	2
total cholesterol (mg)	0	0	0
total sodium (mg)	2188	2181	4375
total fiber (g)	32	49	65
% calories from fat	5	5	5

Italian Pork Bread

The Italians have a great tradition of combining meat with their bread, as in pizza, calzones, and the like. This bread has a great flavor and is best eaten right out of the bread machine while still hot. Because the bread contains fresh pork, it is best to bake only as much as you plan to eat while it is hot and freshly baked.

1 lb	1½ lb	2 lb
5 oz warm water	7½ oz warm water	10 oz warm water
1½ T sugar	2¼ T sugar	3 T sugar
1¾ C bread flour	2⅝ C bread flour	3½ C bread flour
½ t salt	¾ t salt	1 t salt
¼ t black pepper	⅜ t black pepper	½ t black pepper
½ C pork roast, cooked & shredded	¾ C pork roast, cooked & shredded	1 C pork roast, cooked & shredded
1 t active dry yeast	1½ t active dry yeast	2 t active dry yeast

Nutritional Analysis (per loaf, approximate)

Item	1 lb	1½ lb	2 lb
total calories (kcal)	1311	1966	2622
total protein (g)	57	85	114
total carbohydrates (g)	195	292	389
total fat (g)	32	47	63
total saturated fat (g)	11	16	21
total cholesterol (mg)	101	152	203
total sodium (mg)	1410	2116	2821
total fiber (g)	7	11	14
% calories from fat	22	22	22

Lithuanian Potato Bread

Using fresh potato enhances the flavor of this variation of the perennial favorite, potato bread. Note the variety of liquids used here: water, milk, butter, sour cream, and egg.

1 lb	1½ lb	2 lb
1½ T warm water	2½ T warm water	3 T warm water
3 oz milk	4½ oz milk	6 oz milk
1 egg	1 egg	2 eggs
1 T sour cream	1½ T sour cream	2 T sour cream
½ T butter	2½ t butter	1 T butter
¼ t sugar	⅜ t sugar	½ t sugar
2¼ C bread flour	3¼ C bread flour	4½ C bread flour
1 t salt	1½ t salt	2 t salt
¼ C potato, grated	⅜ C potato, grated	½ C potato, grated
1 t active dry yeast	1½ t active dry yeast	2 t active dry yeast

Nutritional Analysis (per loaf, approximate)

Item	1 lb	1½ lb	2 lb
total calories (kcal)	1336	1919	2673
total protein (g)	47	66	95
total carbohydrates (g)	234	338	468
total fat (g)	21	30	42
total saturated fat (g)	9	14	19
total cholesterol (mg)	214	233	428
total sodium (mg)	2302	3436	4604
total fiber (g)	9	13	18
% calories from fat	14	14	14

Olive, Mint, and Onion Bread

This unusual bread originated in Cyprus, where olive trees abound, and stems from the traditional Greek bread called *eliopsomo*.

1 lb	1½ lb	2 lb
5½ oz warm water	8½ oz warm water	11 oz warm water
1 T olive oil	1½ T olive oil	2 T olive oil
¼ t sugar	½ t sugar	½ t sugar
¼ C whole wheat flour	⅜ C whole wheat flour	½ C whole wheat flour
1½ C bread flour	2¼ C bread flour	3 C bread flour
½ t salt	¾ t salt	1 t salt
1 t dried mint flakes	1½ t dried mint flakes	2 t dried mint flakes
4 T onions, chopped	⅜ C onions, chopped	½ C onions, chopped
2 T black olives, chopped	3 T black olives, chopped	¼ C black olives, chopped
1 t active dry yeast	1½ t active dry yeast	2 t active dry yeast

Nutritional Analysis (per loaf, approximate)

Item	1 lb	1½ lb	2 lb
total calories (kcal)	1006	1511	2012
total protein (g)	31	46	62
total carbohydrates (g)	176	265	352
total fat (g)	20	29	39
total saturated fat (g)	3	4	5
total cholesterol (mg)	0	0	0
total sodium (mg)	1374	2061	2747
total fiber (g)	10	15	20
% calories from fat	18	18	18

Turmeric and Caraway Bread

This African-style bread can be made more authentic by substituting red palm oil for the olive oil. If red palm oil is not available, try mixing corn oil with a pinch of paprika.

1 lb	1½ lb	2 lb
6 oz warm water	9 oz warm water	12 oz warm water
1 T honey	1½ T honey	2 T honey
1 T olive oil	1½ T olive oil	2 T olive oil
½ T turmeric	2¼ t turmeric	1 T turmeric
½ t salt	¾ t salt	1 t salt
2 C bread flour	3 C bread flour	4 C bread flour
1¼ t caraway seed	2 t caraway seed	2½ t caraway seed
1½ t active dry yeast	2¼ t active dry yeast	1 T active dry yeast

Nutritional Analysis (per loaf, approximate)

Item	1 lb	1½ lb	2 lb
total calories (kcal)	1212	1819	2424
total protein (g)	36	54	72
total carbohydrates (g)	222	333	444
total fat (g)	19	29	38
total saturated fat (g)	3	4	5
total cholesterol (mg)	0	0	0
total sodium (mg)	1082	1623	2164
total fiber (g)	10	15	20
% calories from fat	14	14	14

TRADITIONAL BREADS

These breads have their roots in the American past and are traditional favorites in various parts of the United States.

Bacon–Cheese Bread

A wonderful variation on white bread that has a moist texture and is great for sandwiches. You can use bacon or cheese substitutes in lieu of the real thing. The nutritional analysis doesn't include the cheese or bacon, since that varies according to the type you use.

1 lb	1½ lb	2 lb
⅔ C milk	1 C milk	1⅓ C milk
1 T butter	1⅓ T butter	2 T butter
2 t sugar	1 T sugar	1⅓ T sugar
½ t salt	½ t salt	1 t salt
2 C bread flour	3 C bread flour	4 C bread flour
1 t active dry yeast	1½ t active dry yeast	2 t active dry yeast

At the mix cycle add:

¼ C shredded cheddar cheese	6 T shredded cheddar cheese	½ C shredded cheddar cheese
¼ C cooked, crumbled bacon	6 T cooked, crumbled bacon	½ C cooked, crumbled bacon

Nutritional Analysis (per loaf, approximate)

Item	1 lb	1½ lb	2 lb
total calories (kcal)	1233	1834	2467
total protein (g)	40	60	80
total carbohydrates (g)	216	324	432
total fat (g)	22	30	43
total saturated fat (g)	11	16	22
total cholesterol (mg)	53	74	106
total sodium (mg)	1269	1351	2538
total fiber (g)	2	3	4
% calories from fat	16	15	16

Blue Ribbon Potato Bread

Here is a simple loaf of potato bread that has very few ingredients to round up, is quick to put together, and is very tasty.

1 lb	1½ lb	2 lb
⅔ C warm water	1 C warm water	1⅓ C warm water
1 t salt	1½ t salt	2 t salt
2½ t butter	1½ T butter	1⅔ T butter
5 t potato flakes	2½ T potato flakes	3⅓ T potato flakes
1 T sugar	1½ T sugar	2 T sugar
2 C bread flour	3 C bread flour	4 C bread flour
1 t active dry yeast	1½ t active dry yeast	2 t active dry yeast

Nutritional Analysis (per loaf, approximate)

Item	1 lb	1½ lb	2 lb
total calories (kcal)	1150	1749	2299
total protein (g)	35	52	70
total carbohydrates (g)	217	325	433
total fat (g)	14	24	28
total saturated fat (g)	7	12	13
total cholesterol (mg)	26	46	51
total sodium (mg)	2245	3397	4491
total fiber (g)	8	12	16
% calories from fat	11	13	11

Colonial Bread

This traditional bread uses ingredients that were commonly found on the colonial farm and has a crunchy texture unique to recipes containing corn meal.

1 lb	1½ lb	2 lb
6 oz warm water	9 oz warm water	1½ C warm water
2½ T molasses	3⅓ T molasses	⅓ C molasses
1½ T butter	2⅓ T butter	3 T butter
2½ T yellow corn meal	3¾ T yellow corn meal	⅓ C yellow corn meal
½ t salt	¾ t salt	1 t salt
1¾ C bread flour	2⅝ C bread flour	3½ C bread flour
¾ t active dry yeast	1¼ t active dry yeast	1½ t active dry yeast

Nutritional Analysis (per loaf, approximate)

Item	1 lb	1½ lb	2 lb
total calories (kcal)	1240	1847	2504
total protein (g)	32	48	64
total carbohydrates (g)	227	335	460
total fat (g)	22	33	43
total saturated fat (g)	11	18	23
total cholesterol (mg)	46	71	92
total sodium (mg)	1270	1912	2543
total fiber (g)	3	5	7
% calories from fat	16	16	16

Eleanor Roosevelt's Whole Wheat Bread

This recipe was adapted from *The White House Cookbook* (Culinary Arts Institute, Chicago, Illinois, 1968). Mrs. Franklin D. Roosevelt liked wheat bread and served it at many White House gatherings. She enjoyed coarse bread and liked to use fresh stone-ground whole wheat flour.

1 lb	1½ lb	2 lb
2 T molasses	3 T molasses	¼ C molasses
½ T butter	1 T butter	1 T butter
6 oz warm water	1 C warm water	1½ C warm water
½ C whole wheat flour	¾ C whole wheat flour	1 C whole wheat flour
½ T brown sugar	2¼ t brown sugar	1 T brown sugar
½ t salt	¾ t salt	1 t salt
1¾ C bread flour	2⅝ C bread flour	3½ C bread flour
1 t active dry yeast	1½ t active dry yeast	2 t active dry yeast

Nutritional Analysis (per loaf, approximate)

Item	1 lb	1½ lb	2 lb
total calories (kcal)	1257	1911	2514
total protein (g)	39	58	77
total carbohydrates (g)	252	377	503
total fat (g)	11	19	22
total saturated fat (g)	4	8	9
total cholesterol (mg)	15	31	31
total sodium (mg)	1156	1762	2312
total fiber (g)	14	21	28
% calories from fat	8	9	8

Farmer Bread

A traditional white loaf made sweeter by dates and nuts.

1 lb	1½ lb	2 lb
1 egg	1 egg	2 eggs
3 T butter	¼ C butter	⅜ C butter
5 oz milk	8 oz milk	10 oz milk
2 T walnuts, chopped	3 T walnuts, chopped	¼ C walnuts, chopped
2 T dates, chopped	3 T dates, chopped	¼ C dates, chopped
1 t salt	1½ t salt	2 t salt
2 C bread flour	3 C bread flour	4 C bread flour
1½ T sugar	2½ T sugar	3 T sugar
1½ t lemon peel	2¼ t lemon peel	1 T lemon peel
1 t active dry yeast	1½ t active dry yeast	2 t active dry yeast

Nutritional Analysis (per loaf, approximate)

Item	1 lb	1½ lb	2 lb
total calories (kcal)	1603	2343	3205
total protein (g)	46	67	92
total carbohydrates (g)	242	366	484
total fat (g)	50	68	100
total saturated fat (g)	26	36	53
total cholesterol (mg)	292	334	584
total sodium (mg)	2610	3838	5221
total fiber (g)	10	15	19
% calories from fat	28	26	28

Honey Barley Bread

The distinctive flavor of barley is evident in this bread that combines three different types of flour.

1 lb	1½ lb	2 lb
1 C warm water	1½ C warm water	2 C warm water
2½ T honey	¼ C honey	⅓ C honey
2 T wheat gluten	3 T wheat gluten	¼ C wheat gluten
1 ⅛ C bread flour	1¾C bread flour	2⅓ C bread flour
⅓ C barley flour	½ C barley flour	⅔ C barley flour
½ t salt	½ t salt	1 t salt
¾ C whole wheat flour	1¼ C whole wheat flour	1½ C whole wheat flour
1½ t active dry yeast	2 t active dry yeast	1 T active dry yeast

Nutritional Analysis (per loaf, approximate)

Item	1 lb	1½ lb	2 lb
total calories (kcal)	1181	1834	2361
total protein (g)	58	88	115
total carbohydrates (g)	229	358	457
total fat (g)	7	10	13
total saturated fat (g)	1	2	2
total cholesterol (mg)	0	0	0
total sodium (mg)	1128	1159	2256
total fiber (g)	13	22	27
% calories from fat	5	5	5

Mormon Rye Bread

A traditional recipe from the 19th century, modernized to include yeast as leavening.

1 lb	1½ lb	2 lb
3½ oz warm water	5½ oz warm water	7 oz warm water
2 T honey	3 T honey	¼ C honey
4 T shortening	⅜ C shortening	½ C shortening
1 T butter	1½ T butter	2 T butter
½ T sugar	2¼ t sugar	1 T sugar
½ C rye flour	¾ C rye flour	1 C rye flour
1½ C bread flour	2¼ C bread flour	3 C bread flour
2 T brown sugar	3 T brown sugar	¼ C brown sugar
½ t salt	¾ t salt	1 t salt
1½ t active dry yeast	2½ t active dry yeast	1 T active dry yeast

Nutritional Analysis (per loaf, approximate)

Item	1 lb	1½ lb	2 lb
total calories (kcal)	1715	2575	3429
total protein (g)	32	48	64
total carbohydrates (g)	250	375	499
total fat (g)	67	101	134
total saturated fat (g)	21	31	41
total cholesterol (mg)	31	46	61
total sodium (mg)	1202	1804	2404
total fiber (g)	14	22	28
% calories from fat	35	35	35

Mountain Rye Bread

This basic rye recipe will give you the taste of rye with a fluffy consistency.

1 lb	1½ lb	2 lb
1 C water	1½ C water	2 C water
1 T vegetable oil	1½ T vegetable oil	2 T vegetable oil
2 T honey	3 T honey	¼ C honey
1 t salt	1½ t salt	2 t salt
1 T caraway seed	1½ T caraway seed	2 T caraway seed
1 C rye flour	1½ C rye flour	2 C rye flour
1¾ C bread flour	2½ C bread flour	3½ C bread flour
3 T nonfat dry milk	¼ C nonfat dry milk	⅜ C nonfat dry milk
1½ t active dry yeast	2¼ t active dry yeast	1 T active dry yeast

Nutritional Analysis (per loaf, approximate)

Item	1 lb	1½ lb	2 lb
total calories (kcal)	1597	2334	3194
total protein (g)	50	73	100
total carbohydrates	305	445	610
total fat (g)	21	31	42
total saturated fat (g)	3	4	5
total cholesterol (mg)	4	7	9
total sodium (mg)	2272	3407	4544
total fiber (g)	6	9	13
% calories from fat	12	12	12

Mustard Grain Bread

This whole-grain bread features 3 different types of flour and the tang of Dijon mustard.

1 lb	1½ lb	2 lb
½ C warm water	¾ C warm water	1 C warm water
2 T butter	3 T butter	¼ C butter
⅓ C Dijon mustard	½ C Dijon mustard	⅔ C Dijon mustard
1 t sugar	1½ t sugar	2 t sugar
½ t salt	1 t salt	1 t salt
¾ C bread flour	1⅓ C bread flour	1½ C bread flour
½ C rye flour	⅔ C rye flour	¾ C rye flour
½ C whole wheat flour	⅔ C whole wheat flour	1 C whole wheat flour
2 t active dry yeast	3 t active dry yeast	1½ T active dry yeast

Nutritional Analysis (per loaf, approximate)

Item	1 lb	1½ lb	2 lb
total calories (kcal)	1014	1622	2026
total protein (g)	31	50	63
total carbohydrates (g)	161	262	321
total fat (g)	30	46	60
total saturated fat (g)	15	22	30
total cholesterol (mg)	61	92	123
total sodium (mg)	2313	4002	4626
total fiber (g)	11	17	24
% calories from fat	26	25	26

Nutmeg Bread

Try this bread for a spicy treat. Excellent as toast.

1 lb	1½ lb	2 lb
⅔ C water	1 C water	1⅓ C water
1 egg	1 egg	2 eggs
1 T orange juice (frozen concentrate)	1½ T orange juice (frozen concentrate)	2 T orange juice (frozen concentrate)
1⅔ T honey	2½ T honey	3⅓ T honey
1 to 3 dashes salt	¼ t salt	½ t salt
⅓ t nutmeg	½ t nutmeg	¾ t nutmeg
2¼ C whole wheat flour	3⅓ C whole wheat flour	4½ C whole wheat flour
1 t active dry yeast	1½ t active dry yeast	2 t active dry yeast

Nutmeg Bread Nutritional Analysis (per loaf, approximate)

Item	1 lb	1½ lb	2 lb
total calories (kcal)	1129	1694	2283
total protein (g)	45	67	91
total carbohydrates (g)	232	348	469
total fat (g)	11	16	21
total saturated fat (g)	3	4	5
total cholesterol (mg)	213	319	425
total sodium	440	661	1237
total fiber	34	51	69
% calories from fat	8	8	8

Parsley Bread

Try this bread for a variation on the white bread theme. The parsley and garlic add zest to this tasty bread.

1 lb	1½ lb	2 lb
7 oz water	1¼ C water	1¾C water
1 T olive oil	1½ T olive oil	2 T olive oil
4 t parsley, chopped	2 T parsley, chopped	2⅔ T parsley, chopped
½ t minced garlic	1 t minced garlic	1 t minced garlic
1 T sugar	1½ T sugar	2 T sugar
2 T wheat bran	3 T wheat bran	¼ C wheat bran
2 T wheat germ	3 T wheat germ	¼ C wheat germ
2 C bread flour	3 C bread flour	4 C bread flour
1 t active dry yeast	1½ t active dry yeast	2 t active dry yeast

Nutritional Analysis (per loaf, approximate)

Item	1 lb	1½ lb	2 lb
total calories	1244	1866	2487
total protein (g)	39	59	79
total carbohydrates (g)	226	340	453
total fat (g)	20	30	40
total saturated fat	3	4	6
total cholesterol (mg)	0	0	0
total sodium (mg)	24	35	48
total fiber (g)	6	8	11
% calories from fat	15	15	15

Polenta–Millet–Sunflower Seed Bread

When my boys were small, they planted some sunflower seeds in our back yard in Arizona. To their amazement, the plants grew over 10 feet (3 m) tall, and had a large sunflower at the top of each stalk. Sunflower seeds are native to the American Southwest and to Mexico, and have become very popular in American baking. This bread is a wonderful blend of grains with cornmeal, millet, and whole wheat. (*Polenta* is actually an Italian mush that is sometimes made from cornmeal.) There is enough bread flour to give the bread a wonderful, smooth texture that makes it excellent for toasting.

1 lb	1½ lb	2 lb
½ C warm water	¾ C warm water	1 C warm water
2 T honey	3 T honey	¼ C honey
1 T vegetable oil	1½ T vegetable oil	2 T vegetable oil
1 egg	1 egg	2 eggs
¼ t sugar	½ t sugar	½ t sugar
½ t salt	¾ t salt	1 t salt
2 T millet, raw	3 T millet, raw	¼ C millet, raw
2 T cornmeal	3 T cornmeal	¼ C cornmeal
½ C whole wheat flour	¾ C whole wheat flour	1 C whole wheat flour
1¼ C bread flour	2 C bread flour	2½ C bread flour
2 T sunflower seeds	3 T sunflower seeds	¼ C sunflower seeds
1 t active dry yeast	1½ t active dry yeast	2 t active dry yeast

(Nutritional analysis is on next page.)

Polenta–Millet Nutritional Analysis (per loaf, approximate)

Item	1 lb	1½ lb	2 lb
total calories (kcal)	1304	1989	2609
total protein (g)	40	60	81
total carbohydrates (g)	228	355	456
total fat (g)	27	39	55
total saturated fat (g)	4	6	8
total cholesterol (mg)	181	181	361
total sodium (mg)	1135	1675	2269
total fiber (g)	15	23	31
% calories from fat	19	18	19

Potica

This traditional bread is a smoothly textured sweet white bread that is excellent for breakfast.

1 lb	1½ lb	2 lb
3½ T milk	⅓ C milk	⅜ C milk
2 T shortening	3 T shortening	¼ C shortening
2½ T warm water	3¾ T warm water	⅓ C warm water
1 egg	1 egg	2 eggs
2 T butter	3 T butter	¼ C butter
2 T sugar	3 T sugar	¼ C sugar
2 T walnuts, chopped	3 T walnuts, chopped	¼ C walnuts, chopped
½ T grated orange peel	2 t grated orange peel	1 T grated orange peel
1½ t active dry yeast	2 t active dry yeast	1 T active dry yeast

Nutritional Analysis (per loaf, approximate)

Item	1 lb	1½ lb	2 lb
total calories (kcal)	661	957	1312
total protein (g)	11	13	21
total carbohydrates (g)	32	47	62
total fat (g)	57	83	113
total saturated fat (g)	23	34	46
total cholesterol (mg)	249	284	496
total sodium (mg)	316	447	624
total fiber (g)	2	3	4
% calories from fat	75	76	75

Pueblo Sage Bread

Since sage grows wild in the Pueblo country of New Mexico, it is a popular herb among the Native Americans of the area. This bread uses some modern ingredients, but has the age-old flavor unique to Southwestern cooking.

1 lb	1½ lb	2 lb
2 T warm water	3 T warm water	¼ C warm water
1 T cooking oil	1½ T cooking oil	2 T cooking oil
½ C cottage cheese	¾ C cottage cheese	1 C cottage cheese
1 egg	1 egg	2 eggs
1¾ C bread flour	2½ C bread flour	3½ C bread flour
1½ t sugar	2¼ t sugar	1 T sugar
2 t dried sage	1 T dried sage	1⅓ T dried sage
¼ t salt	½ t salt	½ t salt
½ t baking soda	¾ t baking soda	1 t baking soda
1½ t active dry yeast	2¼ t active dry yeast	1 T active dry yeast

Nutritional Analysis (per loaf, approximate)

Item	1 lb	1½ lb	2 lb
total calories (kcal)	1197	1702	2393
total protein (g)	52	73	104
total carbohydrates (g)	188	269	376
total fat (g)	25	34	49
total saturated fat (g)	5	7	10
total cholesterol (mg)	190	195	380
total sodium (mg)	1683	2764	3367
total fiber (g)	8	11	15
% calories from fat	19	18	19

Sesame Honey Bread

Sesame seeds always add a nutty flavor to bread, and this is no exception. It is great toasted with jam or jelly.

1 lb	1½ lb	2 lb
⅔ C warm water	1 C warm water	1⅓ C warm water
2½ T honey	¼ C honey	⅓ C honey
2½ T buttermilk	¼ C buttermilk	⅓ C buttermilk
1 t salt	1½ t salt	2 t salt
2 C bread flour	3 C bread flour	4 C bread flour
2 T wheat bran	3 T wheat bran	¼ C wheat bran
⅓ C sesame seeds	½ C sesame seeds	⅔ C sesame seeds
1½ t active dry yeast	2¼ t active dry yeast	1 T active dry yeast

Nutritional Analysis (per loaf, approximate)

Item	1 lb	1½ lb	2 lb
total calories	1474	2229	2948
total protein (g)	46	69	92
total carbohydrates (g)	262	398	525
total fat (g)	29	44	58
total saturated fat (g)	5	7	9
total cholesterol (mg)	1	2	3
total sodium (mg)	2193	3293	4385
total fiber (g)	4	6	7
% calories from fat	18	17	18

Shaker Daily Loaf

The story goes that a 19th century Kentucky Shaker community member named Sister Virginia originated this bread and baked it daily. Her original recipe yielded roughly 5 lb (2.2 kg) of bread and has, of course, been scaled down for the bread machine. This simple but tasty white bread is an excellent staple white bread, fit for putting on the table while still hot.

1 lb	1½ lb	2 lb
3 oz warm water	4½ oz warm water	6 oz warm water
⅓ C milk	½ C milk	⅔ C milk
1½ T shortening	2¼ T shortening	3 T shortening
1 t sugar	1½ t sugar	2 t sugar
½ t salt	¾ t salt	1 t salt
2 C bread flour	3 C bread flour	4 C bread flour
1 t active dry yeast	1½ t active dry yeast	2 t active dry yeast

Nutritional Analysis (per loaf, approximate)

Item	1 lb	1½ lb	2 lb
total calories (kcal)	1237	1855	2474
total protein (g)	37	56	74
total carbohydrates (g)	208	312	416
total fat (g)	27	40	53
total saturated fat (g)	7	11	14
total cholesterol (mg)	11	17	22
total sodium (mg)	1116	1674	2232
total fiber (g)	8	12	15
% calories from fat	20	20	20

Trail Bread

Rye is a popular grain throughout the world because it will grow in many places where less rugged grains will not. It requires less water than wheat and can grow well in soil of much poorer quality. It was first cultivated in Roman times and quickly became a staple in breads throughout Europe, including Scandinavia and Russia. Since rye is naturally low in gluten content, it doesn't rise much. While the original bread tends to be much denser, for the bread machine we have tried to capture the essence of this bread, although we added more wheat flour to give it a better rise. Substituting rye flour for wheat will work, but take care not to overburden the mixing motor of your bread machine with too dense a loaf.

1 lb	1½ lb	2 lb
½ C warm water	¾ C warm water	1 C warm water
1½ T vegetable oil	2¼ T vegetable oil	3 T vegetable oil
1 T honey	1½ T honey	2 T honey
½ T butter	2 t butter	1 T butter
1 T brown sugar	1½ T brown sugar	2 T brown sugar

½ C whole
  wheat flour
	¾ C whole
	  wheat flour
		1 C whole
		  wheat flour

1 C bread flour	1½ C bread flour	2 C bread flour
¼ C rye flour	⅜ C rye flour	½ C rye flour
2 T instant dry milk	3 T instant dry milk	¼ C instant dry milk
¾ t salt	1 t salt	1½ t salt
1 T raisins	1½ T raisins	2 T raisins
1½ t active dry yeast	2¼ t active dry yeast	1 T active dry yeast

(Nutritional analysis is on next page.)

Trail Bread Nutritional Analysis (per loaf, approximate)

Item	1 lb	1½ lb	2 lb
total calories (kcal)	1193	1781	2386
total protein (g)	33	49	65
total carbohydrates (g)	203	304	406
total fat (g)	30	45	61
total saturated fat (g)	7	9	13
total cholesterol (mg)	17	23	34
total sodium (mg)	1722	2307	3444
total fiber (g)	16	25	33
% calories from fat	23	22	23

Texas Bran Bread

This traditional basic bread has a hint of sweetness and a soft bran texture.

1 lb	1½ lb	2 lb
6 oz warm water	9 oz warm water	1½ C warm water
1½ T butter	2 T butter	3 T butter
½ t molasses	¾ t molasses	1 t molasses
1 T brown sugar	1½ T brown sugar	2 T brown sugar
½ t salt	¾ t salt	1 t salt
2 C bread flour	3 C bread flour	4 C bread flour
1½ T bran	2 T bran	3 T bran
1 t active dry yeast	1½ t active dry yeast	2 t active dry yeast

Nutritional Analysis (per loaf, approximate)

Item	1 lb	1½ lb	2 lb
total calories (kcal)	1207	1783	2414
total protein (g)	35	53	71
total carbohydrates (g)	215	322	430
total fat (g)	22	30	44
total saturated fat (g)	11	15	23
total cholesterol (mg)	46	61	92
total sodium (mg)	1257	1856	2514
total fiber (g)	10	15	20
% calories from fat	17	15	17

U. S. Liquid Measure Equivalencies*
and Metric Conversions

1 cup = 8 fluid ounces

1 cup = 16 tablespoons

1 cup = 48 teaspoons

1 cup = 236 mL

4.2 cups = 1 L

1 fluid ounce = 29.5 mL

1 fluid ounce = 6 teaspoons

1 fluid ounce = 2 tablespoons

1 tablespoon = ½ fluid ounce

1 tablespoon = 3 teaspoons

1 tablespoon = 15 mL

1 teaspoon = ⅙ fluid ounce

1 teaspoon = 5 mL

Abbreviations:

C = cup

T = tablespoon

t = teaspoon

oz = ounce

*These are also used for measuring flour and other dry ingredients in this book.

INDEX